MW00637437

ADVANCE PRAISE
for
Lessons from *Walden*

"A reading of Thoreau for the age of Trump—and really for any moment when our courage as individuals and as a polity seems to be flagging. This is a book that will make you think, and perhaps even act!"

—Bill McKibben, author of
The End of Nature and *Falter*

"*Lessons from* Walden delivers exactly what its title promises—an educational guide for an individual life committed to simplicity, moral responsibility, and ethical integrity. Like Thoreau, Taylor's goal is to wake us up."

—Sandra Harbert Petrulionis, author of
Thoreau in His Own Time

"*Lessons from* Walden is a welcome tonic in this moment of political and environmental crisis. Bob Pepperman Taylor's always-trenchant and insightful analysis reveals Thoreau's enduring relevance for modern democracies. His lessons are both important and timely."

—Kimberly Smith, author of
The Conservation Constitution

"Bob Taylor's measured and fair-minded mediation on *Walden* allows the fullness of Thoreau's stance to appear to the reader with all his contradictions intact. The result is a true conversation in which Thoreau becomes the springboard to further deliberation."

—Laura Dassow Walls, author of
Henry David Thoreau: A Life

"Bob Taylor's *Lessons from* Walden brings Thoreau's classic text to bear on the present moment, into Trump's America, into an age of environmental degradation, into a time of cultural self-absorption, instrumental rationality, and neoliberal indifference to what is local, communal, and particular."

—Shannon Mariotti, author of
Thoreau's Democratic Withdrawal

LESSONS

FROM

WALDEN

LESSONS
FROM
WALDEN

Thoreau and the Crisis of
American Democracy

BOB PEPPERMAN TAYLOR

University of Notre Dame Press
Notre Dame, Indiana

Copyright © 2020 by the University of Notre Dame
Notre Dame, Indiana 46556
undpress.nd.edu
All Rights Reserved

Published in the United States of America

Library of Congress Control Number: 2019054909

ISBN: 978-0-268-10733-8 (Hardback)
ISBN: 978-0-268-10736-9 (WebPDF)
ISBN: 978-0-268-10735-2 (Epub)

CONTENTS

Henry David Thoreau occupies two critical positions in the American story, one as an advocate of "civil disobedience" to unjust political authority, and the other as an advocate for nature and its appropriate role in our economic, moral, and spiritual lives. Both of these matters are central to what Thoreau has offered our American literary, political, and environmental traditions. The most expansive expression of his views is found in his masterwork, *Walden*.

When we begin probing these contributions we find, not surprisingly, that they are more complex and challenging than may first appear. In what follows, I will discuss three central claims found in *Walden*, each of them familiar even to those only casually familiar with Thoreau's book. (1) He believes we need to simplify our lives and that we may, in fact, need to cultivate what he calls "voluntary poverty"; (2) he encourages us to follow our moral intuition (to follow our own "drummer") for the sake of maintaining our moral integrity; and (3) he recommends that we live close to and learn from the natural world. All three of these pieces of advice have been embraced (or criticized) with more or less enthusiasm (or vitriol) by generations of *Walden* readers, even as what these recommendations might mean has not always been clear. My purpose in this book is to explain what I think Thoreau had in mind, what I believe his ideas demand of us, and the ways in which these demands resonate in our own time.

ACKNOWLEDGMENTS

Ben Minteer, Patrick Neal, Fran Pepperman Taylor, and Alex Zakaras all read an early draft of this book and provided comments that were (as always) of great value to me. Three anonymous reviewers for the University of Notre Dame Press offered equally interesting, provocative, and helpful reports that guided me as I worked my way through another draft of the manuscript. Stephen Wrinn, director of the press, was the source of both insightful comments and encouraging support for the project. I am, once again, overwhelmed by the thoughtfulness, scholarship, and generosity of my friends and colleagues. My heartfelt thanks to all.

The bulk of the writing for this book was completed during a sabbatical leave for 2017–18. I am grateful to the College of Arts and Sciences at the University of Vermont for providing me with the leisure to work on this project. I would also like to thank the library staff at Saint Michael's College for greeting me with such good cheer each morning as I sought a quiet writing space in their lovely facility.

INTRODUCTION

The Challenge of *Walden*

To spend even a little time with Henry David Thoreau's *Walden* is to recognize that an overriding image of the book—perhaps *the* overriding image—is that of awakening. Early on, Thoreau boasts that he hopes to crow like a rooster, like chanticleer, in order to wake his neighbors up.[1] He reminds us that "we are sound asleep nearly half our time,"[2] and suggests that, in truth, this slumber extends, all too often, to our so-called waking hours: "The commonest sense is the sense of men asleep, which they express by snoring."[3] Walden Pond is asleep (perhaps even dead) for three months at a time under the ice of winter, resurrected by the warming of spring ("Walden was dead and is alive again"[4]), and this reawakening becomes Thoreau's metaphor or symbol for our own moral awakening (he confides that he is "thankful that this pond was made deep and pure for a symbol").[5] All reform, he suggests, is an effort to "throw off sleep,"[6] and, in the final sentences of the book, he shifts from speaking of the dawn of spring to the dawn of morning in the hope of inspiring us to wakefulness: "Only that day dawns to which we are awake. There is more day to dawn. The sun is but a morning star."[7]

Even those who have not spent any significant time with *Walden* may have heard that Thoreau believed that most of his neighbors lived lives of "quiet desperation."[8] He thought his contemporaries were discontent, were alienated not only from their society but from themselves, that they were unhappy, confused, and in grave danger of losing control of their lives even while enjoying great, even unprecedented, social and political freedom; his audience, of course, consisted primarily of white citizens of Massachusetts in the mid-nineteenth century, living in the wake of the Jacksonian expansion of democratic sentiments and practices. He even audaciously suggests that his neighbors were less free than African Americans held in servitude in the American South.[9] But it is less widely recognized that Thoreau did not spare himself in this critique. He explains in the opening passages that he will write autobiographically, as he believes that a responsible author must, indeed, can't help but give an account of him- or herself: "Unfortunately, I am confined to this theme by the narrowness of my experience."[10] He explains that he has "travelled a good deal in Concord,"[11] his native town, and has observed not only himself but his neighbors and surroundings. He writes, however, not as one condescending to those around him—although he is accused of this often enough.[12] Overall, he is writing to the "discontented" not because he is superior to them, but because he is one of them and has learned some significant lessons about how to address this discontent.[13] That is, he is offering advice to his peers. Make no mistake about it: Thoreau, like those he addresses, has experienced loss and sorrow, even if he is rather oblique about the nature of these troubles.[14] He explicitly denies any moral class distinction between himself and others; he'll never know, he bluntly admits, a man worse than himself.[15] He offers advice, as from one who knows discontent but has learned something about how to address it, to others whom he assumes understand what discontent is and who are equally capable of not only coping with, but perhaps even of transcending, their own "quiet desperation." He suggests that if he brags from time to time, it is on the account of all humanity. He thinks of himself in significant ways as a representative man, and speaks as such.[16] His outlook is egalitarian and democratic: "When one man has reduced a fact of the imagination to be a fact to his understanding, I foresee that all men will at length establish their lives on that basis."[17] That is, if one man can willfully and positively transform his life on the strength of an imagined alternative, all people have an equal potential to do the same.

The initial concern that *Walden* addresses, therefore, is explicitly private and personal. Thoreau makes clear that he went to Walden Pond to transact some *private* business.[18] His assumption is that his audience also has private concerns to address. And his message is deeply optimistic and inspirational. To his audience, who he believes is desperate, his concluding message enthuses that for one who lives boldly, who breaks out of the "ruts of tradition and conformity,"[19] the world will present opportunities for "success unexpected in common hours."[20] Our tendency is to think the life we currently live is our only option, but Thoreau suggests how wrong it is to "think that we can change our clothes only."[21] Brian Walker has nicely tied *Walden* to an entire genre of Jacksonian period self-help literature,[22] and it is certainly true that the book builds to an inspirational crescendo in which Thoreau assures us that we can live simpler, more imaginative, more independent, and profoundly more satisfying lives.

There is a subtext here, however, that is less obvious but equally important. Thoreau goes to pains to tie his experiment at Walden not only to the private concerns he believes he shares with many of his neighbors, but also to the public and collective nature of our society and nation. He notes that he moved to his cabin on the Fourth of July (ironically suggesting that this was an "accident"), tethering his private act to our collective Independence Day.[23] He believes that in addition to producing alienated and desperate individuals, our society also produces, not coincidentally, grave and destructive inequality: "The luxury of one class is counterbalanced by the indigence of another."[24] There are other hints that he has real interest in producing a healthier public life. Consider this famous passage from the conclusion to the chapter entitled "Reading":

In this country, the village should in some respects take the place of the nobleman of Europe. It should be the patron of the fine arts. It is rich enough. . . . To act collectively is according to the spirit of our institutions; and I am confident that, as our circumstances are more flourishing, our means are greater than the nobleman's. New England can hire all the wise men in the world to come and teach her, and board them round the while, and not be provincial at all. That is the *uncommon* school we want. Instead of noblemen, let us have noble villages of men. If it is necessary, omit one bridge over the river, go round a little there, and throw one arch at least over the darker gulf of ignorance which surrounds us.[25]

In Thoreau's imagined future, our "noble villages of men" would have their spiritual and philosophical priorities settled in favor of learning and deliberation, and against the endless and frenetic pursuit of wealth. We know, from a comment about helping move a runaway slave along the Underground Railroad to Canada, to say nothing of what he writes in any number of his abolitionist writings,[26] that Thoreau ties his imagined and potentially more thoughtful, less materialistic neighbors to a significantly more just and egalitarian society. The focus of *Walden* is on private awakening, but we know Thoreau thinks such awakenings have deep significance for our public affairs. Political reform results from private reform, however, and can't be the primary focus of the reform process. First things first.

There are two essential elements of Thoreau's project that interest us here. The first is that his concern about the character of his neighbors ties him to an ancient tradition of disquiet about the nature of democratic citizens, a worry with profound resonance in our own time. The second is that these worries are integrally tied to a set of claims about our relationship with the natural world, another matter with profound resonance today. The contention of this book is that these interrelated elements of Thoreau's discussion constitute strong reasons to pay attention to Thoreau's project in *Walden*. The first claim is that Thoreau's book is one of America's most significant and influential meditations on the moral character of (relatively) free peoples, and, by implication, their relation to (relatively) free societies. The second claim is that Thoreau closely ties this set of observations to a deep interest in and concern about nature. His view is that to be responsible and happy individuals, individuals capable of cultivating freedom for the sake of the most humane and satisfying lives available, we must tame our current passions, impulses, and desires and rechannel them in more humane and satisfying ways; that in order to do this, we must learn from the natural order of the world around us; and that these developments are the preconditions for a genuinely free and equal—that is, democratic—society. Put another way, *Walden* is a central American text for addressing two of the central crises of our time: the increasingly alarming threats we now face to democratic norms, practices, and political institutions, and the perhaps even more alarming environmental dangers confronting us. It is not merely that Thoreau had a set of political opinions, and a set of opinions about nature, and that we can learn from these separate but equally interesting matters. On the contrary, these matters were essentially related for Thoreau, constituting different ways of talking about the same moral problems and moral order. The challenge of *Walden* could not be more relevant to both our private and public conditions today. Given his influence on later generations, and his centrality to the debates as they have emerged in American political culture, Thoreau, at the very least, helps us think seriously about the grave challenges before us more than 200 years after his birth.

The ultimate aim of *Walden*, and of so much of Thoreau's work, is to promote personal character and responsibility. As suggested already, there are for Thoreau two reasons to worry about this problem: the private satisfaction of individuals, and the public good of society. Our private desperation and our public irresponsibility both grow from a lack of reflection and self-discipline, which is another way of saying, from our lack of genuine independence. In *Civil Disobedience*, Thoreau is so disgusted by the voting behavior of American citizens that he casts significant doubt on the moral significance of elections (he refers to voting as "a sort of gaming"), and he pleads for individual citizens to stand and forthrightly reject the institutions of slavery and imperial war: "O for a man who is a *man*, and, as my neighbor says, has a bone in his back which you cannot pass your hand through!"[27] As Jane Bennett notes, "What haunts Thoreau about civil disobedience is not, as one might expect, the question of its justification. It is, rather, the fact of its infrequency."[28] If *Walden* is a plea to take control of one's own life primarily for one's own sake, *Civil Disobedience* and other writings suggest that Thoreau believes such independence will have desirable political repercussions. We will not be good (which, given the unjust condition of our politics, will not infrequently mean rebellious) citizens until we have the courage of our convictions, and such courage cannot emerge for individuals who do not control and assess these convictions for themselves. The problem of free individuals is the problem of responsible individuals and is relevant to both our public and our private lives.

THOREAU IS CERTAINLY NOT the first person to worry about this problem. In fact, it is among the most ancient concerns of political philosophy. The fear has always been that democratic citizens will lack self-discipline and self-knowledge, that they will be governed not by their deliberate and rational choice but, instead, by arbitrary custom, habit, impulse, and whim. Perhaps the greatest, and among the most pessimistic (and the oldest) set of reflections along these lines is found in the later passages of Plato's *Republic*. In books 8 and 9, Plato presents a discussion of how he believes even the best regime—rule by philosopher-kings, if that were even possible, an unlikely event at best—will deteriorate over time into increasingly unattractive regimes, ultimately culminating in the establishment of a pure and vicious tyranny. The key to this unhappy story, from Plato's perspective, is to understand the rebellion of sons against their fathers, and the way these generational rebellions mark a decline in the citizen virtue required to maintain any given political community. In Plato's view, even if we are lucky enough to be governed by true philosophers, the world is a sorry enough affair that we should expect, over time, the children of philosophers to be incapable of fully understanding the values, commitments, and knowledge of their parents. For Plato, the first moment of this decline from an ideal society will be marked by the replacement of a generation of philosopher-rulers, who are guided solely by their love of knowledge and the truth, by their unphilosophical sons, who are driven instead by a love of honor and reputation. These "timocrats" (Plato's term for these honor-loving rulers), in turn, eventually produce a generation that comes to view their fathers' preoccupation with honor as either foolish or hypocritical, and they themselves become animated instead by riches.

For those of us concerned with and committed to democracy, the critical moment in Plato's story comes when the sons of these oligarchs become impatient with their fathers' preoccupation with wealth. The democratic son finds the oligarchic father remarkably narrow and obtuse to all the various and beautiful possibilities in life. He, in contrast, is drawn to the full universe of human potentiality and insists on cultivating a wide array of human goods. The democratic city that grows from this rebellion looks, at first glance, extremely attractive: "Then it looks as though this is the finest or most beautiful of the constitutions, for, like a coat embroidered with every kind of ornament, this city, embroidered with every kind of character type, would seem to be the most beautiful."[29] A problem arises, however, insofar as the diversity of interests and characters generated by this democratic world lead the democratic citizen away from the disciplined life of the oligarch, who may have been narrow but was at least morally constant and focused. The democrat, in contrast, cultivates a life of continual motion, change, and free movement from interest to interest. Plato critically observes, "There's neither order nor necessity in his life, but he calls it pleasant, free, and blessedly happy, and he follows it for as long as he lives."[30]

In Plato's view, once this dynamic is set in motion, life in democratic society becomes increasingly extravagant and unpredictable. The oligarch's life looks stunted, even repressed and constricted. As the democrat is drawn to a variety of activities and objects, so he becomes unwilling to draw (perhaps he is even unable to draw) moral distinctions between different activities and commitments and beliefs. He "declares that all pleasures are equal and must be valued equally."[31] At this point the moral flood gates are opened and the democrat insists that whatever he wants, no matter what it is, should be respected and valued. He views restrictions on his liberty as unjustifiable attempts to impose one morally arbitrary set of values on whatever values he happens to hold. He becomes, in our language, a "moral relativist," who chaffs at all moral claims and all restrictions on personal liberty. Indeed, from this perspective the democrat resists the very idea of governance and authority: "In the end . . . [the democrat] take[s] no notice of the laws, whether written or unwritten, in order to avoid having any master at all."[32] Any sense that we should draw meaningful moral distinctions between different values or ways of life is viewed as tyrannical, as indefensibly impositional. Demands for self-sacrifice or self-restraint for the good of others or the community at large are viewed as insidious. For Plato, the logic of democracy is anarchic, but this is not an ordered anarchy; ultimately it produces a political chaos of morally unrestrained and demanding individuals, all claiming the right to follow their own whims and impulses undeterred and blind to the needs of others or the good of the community as a whole.

Plato's "cycle of regimes" is not presented as a history. It is, rather, an abstract schema of what he takes to be the fundamental characteristics and weaknesses of different regimes and how, in general, these relate to one another. The moral of the story is, obviously, not a happy one: the inevitable end point for a society with such ungoverned and self-centered individuals is a breakdown of order so great that political tyranny—the establishment of law and order at all costs—comes to look attractive from the perspective of those at risk of ruin from democracy's excesses. Just as oligarchy's sons demand democratic freedom and equality, democracy's sons will eventually turn to the seeming (but false) comfort and stability of tyrannical rule: "And isn't democracy's insatiable desire for what it defines as the good also what destroys it?"[33] If Plato is right, democratic citizens will develop characters that threaten the stability of democracy itself.

The problem Plato raises, or we might rather say variants of this problem, echo resoundingly through the tradition of American political thinking. Horace Mann, the great nineteenth-century American educator and Thoreau's contemporary,[34] was, unlike Plato, deeply committed to democratic government. He contended, however, that although democracy is potentially the most just and free of all political orders, it also ironically has the potential to become the most unjust and tyrannical—for reasons not incompatible with Plato's analysis. In conventional tyrannies, Mann argues, "a few men, whom we call tyrants and monsters, having got the mastery, have prevented thousands of others from being tyrants and monsters like themselves." Once these tyrants have been deposed, however, and democracy established, the tyrannical impulses of the whole population are in danger of being unleashed: "Should all selfish desires at once burst their confines, and swell to the extent of their capacity, it would be as though each drop of the morning dew were suddenly enlarged into an ocean."[35] Mann maintained great hope for democracy, but he also feared that critics such as Plato were right to warn about the dangers of an undisciplined and unlawful democracy. John Locke famously drew a distinction between liberty—the self-control of the autonomous individual to willfully and self-consciously act lawfully—and what he called "license"—the impulsive pursuit of every selfish whim and desire.[36] The enemies of democracy have always asserted, one way or another, the inevitability of democratic citizens succumbing to disorder, to Locke's feared "license." Democracy's friends have also feared it.

Ralph Waldo Emerson, Thoreau's friend and mentor, identifies Napoleon Bonaparte as the "incarnate Democrat"[37] the "agent or attorney of the middle class of modern society; of the throng who fill the markets, shops, counting-houses, manufactories, ships, of the modern world, aiming to be rich."[38] This social type, Emerson believes, is not distinguished simply by the aspiration for wealth, but by a total lack of "any stipulation or scruple concerning the means."[39] Ultimately these democrats, driven by "sensual and selfish" aims, must fail: "As long as our civilization is essentially one of property, of fences, of exclusiveness, it will be mocked by delusions.

Our riches will leave us sick; there will be bitterness in our laughter; and our wine will burn our mouth. Only that good profits, which we can taste with all doors open, and which serves all men."[40] Like Mann, Emerson fears that the modern democrat is selfish, unprincipled, and drawn to despotic champions such as Napoleon. The degree to which his fears have merit is the degree to which he foresees poor and dangerous outcomes for democratic society.

American political culture has been plagued by strong and nagging doubts about these matters throughout our national history. The early years of the republic saw two developments that greatly alarmed the founding generation: the growth of political parties and the unprecedented unleashing of private commerce. Rough and tumble partisan politics, combined with a growing capitalist economy, encouraged early Americans to think of the aggressive promotion of private and individual interests as the best manner in which the public good would be promoted. Andrew Delbanco has observed, "This instillation of ambition as the one common good was the great transformation of nineteenth-century American life. By 1850, Americans found themselves both liberated and imprisoned by the enormously compelling idea—once decried as pride—of the striving self. There could be no place for the old devil in this new world, whose religion was pride of the self."[41] This emergence of the "striving self" as the image of the American par excellence, in both political and economic life, helps to explain why Founders such as Jefferson and Madison were deeply concerned that the political life in the new nation was discouraging the kind of virtues required by citizens in a free republic. Gordon Wood reports that Jefferson "loathed the new democratic world that America had become."[42] Lance Banning documents not only Jefferson's and Madison's concerns about the emerging character of American citizens, but he muses that we, too, "simply do not like, or trust, or listen to each other in the way they thought essential."[43] The fear that Banning identifies, and that continues to arouse concern today in so many different contexts, is that American citizens are now so self-preoccupied as to have become blind to the needs of others, the fact of our interdependency as citizens, the collective goods we share, and the need to compromise and cooperate in democratic political and social life.

These nineteenth-century American citizens, driven by the "pride of the self," appeared particularly vulnerable to the flattery and manipulation of political elites. In 1838, James Fenimore Cooper wrote that the "peculiar danger of a democracy, arises from the arts of demagogues,"[44] and a critic from our own time takes this claim a step further to express a view that is perhaps quite widely shared: "Put bluntly, rule by demagogues is not an aberration. It is the natural condition of democracy."[45] The supposed reasons for this, in most cases, are the foolishness and the blinding self-interest driving the vast majority of democratic citizens. Toward the end of the nineteenth century we witness the rise of patriotic societies, suggesting an anxiety about the ability of American democracy to survive unless a way is found to nurture a more robust sense of civic obligation—a fear that was not without reason, given the profound upheavals and violence of the recent civil war. This is the period during which the Pledge of Allegiance appears, and "America the Beautiful" is written and popularized. The former becomes the only oath routinely requested of children in any modern liberal democracy; the latter reminds democrats of the Pilgrims' "self-control" and that "liberty" can only be properly understood as freely chosen submission to law ("God mend thine every flaw / Confirm thy soul in self-control / Thy liberty in law!").[46] These movements and cultural artifacts, along with the growth of the common (public) school movement, convey a deep anxiety about the virtue and public spiritedness of average American citizens.[47] Great efforts would be required to bring Americans to an acceptable level of civic commitment, responsibility, and military vigor. One need only look at Theodore Roosevelt's essay "The Duties of American Citizenship," written in 1883, to sense the concern that we were losing the qualities required for self-governance.[48] William James, in his famous 1906 essay "The Moral Equivalent of War," argued that a "permanently successful peace-economy cannot be a simple pleasure-economy," because citizens require a more morally inspiring and physically vigorous set of commitments if they are to keep from becoming decadent and publicly disengaged.[49]

Mark Twain's comments in his *Autobiography* about President Theodore Roosevelt, as "one of the most impulsive men in existence," are very much to the point here. With characteristic dry exaggeration, Twain suggests that Roosevelt "probably never thinks of the right way to do anything." This leads to a discussion of the president's character, with comments remarkable enough to warrant lengthy quotation:

Mr. Roosevelt is one of the most likable men that I am acquainted with. I have known him . . . for certainly twenty years. I always enjoy his society, he is so hearty, so straightforward, outspoken, and so absolutely sincere. These qualities endear him . . . to all his friends. But when he is acting under their impulse as President, they make of him a sufficiently queer president. He flies from one thing to another with incredible dispatch—throws a somersault and is straightway back again where he was last week. He will then throw some more somersaults and nobody can foretell where he is finally going to land after the series. Each act of his, and each opinion expressed, is likely to abolish or controvert some previous act or expressed opinion. This is what is happening to him all the time as President. But every opinion that he expresses is certainly his sincere opinion at that moment, and it is as certainly not the opinion which he was carrying around in his system three or four weeks earlier, and which was just as sincere and honest as the latest one. No he can't be accused of insincerity—that is not the trouble. His trouble is that his newest interest is the one that absorbs him; absorbs the whole of him from his head to his feet, and for the time being it annihilates all previous opinions and feelings and convictions. He is the most popular human being that has ever existed in the United States, and that popularity springs from just these enthusiasms of his—these joyous ebullitions of excited sincerity. It makes him so much like the rest of the people. They see themselves reflected in him. They also see that his impulses are not often mean. They are almost always large, fine, generous. He can't stick to one of them long enough to find out what kind of a chick it would hatch if it had a chance, but everybody recognizes the generosity of the intention and they admire it and love him for it.[50]

Twain's description may be more or less accurate, more or less extravagant, as a portrait of our twenty-sixth president. The key point is not, however, the issue of whether Twain is a reliable biographer. Rather, consider what it is that Twain is humorously but pointedly saying about the citizens of the United States when he wrote this passage early in 1906 (a half century after the publication of *Walden*). Roosevelt, he suggests, is a very attractive man in significant ways—he is sincere, energetic, enthusiastic, straightforward, and very likeable. He is also, however, impulsive, unpredictable, even anarchic in his opinions, and, therefore, in the behavior that unselfconsciously grows from these opinions; he never sticks to one of his "joyous ebullitions" long enough to "find out what kind of a chick it would hatch if it had a chance." As striking as this is as a description of a U.S. president, the critical point is that these qualities of character are not merely peculiar to Roosevelt. Rather, the very source of the president's success, the reason he is so popular, well loved, and has enjoyed such public recognition and reward, is that he mirrors so perfectly American citizens themselves. Roosevelt's political career hasn't grown from his heroic distinctiveness; instead it has grown from the degree to which he embodies in pure and exaggerated form certain personality traits common—although usually, without a doubt, in less impressive form—in the American people themselves. The democratic character looks interesting, enthusiastic, and full of energy, but it also looks significantly capricious, unreflective, and inconsistent. The American citizens Twain describes are appealing, as is the president, but, like Roosevelt, they are not terribly self-conscious about their own commitments, beliefs, and projects. Nor do they seem aware of the degree to which these commitments, beliefs, and projects appear to be both arbitrary and unpredictably subject to change.[51]

These comments by Twain are more humorous and affectionate than Thoreau's prose in *Walden*, less morally aghast than Emerson and Mann. Twain is most intrigued by impulsiveness, and Thoreau by conformism, while others worry about demagogues and the manipulation of public passion. For all their differences, however, these and similar observations build in some way on Plato's concern, from 2,400 years earlier, that the democratic world is morally obtuse. It is not just that democratic citizens are ignorant, though this is a common enough concern. Even worse, democratic citizens appear to be of bad character, or at least of character inadequate to the demands of freedom. All these authors follow Plato in suggesting that democratic citizens are remarkably unselfconscious about their own best interests. They are moved more by desire than by reflection, and as such are more the playthings than the rulers of their own desires and impulses.

Twain gives no suggestion in this passage that he finds the democratic qualities he identifies as deeply destabilizing in the same way Plato does, and Thoreau finds the problem more conducive to private discontent and social injustice than to carefree impulsiveness, but both share with the ancient writer a sense of the moral blindness of democrats. In addition, these observations are in no way idiosyncratic to these authors so dramatically separated by time and space. What all three allude to is a set of observations and apprehensions that are common among democracy's friends and foes alike.

Voices expressing similar worries in our own time are extensive and offered by individuals from across the political spectrum. Consider, just as examples, the concerns of the following contemporary scholars. In the wake of 9/11, one editorial writer, a humanities professor, raises the Rooseveltian concern that American youth have become too soft and decadent to assume the military responsibilities of citizenship.[52] Law professor Stephen Carter laments the "unhappy political spirit of our selfish age,"[53] and worries that "living in a democracy requires hard work that we seem less and less willing to do."[54] Political scientist Robert Dahl fears that consumerism has replaced the concerns and perspective of citizenship in our public life, and hopes for a shift back to civic engagement and commitments.[55] Political sociologist Alan Wolfe observes the degree to which the virtue of compromise is being lost in our political culture, as ideologues and polarized political debate replace the pragmatic democratic arts of negotiation.[56] Philosopher Michael Sandel believes that our moral fabric is unraveling, and that the contemporary conception of democracy "lacks the civic resources to sustain self-government."[57] Jean Elshtain, from the University of Chicago Divinity School, declares that "our American democracy is faltering" as a result of the deterioration of necessary "democratic dispositions."[58] A group of legal scholars generally friendly to liberal and expansive understandings of the First Amendment issue a volume of essays expressing great alarm at the way the Internet frequently becomes a vicious tool for attacking women, racial minorities, and other minority groups; the conclusion is clearly that a significant number of citizens do not have the character or restraint required to use this tool responsibly.[59] Intellectual historian Mark Lilla, analyzing the Tea Party phenomena a number of years ago, paints a picture of at least a significant minority of American citizens that comes remarkably close to that we have seen given by Plato of democrats in general:

> For half a century now Americans have been rebelling in the name of individual freedom. . . . Now an angry group of Americans wants to be freer still—free from government agencies that protect their health, wealth, and well-being; free from problems and policies too difficult to understand; free from parties and coalitions; free from experts who think they know better than they do; free from politicians who don't talk or look like they do (and Barack Obama certainly doesn't). They want to say what they have to say without fear of contradiction, and then hear someone on television tell them they're right. They don't want the rule of the people, though that's what they say. They want to be people without rules—and, who knows, they may succeed. This is America, where wishes come true. And where no one remembers the adage "Beware what you wish for."[60]

This catalog of concerns by distinguished scholars of American politics and public life could be expanded more or less indefinitely.

The above examples and illustrations all date from before the 2016 U.S. presidential campaign, which culminated in the election of Donald Trump. If there were worries prior to Trump's election, imagine how this event amplifies the concerns. Public rage and foreign meddling combined to elect a reality TV star and amoral (at best) real-estate mogul with clear misogynous swagger and a pattern of shamelessly inflaming and exploiting racist passions. Who could deny that that acrimonious and angry electoral season didn't reflect precisely the kind of pathologies, even to a surprisingly exaggerated degree, captured by the above worries? I write during the first years of the Trump presidency, and in the shadow of growing political violence;[61] anger and chaos in our political order are all that has been feared and a great deal more. Much ink has been spilled to explain how reality itself has become unhinged in the American political experience, as when the new president's advisor defended his (extraordinarily) routine lies by referring to "alternative facts." There is good reason to think that this assault on reality is, to use a popular term, "unsustainable" in the long term, but we have seen that what began as an assault on science by previous presidential administrations (primarily in the service of attempting to delegitimize environmental concerns) has grown to the cultivation of such extreme levels of irrationality that Russian hackers appear to have had a field day during the election in providing "fake news" that was gobbled up by ideological partisans. Certainly, we might believe, a thoughtful and public-spirited citizenry would never succumb to such cartoonish and vicious demagoguery as we have seen of late, to such divisive and cynical political tactics, to support for a presidential administration responsible, by one respected count, for an unprecedented 5,000 well-documented lies or cynically misleading claims in less than two years in office.[62] The dysfunction and cynicism of contemporary politics appears to suggest that concerns about the American civic culture may have been, if anything, understated in the past. Law professor Cass R. Sunstein begins a recent book with the claim that "in a well-functioning democracy, people do not live in echo chambers or information cocoons."[63] The point is that it is precisely such echo chambers and information cocoons that characterize our current acrimonious, bitter, and deeply troubled politics. U.S. citizens (especially, but not only, those on the Right) appear to believe what they want to believe, evidence be damned.[64] Communication across our partisan divide appears almost impossible. Democratic debate and deliberation seem at the moment quaint and nostalgic notions, far removed from our current fractious political behavior.

Contemporary concerns about the self-discipline of U.S. citizens extends beyond our political behavior and reaches deep within our culture. A number of years ago, journalist Daniel Akst addressed these matters in striking detail. It is clear, Akst believes, that contemporary society presents us with unprecedented freedom and affluence, and that we are poorly equipped to cope with the possibilities these realities lay before us. He notes, "Modern life simply requires an unnatural degree of self-control, and one of its side effects is self-control fatigue."[65] The evidence for this "self-control fatigue" is overwhelming: Akst documents our failures of restraint in matters concerning our diet and health, our sexual and family lives, our consumer and financial habits, our tendency toward addiction, even our ability to resist impulse suicide if we find a handgun close by. His data is not entirely surprising (he is, after all, describing behavior we see every day in our own lives and the lives of those around us), but it is certainly sobering and impressive when brought together in a book such as his. What we are witnessing, Akst argues, "is nothing less than the democratization of temptation."[66] In previous epochs, such temptations were confined to the elite few. Although these elite classes never provided a great deal of evidence that they could themselves manage these temptations with restraint and discipline, the consequences of their excesses were at least limited by the number of individuals involved. Now, in contrast, society has widely dispersed these opportunities, and "the many" prove themselves at least as vulnerable to excess as "the few" had been: "Democracy suffers from an essential contradiction concerning self-control, which it depends upon, reinforces, and undermines all at the same time."[67] Akst believes that government power must be used to "shape the public realm in ways that promote healthy choices."[68] Quite simply, we do not have the willpower we need when confronted by unwise opportunities, and government needs to assume responsibility for shaping our choices more aggressively, since "individuals cannot adequately regulate themselves."[69] From Akst's perspective, the paradox is that we need to democratically chose to revoke certain freedoms granted by democratic society in order to maintain the discipline and restraint required by democracy in the first place.

Jonathan Franzen's novel *Freedom* was released in 2010 to great fanfare and excitement. Franzen found himself on the cover of *Time* magazine with the proclamation that he is our generation's "great American novelist"; *Freedom* is also the novel that President Obama selected for his vacation reading that summer, but there is no public record, to my knowledge, of his having succeeded in plowing through the entire book. The story chronicles the disintegration of a family, the personal and collective inability of the characters to resist temptation or temper their decisions with prudent foresight, and additionally the moral and ecological irresponsibility of the American political order as a whole. The heroine, composing a journal to reflect on her disasters as a mother, wife, neighbor, worker, and citizen, writes: "She had all day every day to figure out some decent and satisfying way to live, and yet all she ever seemed to get for all her choices and all her freedom was more miserable. The autobiographer is almost forced to the conclusion that she pitied herself for being so free."[70] The increasingly successful musician, Richard, faces a similar problem: "He was at once freer than he'd been since puberty and closer than he'd ever been to suicide. In the last days of 2003, he [abandoned his music career and] went back to building decks."[71] The son, insisting on freedom from his parents' governance, finds himself burdened by his own successful rebellion: "He'd asked for his freedom, they'd granted it, and he couldn't go back now."[72] And on and on: although there are genuine moments of virtue and decency in the novel, and Franzen provides an almost comically (certainly unlikely) happy resolution to the novel's crises in the end, the real message of the book appears to be the incompetence of normal people to live happy, well-ordered, free lives. Walter, the hero, finds his brother reduced to alcoholism, estranged from his family, and homeless. He remarks to him, "You're a free man"; the brother simply responds, "That I am."[73] If there is any message to take away from Franzen's vision of American society it is that American citizens are overwhelmed, perhaps terrifyingly overwhelmed, by their own freedom. There is little hope for dignified self-governance here. Indeed, there is a frank skepticism about such a possibility, and the popularity of the book, the degree to which it resonates in the American popular culture, reflects the degree to which such skepticism is at least viewed as plausible, even if it is not fully shared by readers.

Our anxiety about such matters has obviously taken many forms and focused on a variety of issues over the course of our history. It consistently reflects, however, a general concern that democratic citizens are threatened by a kind of character flaw, an unwillingness to control and discipline themselves, a blindness to the question of whether their own wants and desires reflect reasonable projects and the degree to which their personal demands respect the needs and obligations of the community at large. Such concerns, as we have suggested above, are long-standing themes in American political thought. For all the variation in how different democratic thinkers propose to manage these anxieties and what they view as potential pathologies of democracy, there is a strong undercurrent of agreement about the general threat that this problem poses to the health and stability of democratic society and politics. Simply put, without appropriately restrained, disciplined, moderate, reasonable, and publicly spirited citizens, the fear is that democracy will succumb to a kind of moral incompetence, even perhaps to the tyrannical impulses Mann and Emerson feared, and that it will become an unstable contest between irresponsibly aggressive, selfish, and dangerously tribalized citizens. It is feared that such a political community will find it impossible to discover and promote the public good, let alone provide stable relations between citizens or ensure wise public policy. The concern is that to some degree or another, this potential disease of democracy threatens the stability and well-being of the democratic order as a whole. Plato's prognosis may have been exaggerated, but it is certainly not unique or of an entirely different order from the nightmare haunting democrats themselves. One nineteenth-century Western settler in America is reported to have said, "When without a king, [one] doeth according to the freedom of his own will."[74] The concern is about the content of this will. Will it lead to responsible action in accord with Locke's "liberty," or will it become an expression of an irresponsible "license"?

This is not to say that concerns such as these are the most prominent element of our political self-consciousness in the United States. Walt Whitman, the great poet of American democracy, captures in unusually powerful language a strong and conventional American faith in American democracy when he writes that democracy "has fashion'd, systematized, and triumphantly finish'd and carried out, in its own interest, and with unparallel'd success, a new earth and a new man."[75] Regardless of the dangers posed by democracy, Whitman expresses a profound and recognizable pride and confidence in the emergence of democratic individuals: "Political democracy, as it exists and practically works in America, with all its threatening evils, supplies a training-school for making first-class men."[76] Whitman writes of the "banner of the divine pride of man in himself" encouraged by democracy, and contrasts this with the past, when common people were encouraged to think of greatness as found only in the aristocratic and governing classes: "Long enough have the People been listening to poems in which common humanity, deferential, bends low, humiliated, acknowledging superiors. But America listens to no such poems. Erect, inflated, and fully self-esteeming be the chant; and then America will listen with pleased ears."[77] Although such pride can easily take chauvinistic and imperialist forms (and, sadly, often has, throughout the course of our history), many have shared with Abraham Lincoln the belief that American democracy represents the "last best hope of earth," less as a claim to American superiority than as a profession of faith in the power and potential of democracy itself.[78] And regardless of the justification for such views, or the full moral implications of them, there has been a strong, even dominant, element of self-confidence in the American psyche from very early on in our history. Alexis de Tocqueville complained, in fact, that the overpowering sense of self-importance and virtue in

Americans he met in the early years of the republic was one of the least attractive elements of "democracy in America" (he referred to the "irritable patriotism of Americans"[79]). At the very least, it is a commonplace that American democracy has produced all manner of self-confidence in the virtue and wisdom of democracy, and a strong conviction that the United States is itself the original home[80] and continuing epicenter of democratic possibility.[81]

Despite our aggressive patriotism and self-confidence, however, the concerns I've raised are obviously not unusual, nor are they unique to the individuals and illustrations discussed. They are common in writings and public statements both sympathetic and hostile to democratic society and political organization, and they represent what we might think of as among the gravest concerns raised by democratic life.[82] In some ways, this is very discouraging: in the early years of the twenty-first century we were reminded, by the optimism and idealism of the "Arab Spring" of 2011, that democracy remains the great dream and hope of those suffering at the hands of tyrants and kings. The freedom of democracy promises relief from the terror of secret police and all forms of irresponsible political power; it holds out the hope for free speech and for the freedom to participate in and petition the government without fear; it represents a possible challenge to graft and favoritism in economic life; it imagines a world of equality for women; it promotes tolerance for religious and lifestyle variety; these and so many other positive goods are promised by democracy and longed for by victims of all forms of authoritarianism. Participants in democratic resistance movements are not always aware of, or realistic about, the kinds of concerns I have raised, even if their opponents, religious authoritarians and theocrats especially, can be very vocal about the decadence and—in their view, repulsive—moral tolerance of democratic societies. It is not for the sake of discouraging those who struggle against undemocratic regimes that I raise these matters here. Rather, honest democrats need to realistically face these concerns and evaluate the degree to which they constitute real threats to democratic stability, and to think clearly about how these problems can be mitigated while maintaining respect for democratic values and practices.

As I have been suggesting, these concerns have informed American political thought from the very beginning and have generated an array of responses for mitigating or controlling problems endemic to democracy. The most well-known of these was proposed by the Founders, who were clearly worried about these democratic pathologies and determined to prevent them from shaping the politics of the new nation. James Madison famously notes, in Federalist 10, that all free governments produce factions, self-interested groups consolidating primarily around economic (property) interests, but possibly around other strong ideological or material concerns. These factions, in turn, reflect their members' narrow and particular perspective, and place them in competition with other factions. Politics becomes a struggle between these rival groups. Democracies, or small communities of equal and self-governing citizens, cannot solve the problem of faction; the strongest among them, the majority faction, simply dominates the rest. Madison and his fellow Federalists championed their national Constitution as the solution to "the mischiefs of faction."[83] The key, they argue, is to turn away from small republics and democracies and embrace a large republic. Such a republic allows, most importantly, for the multiplication of faction as the community grows in size and complexity: "Extend the sphere and you take in a greater variety of parties and interests; you make it less probable that a majority of the whole will have a common motive to invade the rights of other citizens; or if such a common motive exists, it will be more difficult for all who feel it to discover their own strength and to act in unison with each other."[84] In addition, because republics rely on representation rather than direct citizen participation, larger republics are more likely than smaller republics to produce elites who take a broad view of the public good. Representation in the new political order, they believe, promises to "refine and enlarge the public views" of the representatives by giving them a more expansive perspective on the whole than is available to an individual citizen.[85] And even if these hopes for enlightened political leadership fail, we learn in Federalist 51 that when faction is reflected in the wills and interests of representatives, these factional impulses will be disciplined by the checks and balances of constitutionally divided power. "Ambition must be made to counteract ambition," and the genius of the Constitution is to channel even tyrannical impulses into the public good by forcing factious representatives (and branches of government) to compromise and cooperate with one another.[86]

For all its ambition and brilliance, however, the constitutional order of 1787 has failed, at least in the judgment of many American citizens, to control the factional impulses it hoped to tame and channel into the public good. Jefferson and Madison were deeply discouraged by the developments they witnessed during the later years of their lives. As American politics evolved during the Jacksonian years, democracy was expanding along with the factiousness of political competition. Once again, consider Horace Mann, who blamed the Founders for believing they could address these problems of political discipline through the genius of constitutional mechanisms alone:

> On what grounds of reason or of hope, it may well be asked, did the framers of our National and State Constitutions expect, that the future citizens of this Republic would be able to sustain the institutions, or to enjoy the blessings, provided for them? And has not all our subsequent history shown the calamitous consequences of their failing to make provision for the educational wants of the nation? . . . They did not reflect that, in the common course of nature, all the learned and the wise and the virtuous are swept from the stage of action, almost as soon as they become learned and wise and virtuous; and that they are succeeded by a generation who come into the world wholly devoid of learning and wisdom and virtue.[87]

For Mann, and for many others from his generation to ours, methods more direct than constitutional design and the formal structure of political institutions are required to bring the pathologies of democracy under control. President Obama observed, in his Farewell Address, that "our Constitution is a remarkable, beautiful gift. But it's really just a piece of parchment. It has no power on its own."[88] His point was that the Constitution is not self-executing, that it requires the people themselves, through their acts and commitments, to make "a more perfect union." When asked in the summer of 1787 what the convention in Philadelphia had given the American people, Benjamin Franklin answered, "A republic, if you can keep it."[89] Even at the moment of its birth, it was clear to many that the Constitution would only succeed if American citizens where of a certain character.[90]

THE GOAL OF *WALDEN* is to promote a kind of personal responsibility, both for the sake of individuals and for the good of the community at large. I've noted that Thoreau appears to differ from both Plato and Twain to the degree that he seems more concerned about conformity than he does about impulsiveness. Indeed, Thoreau appears on one level to be on the side of the individuality Plato criticizes; he suggests, after all, that we need to march to the rhythm of our own drummer.[91] As we will see in chapter 2, however, this observation can be misleading. Thoreau is far from promoting the kind of moral relativism we find cultivated by Plato's democratic man. On the contrary, he hopes to encourage us to have the courage to conform to general and timeless law, rather than the habits, inclinations, and prejudices of our society. Such an individual will appear eccentric from the perspective of his or her contemporaries, but not, in Thoreau's opinion, when seen from a longer view.

Another way of thinking about Thoreau's difference with the Platonic critique of democracy is that it is, at its deepest level, a concern about what it is that will seduce and derail democratic citizens. The Platonic democratic citizen flits from desire to desire, impulse to impulse, one minute drawn in one direction, the next in another. For Thoreau, the fear is that free people will succumb to a much less interesting, and morally deadening, utilitarianism. If only we *would* sometimes be seduced by the beauty of art, or of other pleasures incapable of being captured in the crass calculation of monetary value! Thoreau cries against the "incessant business" of his society,[92] the degree to which we appear to be subjecting ourselves to the market as the ultimate arbiter of all value. Rather than riding the railroad, as he tells us in *Walden*, the railroad rides upon us, and our enslavement to the market makes us the tool of our tools.[93] If it were not that Thoreau promotes a form of moral universalism (again, see chapter 2), it would appear that he is Plato's democratic son rebelling against the oligarchic fathers. Instead, he appears to have a slightly different set of fears than does Plato about how freedom can be coopted and perverted.

What Thoreau offers is related to, but also significantly different from, what is offered by conservative critiques of liberal society. Thoreau shares with conservatives a belief in the need to build personal character, to strengthen our ability to take personal responsibility, and to distrust liberal flirtations with moral relativism. Thoreau, too, is distrustful of the degree to which utility has become the measure of moral concern in modern society, unleashing the market to serve the pleasures of individuals.[94] Yet conservatives aim for restoration of tradition and conventional forms of life, while Thoreau aims to stimulate an individual responsibility that will be rebellious, a breaker of traditions, and civilly disobedient. Conservatism demands that the individual learn to responsibly submit to the needs and conventions of society,[95] but Thoreau insists that we submit to principles that will make us nonconforming in our unjust world. Patrick Deneen, defending conservatism from what he takes to be the ravages of liberal individualism, writes that the "great task of civilization has been to sustain and support familial, social and cultural structures and practices that perpetuate and deepen personal and intergenerational forms of obligation and gratitude, of duty and indebtedness."[96] The emphasis in Thoreau's writing, in contrast, is on the reform of conventional relationships and institutions, the building of a future society more just than what has been experienced in the past. In this sense, Thoreau speaks to the concerns of the Left in a way that much conservatism cannot. He offers insights into a progressive politics that will not shy away from questions of personal character, commitment, and sacrifice for the sake of justice (rather than with the aim of restoration). For all that Thoreau shares with conservatives—the distrust of liberal market society, the appeal to a natural moral order—the differences in focus are profound.

Thoreau and the tradition he has sparked speaks to egalitarian and environmental values in ways that contemporary conservatism does not and probably cannot.

Each of the three chapters that follow is organized around an obvious and widely recognized trope or theme from *Walden*: the virtue of simplicity, the need to follow the beat of our own drummer, and the attractions and lessons of the woodsy outdoors Thoreau embraces at Walden Pond. I do not intend to provide a complete or general interpretation of *Walden* or a reading of Thoreau's ideas as a whole.[97] I will have to explain what I believe Thoreau has in mind when he develops these three themes, but my intention is less to focus on Thoreau than to use his great book—a book Nancy Rosenblum refers to as "American Scripture"[98]—as a springboard for thinking how we and our contemporaries wrestle, for better or worse, with the issues Thoreau raises, sometimes self-consciously responding to Thoreau, most often probably not even having him much in mind at all. My contention is that Thoreau frames essential problems and questions for us, but not that he always gives us the final or fully satisfactory answers to these questions. He serves as a guide for considering important elements of our public and private lives; he is certainly not a savior who provides us with all we need to know. He is, however, the founder of a particular strain of environmental thinking that continues to resonate, even as a minority tradition, within American society. Given the dual political and environmental crises we face, it is well to focus some sober thoughts on the lessons this tradition offers. I am more than happy, when I think necessary, to defend a particular reading of Thoreau's writings, but even if from time to time I stray from persuasive interpretation, the questions I think I discover in Thoreau's work speak powerfully to our contemporary environment. The assaults on our democracy have some significant similarities with the Jacksonian politics of Thoreau's lifetime, but demagoguery has its own special qualities in an age of tweets and the Web-driven undermining of shared reality. Thoreau was well aware of the threats to the natural environment in his own time, but he could hardly have imagined the dangers of climate change and the onset of the Anthropocene.

The questions Thoreau raises are ones we do well to ask along with him. We will learn from Thoreau and those who follow him, but any answers will have to be our own.

Although I am writing this book because I am persuaded that Thoreau and the tradition he informs have much to offer as we face our peculiar political and environmental challenges, honesty requires that I admit to having little to say about our current emergencies. It can only be hoped that contemporary citizens and leadership will, at the end of the day, have the prudence and courage to protect our democratic institutions from the most egregious assaults they are now experiencing, and that we will find some short- to medium-term answers to the challenges of climate change and political instability. Both of these fronts present grave and potentially catastrophic dangers, and there is increasing reason to fear the worst from our current presidential leadership and political class. In the short term, however, there is little to do other than to push back against the threats as strongly and as prudently as possible with both the ballot and conventional protest politics. The lessons of *Walden* are not particularly helpful for political and environmental crisis management. Rather, they aim at the longer-term construction of a just, stable, and environmentally sound nation. That is the focus of the discussion that follows. To engage in such a discussion is nothing less than an act of faith, justified or not, that a life beyond our current crises is worth imagining.

ONE

SIMPLICITY

Simplicity, simplicity, simplicity!
    —Thoreau, *Walden*

John Adams once wrote, "The love of poverty is a fictitious virtue, that never existed,"[1] but Henry Thoreau was
unpersuaded. The call to simplicity is probably Thoreau's
most famous comment in *Walden*, and this is just one of
many that promote what he calls voluntary poverty: "With
respect to luxuries and comforts, the wisest have ever lived a
more simple and meagre life than the poor."[2] And while this
concern is central to *Walden*, it is certainly not confined to
it. Thoreau tells us in *Civil Disobedience*, "The opportunities of living are diminished in proportion as what are called
the 'means' are increased," and that a reliable rule of thumb
is "the more money, the less virtue."[3] He recommends that
to live well, "it will not be worth the while to accumulate
property. . . . You must hire or squat somewhere, and raise
but a small crop, and eat that soon."[4] In "Life without Principle," he suggests, "The ways by which you may get money
almost without exception lead downward."[5] Such briefs
for voluntary poverty, with their accompanying attacks on

trade ("trade curses everything it handles"[6]) and wealth ("The luxuriously rich are not simply kept comfortably warm, but unnaturally hot; as I implied before, they are cooked, of course *a la mode*."[7]) are sprinkled generously throughout his works.

Simplicity is not a minor concern in *Walden*. The first chapter, "Economy," constitutes almost a quarter of the entire book. Thoreau clearly believes that if we are to think seriously about the causes of our "quiet desperation," and to imagine ways of awakening from our moral stupor and learn that we can change more than our clothes,[8] we must confront and significantly adjust our economic life. Thoreau's discussions in "Economy" and elsewhere suggest that wealth and affluence are problems for at least four significant reasons. First, wealth is simply a distraction from more important things. He believes that "a man is rich in proportion to the number of things which he can afford to let alone."[9] Most importantly, if we spend all our time and attention caring for what he calls the "necessaries" of life, we are to that degree turned away from those humane pursuits he believes constitute greater goods. We'll return below to what he has in mind about these higher goods, but for now it is sufficient to simply note that the imagery is of turning away from the trivial to the important, from the mundane to the meaningful: once the necessities are cared for, an individual is "to adventure on life now, his vacation from humbler toil having commenced."[10] In a famous image, he writes, "He was a lucky fox that left his tail in the trap,"[11] suggesting one should minimize the needs of the body as much as possible for the sake of higher goods. He claims that he has learned to meet all his economic expenses, through good planning and learning to live simply, by working a mere six weeks annually.[12] When we get caught in the trap of making our living, earning our way becomes a hardship rather than a pastime.[13] As we mentioned in the introduction, Thoreau rants in "Life without Principle": "It would be glorious to see mankind at leisure for once. It is nothing but work, work, work . . . I think there is nothing, not even crime, more opposed to poetry, to philosophy, ay, to life itself, than this incessant business."[14] At its simplest, Thoreau's defense of voluntary poverty grows from his fear that attending too much and too seriously to economic affairs is both trivial and wasteful: "Super-fluous wealth can buy superfluities only."[15] He equates luxury with dissipation.[16] Cut away the waste and attend to more important matters. Thoreau comments that he went to Walden to "live deliberately, to front only the essential facts of life, and see if I could not learn what it had to teach, and not, when I came to die, discover that I had not lived."[17] Voluntary poverty is not an end in itself, but it allows us to concentrate on those things that are.

Related to this concern about distraction is a claim about what we might call alienation, or control. In two famous passages, Thoreau writes, first, of men becoming "tools of their tools," and, second, "We do not ride on the railroad; it rides upon us."[18] The idea is simply that the economy (including our technologies) has become a power over us rather than a set of practices and technologies we control as we wish. Similar observations are found in Marx's (and others') writings from the same period and suggest the degree to which modern economic development was taking on a life of its own, seemingly beyond the control of individuals or even social classes. The only cure for losing control of our individual, and even our collective, lives lies "in a rigid economy, a stern and more Spartan simplicity of life and elevation of purpose."[19] Chasing after wealth is not only a distraction, but the economy takes on a life of its own and becomes our master—reversing the appropriate relationship between workers and tools, the economy and the society it should serve.

A powerful third concern relates to the problem of justice. Thoreau is convinced that any society committed to the enthusiastic pursuit of wealth will necessarily generate economic inequality and injustice. He brags that his cabin "was more respected than if it had been surrounded by a file of soldiers," despite there being no lock on the door. It is true that during his stay at Walden a single volume of Homer was taken from his cabin, but Thoreau is nonetheless "convinced, that if all men were to live as simply as I then did, thieving and robbery would be unknown."[20] Property crimes grow from inequality, and if we all lived simply, such inequality would evaporate. In American society, however, such inequality is essential to the economy itself: "The luxury of one class is counterbalanced by the indigence of another."[21] These points about justice received greater development in Thoreau's earlier *Civil Disobedience*. Two of the problems he identifies with wealth in that essay are germane to the problem of justice raised in *Walden*. First, wealth inevitably entangles us with unjust institutions and relationships. Thoreau makes it very clear, for example, that individuals in Massachusetts engaged in business with Southern states simply cannot avoid becoming implicated in the injustices of slavery. Second, these relationships require the mediation and protection of governments, which are themselves thereby implicated in the injustices under consideration. Thoreau sees no way to be actively involved in the pursuit of wealth, in the real world, without requiring the protection of unjust governments, in part for the sake of doing business with unjust partners. In the passage partially referred to above, he explains this interrelationship between economic and political corruption:

> This makes it impossible for a man to live honestly, and at the same time comfortably, in outward respects. It will not be worth the while to accumulate property; that would be sure to go again. You must hire or squat somewhere, and raise but a small crop, and eat that soon. You must live within yourself, and depend upon yourself always tucked up and ready for a start, and not have many affairs. A man may grow rich in Turkey even, if he will be in all respects a good subject of the Turkish government. Confucius said: "If a state is governed by the principles of reason, poverty and misery are subjects of shame; if a state is not governed by the principles of reason, riches and honors are the subjects of shame."[22]

The state in the antebellum United States, of course, was no more governed by "principles of reason" than was the "Turkish government": slavery, imperial war with Mexico, and the genocidal treatment of the Indians were all monstrous injustices stimulated by greed and promoted by the U.S. government. Only voluntary poverty, Thoreau is suggesting, allows individuals to withdraw their support from such injustices and develop just relations with one another. He says in *Walden*, when discussing the arrest that would become the focus of *Civil Disobedience*, that he "was never molested by any person but those who represented the State."[23] For Thoreau, wealth produces unjust inequalities, which inevitably produce hostilities and conflicts between individuals. These, in turn, require the power of the state to impose order and protect unjust relationships. No wonder he believes that the "ways by which you may get money almost without exception lead downward."[24]

A final concern about wealth relates to the problem of personal independence. We know from the above comments by Thoreau that only voluntary poverty can free us from being dependent on the protection of the state. It can also promote our independence in more obviously economic ways. Thoreau greatly distrusts the division of labor, "a principle which should never be followed but with circumspection."[25] When he considers the extreme division of labor promoted by market society, he worries that the logic of this situation could lead even to having others think for us.[26] Instead, he believes we would be much better off if we control our own economic life by making as many goods as we can for ourselves. He was by no means a fanatic or purist on this issue: he would, after all, sell beans raised at Walden Pond for the cash to purchase rice (which he much preferred).[27] Nonetheless, his belief was that the two keys to independence were to care for one's own needs as much as is reasonable, and to need little so these needs can be easily met. Thoreau himself was very skilled with his hands (unlike his friend Emerson, who often relied on Thoreau's help with household tasks and odd jobs), so it did not seem burdensome to him to perform his own gardening and carpentry, for example. It is worth noting, however, that the concern for independence is in some tension with his concern about not letting one's economic life become too burdensome. After all, there are times when hiring others to perform tasks for us both frees our time and (at least potentially) our focus on noneconomic activities; wealth may increase our dependence on others, but it can potentially simplify at least certain aspects of our life. Be that as it may, Thoreau is jealous of his independence, and is proud that he was "more independent than any farmer in Concord."[28]

If these are the four primary reasons Thoreau gives for pursuing a life of voluntary poverty—to focus on what is important, to
maintain control of one's economic life, to promote just relations
with others, and to cultivate personal independence—the question
remains about the focus of the life being freed by this poverty. Here
Thoreau is quite clear, and also somewhat likely to lose the attention
of a present-day audience: the purpose is to focus on the timeless,
the eternal, and the true. In the first volume of his *Journal*, Thoreau had written, "Let us know and conform only to the fashions
of eternity."[29] The second volume contains the comment, "I see
nothing permanent in the society around me";[30] and in a poem, he
writes, "I do not fear my thoughts will die."[31] This preoccupation
with the timeless, eternal, and universal finds full mature expression
and development in *Walden*. He tells us, "In any weather, at any
hour of the day or night, I have been anxious to improve the nick
of time, and notch it on my stick too; to stand on the meeting of
two eternities, the past and the future, which is precisely the present moment; to toe that line."[32] Living in the present makes time
disappear, and allows one the experience of eternity. Contemporary
life in American society, however, is preoccupied with the transient
and the ephemeral: "I perceive that we inhabitants of New England
live this mean life that we do because our vision does not penetrate
the surface of things." If contemporary life did achieve this pene-
tration, it would see our daily affairs as "shams and delusions," in
contrast to the "true and sublime" found in "eternity."[33] As he suggests, "Time is but the stream I go a-fishing in. . . . Its thin current
slides away, but eternity remains."[34] Thoreau is not afraid to use
overtly religious language to make this most important point: "God
himself culminates in the present moment, and will never be more
divine in the lapse of all the ages."[35] *Walden* opens with an extended
discussion of economic life and the need to restrain and simplify our
bodily wants, needs, and concerns; it culminates in an awakening
to the eternal and the true. Indeed, we can think of his position as
a gloss on and elaboration of the claim in the Gospel of Matthew,
"You cannot serve God and mammon."[36] Make no mistake about
this point: for Thoreau, what is at stake in this transcendence of

conventional economic, social, and political life is participation in the immortal: "In accumulating property for ourselves or our posterity, in founding a family or a state, or acquiring fame even, we are mortal; but in dealing with truth we are immortal, and need fear no change nor accident."[37] It requires faith to believe that our material needs will be sufficiently cared for, were we to take his advice and submit to voluntary poverty. But, as Thoreau tells us early in "Economy," "I think that we may safely trust a good deal more than we do."[38] The stakes, obviously, couldn't be higher for him.

Two images from *Walden*'s "Conclusion" illustrate and drive Thoreau's point home. The first, about the artist in the city of Kouroo, is the tale of a man seeking perfection. Having decided to make a staff, he seeks to devote the rest of his life to making it perfect: "His singleness of purpose and resolution, and his elevated piety, endowed him, without his knowledge, with perennial youth. As he made no compromise with Time, Time kept out of his way, and only sighed at a distance because he could not overcome him." His work was so purely motivated and focused that he remained young while his friends grew old and died, cities rose and fell, and "Brahma had awoke and slumbered many times." The completed staff turns out to be ideally formed, representing not only the staff but a new system for understanding how perfection comes into being: "And now he saw by the heap of shavings still fresh at his feet, that, for him and his work, the former lapse of time had been an illusion, and that no more time had elapsed than is required for a single scintillation from the brain of Brahma to fall on and inflame the tinder of a mortal brain. The material was pure, and his art was pure; how could the result be other than wonderful?"[39]

The second image, from the book's penultimate paragraph, is about a story his contemporaries in New England were likely to have heard, of a "strong and beautiful bug" that emerged from the wood of an apple tree that had been made into a table that stood for sixty years in a farmer's kitchen. "Who does not feel his faith in a resurrection and immortality strengthened by hearing of this? Who knows what beautiful and winged life, whose egg has been buried for ages under many concentric layers of woodenness in the dead dry life of society ... may unexpectedly come forth from amidst society's most trivial and handselled [given as a gift] furniture, to enjoy its perfect summer life at last!"[40] Both of these passages suggest the need to cut away the trivial, to focus on the pure and the timeless, and in this way stimulate a kind of resurrection. When Thoreau repeatedly demands an "elevation of purpose," it is this focus on the present he has in mind. This is the realm of thoughtfulness, of poetry and art, of philosophy and timeless ideas Thoreau charges us to turn to in "Life without Principle" when he puns, "Read not the Times. Read the Eternities."[41] This is why, in the concluding passages of *Walden*, he writes, "I delight to come to my bearings,—not walk in procession with pomp and parade, in a conspicuous place, but to walk even with the Builder of the universe, if I may,—not to live in this restless, nervous, bustling, trivial Nineteenth Century, but stand or sit thoughtfully while it goes by."[42] Voluntary poverty opens the possibility of changing our focus from the lower to the higher, from the transient to the timeless, from the false to the true, from the profane to the sacred. Again, Thoreau's project of voluntary poverty is nothing if not ambitious to the extreme.[43]

Thoreau's desire to shift his, and our, focus from the transient to the permanent is of a piece with the moral theory we find imbuing all his works. When he declares that "men labor under a mistake" in *Walden*, this is a practical error, but also a moral mistake through and through. It causes us to focus on the less important elements of life and thereby profoundly distorts our moral sense. If we focus our moral attention on the world of ever-shifting relationships and events—what he refers to in the above-noted passage from "Life without Principle" as all the knowledge we find in the "Times," our newspapers—our moral calculation will reflect these realities; it will be utilitarian and consequentialist, or, in the language used in *Civil Disobedience*, it will be "expedient." Thoreau clearly ties voluntary poverty to living philosophically, or, what is the same in his view, morally. Recall the passage from *Civil Disobedience* referred to above, "You must hire or squat somewhere, and raise but a small crop, and eat that soon." The case Thoreau makes against wealth, and politics, is that when we allow the press of events to shape our moral thinking, we inevitably lose sight of the deeper moral principles in play and succumb instead to moral opportunism. In *Civil Disobedience* he explicitly attacks the utilitarianism of William Paley, who taught that moral evaluation was best thought of as "a computation of the quantity of the danger and grievance on the one side, and of the probability and expense of redressing it on the other," and the selection, at the end of the day, of the least bad outcome. Such reasoning, Thoreau suspects, becomes a cover for opportunism, a willingness to cut one's losses and compromise with evil for the sake of security and peace. Put bluntly, it becomes a rationalization for accepting the world as it is—even in its most unjust forms. Moral choice, however, requires a willingness to sacrifice for the good, to do what's right, consequences be damned: "Paley appears never to have contemplated those cases to which the rule of expediency does not apply, in which a people, as well as an individual, must do justice, cost what it may. If I have unjustly wrested a plank from a drowning man, I must restore it to him though I drown myself. This, according to Paley, would be inconvenient. But he that would save his life, in such a case, shall lose it."[44] To the degree we become consequentialist choosers in our public life, Thoreau believes, we blind ourselves to the essential moral facts. This is why he charges politicians such as Daniel Webster with failing to "face the facts" concerning the evils of slavery:

> Statesmen and legislators, standing so completely within the institution, never distinctly and nakedly behold it. They speak of moving society, but have no resting-place without it. They may be men of a certain experience and discrimination, and have no doubt invented ingenious and even useful systems, for which we sincerely thank them; but all their wit and usefulness lie within certain not very wide limits. They are wont to forget that the world is not governed by policy and expediency. Webster never goes behind government, and so cannot speak with authority about it. His words are wisdom to those legislators who contemplate no essential reform in the existing government; but for thinkers, and those who legislate for all time, he never once glances at the subject.[45]

It is the "resting-place without it," a moral position outside the press of events, uncorrupted by these events, that Thoreau seeks. Only such a resting-place will allow us to both see and cherish the timeless principles that, in fact, govern the world. Without it, we are blinded by our interests and rationalize our privileges in an unjust society. Thoreau's point about personal life is the same: when we are invested in the broader economy, we are unable to gain a moral perspective sufficient to make clear our own participation in unjust relationships and institutions. As we've seen, "this makes it impossible for a man to live honestly, and at the same time comfortably, in outward respects." To prevent this corruption of our interests, we must withdraw from these powerful forces. The case for voluntary poverty is a case for clarity of moral vision, a case for avoiding the circumstances that inevitably confuse, blur, and compromise this vision.

It is important to note that this voluntary poverty, for Thoreau, is neither primitive nor ascetic, at least in any sense of reveling in loss and hardship. Regarding the first point, he asks why we shouldn't combine the "hardiness" of "savages" with the "intellectualness" of "civilized man."[46] He is not promoting a return to "uncivilized" or premodern modes of life; he is instead proposing a radical simplification of our economic life for the sake of cultivating the best that civilization has to offer: "It is asserted that civilization is a real advantage in the condition of man,—and I think that it is, though only the wise improve their advantages."[47] This is a personal observation parallel to his plea at the end of "Reading," referred to in our introduction (and returned to again in our conclusion), for American villages and towns to become patrons of philosophy and culture. For both individuals and villages, Thoreau's desire is a world with the highest achievements of civilization. His argument is for a correct prioritizing of the values that civilization, properly understood, represents. Regarding the question of sacrifice or self-denial, he is never promoting a melancholy or self-punishing attitude. On the contrary, Thoreau explicitly condemns the "melodious cursing of God and enduring him forever" that he believes he finds in New England's hymn books. "Our manners have been corrupted by communication with the saints," by which he means those who "had rather consoled the fears than confirmed the hopes of man." Indeed, he claims, "There is nowhere recorded a simple and irrepressible satisfaction with the gift of life, any memorable praise of God."[48] His goal is a deeply pleasurable and rewarding life, one to be embraced with enthusiasm as the greatest good available to mortal persons. Thoreau would have us believe that the wealth that makes us "rich in proportion to the number of things" we "can afford to let alone"[49] is the deepest and most rewarding form of wealth. A life lived according to the principles of voluntary poverty would provide the greatest pleasure and satisfaction, and not merely provide consolation or comfort for our sorrow. Voluntary poverty opens the door to the possibility of experiencing the highest human goods. It is not only our duty, but most importantly our satisfaction, he believes he is promoting.

It is worth noting that the position Thoreau is defending is informed by a conception of ethical life many today will find odd, or perhaps even antithetical to a proper understanding of what ethics demands of us. At a recent lecture at a state university, a philosophy professor was presenting the famous thought experiment discussed by Peter Singer about a boy in danger of drowning in a pond: An individual witnessing this is in a position to save the boy but will ruin his expensive shoes in the process. Should he save the boy or his shoes? Clearly, he should save the boy, since the value of the shoes is trivial compared to the value of a human life. Singer uses the example as a device for beginning to think about our obligations to make small (and perhaps not so small) sacrifices for the sake of larger goods. What was interesting in this lecture was that the philosopher asked the audience to give reasons for why they would feel obliged to save the boy in the pond. One student suggested that he would have to save the boy because he "couldn't live with himself" if he didn't. The philosopher responded (humorously!) by accusing the student of "narcissism," worrying about himself, when he should be worried about others.

This response, even given the humor with which it was delivered, was telling and significant. For the contemporary academic philosopher, and for many in the community at large, ethics is fundamentally a discipline concerned with decision-making procedures and principles for dealing with dilemmas and competing values that arise in the regular course of affairs. Such a conception suggests that we must evaluate these dilemmas from a disinterested and impersonal perspective according to either utilitarian (as in Singer's case) or deontological (in the case of neo-Kantian philosophers) principles. When the student implied that he was beginning from a conception of who he was, he was violating the very starting point—disinterestedness—that the philosopher was assuming as the first move in any ethical analysis.

Thoreau, on the other hand, represents an older conception of ethics that would be much more sympathetic to the student's comment. From this perspective, the first questions of ethics concern ourselves, the kind of person we wish to be, the kind of life we wish to live. Ethical analysis first asks who we are, and only then turns to what we should do. For Singer and the philosopher referred to above, we must approach ethics by first forgetting ourselves. For Thoreau, we must approach it by first asking what a successful— happy, decent, satisfying—human life would look like. There are no algorithms (utilitarian or otherwise) that will solve particular dilemmas. Instead, there are sensibilities and values to be cultivated for the sake of a good life, which will inform our responses to moral choices when they arise. Thoreau's sympathies lie much more with the ancient (or today, "virtue ethics") conception of the ethical life than the contemporary perspective. Not only does this approach not insist upon disinterestedness; it requires, on the contrary, a strong conception of the self and what it is that will make that individual flourish in the most humane and rewarding ways. Contemporary ethics focuses on restraint and limitation; Thoreau's ethics focus on human flourishing. The former has a constrained and uninspiring conception of what the human self in fact is ("selfish" in the most mundane ways, which is why disinterestedness is essential to ethical calculation); the latter has a conception of what the human self can be if we have an expansive conception of our most ennobling possibilities. Even if these different moral perspectives would suggest similar courses of action in a given case—for example, pulling the drowning child out of the pond—it is clear that the philosopher mentioned above has a very different conception of the first requirements of an ethical life than does Thoreau (or, for that matter, Aristotle). It is this difference that allows Thoreau to conceive of his ethical project as one of personal fulfillment rather than renunciation.[50]

Voluntary poverty is clearly a central component of Thoreau's conception of an ethical life. Yet there are two passages in *Walden* that raise questions about all we have said about Thoreau's defense of voluntary poverty thus far. The first of these concerns the "Complemental Verses. The Pretensions of Poverty," verses from a masque by Thomas Carew that Thoreau inserts between the end of "Economy" and the beginning of the next chapter, "Where I Lived, and What I Lived For." In these lines, the god Mercury criticizes what he takes to be the pretentiousness of a personified Poverty: "Thou dost presume too much, poor needy wretch, / To claim a station in the firmament, / Because thy humble cottage, or thy tub, / Nurses some lazy or pedantic virtue." The true heroes of the world, such as Hercules, Achilles, and Theseus, are unbounded, active creatures, but poverty makes us docile and withdrawn: it "degradeth nature, and benumbeth sense, And, Gorgon-like, turns active men to stone." Mercury orders Poverty back to "thy loath'd cell" (earlier called "thy tub") to "study to know but what those worthies were."[51] What are we to make of this challenge to the poverty Thoreau has been championing here? Perhaps no more than to recognize that Thoreau is as sensitive to the "pretentions of poverty" as he is to the possibilities it presents. Just before the end of "Economy," he charges the reader to become "one of the worthies of the world,"[52] so he is well aware of the concern raised by Carew: that his project can lead to a passive self-righteousness that is, in fact, impotent and presumptuous, rather than an active, direct and energized engagement with life. He is proposing no disengagement with what is essential and is aware that it would be easy for the poverty he promotes to become an end in itself, a "lazy or pedantic virtue" well pleased with itself. By including these "Complemental Verses," Thoreau is warning his reader not to confuse the method with the purpose or end aspired to. Voluntary poverty, as he defends it, must be a means to allow vigorous and joyful living, to help us to become "worthies of the world." We must beware of allowing this poverty to become a self-righteous end in itself, an outward sign of what would actually be, in truth, "low" and "abject" and mediocre, in addition to passive. This insertion of these verses is Thoreau's honest warning about possible pitfalls of his own project.

More troubling is the passage from "Baker Farm," where Thoreau tells of his meeting with John Field, an Irish laborer living in a previously abandoned shack with his wife and "several children" (including a "wrinkled, sibyl-like, cone-headed infant").[53] Thoreau, on a fishing expedition, gets caught in a rainstorm and takes cover in Field's home. The portrait is bleak: the roof leaks, the family is good-natured and brave yet clearly short of food; Field is obviously an honest and hard-working man, but plainly "shiftless."[54] The family shares their hut with their chickens, and they are apparently unable to win any battles against the prevailing dirt and disorder. Field supports his family by "bogging," that is, cutting the turf in meadows with a spade for farmers who want to bring the land into cultivation. The work is hard, poorly paid, and requires heavy clothes and boots. Thoreau recognizes that he cuts a very different figure than Field. He appears as a "loafer," in lighter clothing, who lives in a "tight light and clean house," without great effort or exertion. He explains to Field that as his (Thoreau's) work is less strenuous, he requires less meat, butter, and milk to renew his energy, and he can wear less durable clothing. Field could do the same: "If he and his family would live simply, they might all go a-huckleberrying in the summer for their amusement."[55] Field sighs at this idea, but he and his wife are unable to fully imagine how Thoreau's discoveries could possibly apply to their lives. In fact, despite their poverty, they consider their move to America to have been a success, as here they have access to the beef, milk, coffee, and tea Thoreau counsels them to consider living without. Thoreau prissily criticizes their judgment: "But the only true America is that country where you are at liberty to pursue such a mode of life as may enable you to do without these, and where the state does not endeavor to compel you to sustain the slavery and war and other superfluous expenses which directly or indirectly result from the use of such things."[56] He did what he could to be a good guest (he drank the dirty water that was offered, since he was "not squeamish in such cases where manners are concerned"),[57] and set off after the storm to resume his expedition. Although Field had declined Thoreau's offer to join him fishing, he changed his mind in the end: "But he, poor man, disturbed only a couple of fins while I was catching a fair string, and he said it was his luck; but when we changed seats in the boat luck changed seats too. Poor John Field!"[58] Thoreau concludes he was "born to be poor, with his inherited Irish poverty or poor life, his Adam's grandmother and boggy ways, not to rise in this world, he nor his posterity, till their wading webbed bogtrotting feet get *talaria* to their heels."[59] Thoreau had determined, he tells us, to speak with Field as "if he were a philosopher, or desired to be one,"[60] but he recognizes that Field was unlikely to read his account of their encounter, and to be improved by it.[61] Even though Thoreau had persuaded him to take the afternoon off from bogging, Field's poverty looked more intractable than Thoreau's—more an inheritance than a choice, something that shaped him rather than something he could himself freely shape. Thoreau appears genuinely baffled by Field: *Could* he live as Thoreau does, after all? Or is there something about Field's poverty, or his Irish heritage, that makes this impossible?

This passage can obviously make one quite uncomfortable about Thoreau's attitude toward individuals whose poverty is significantly less voluntary than his own. Gavin Jones, for example, writes that Thoreau appears to be frustrated by those for whom "the culture of the poor might be a response to their social situation rather than an effort to transcend it":

> His anger emerged from the seemingly fixed values of the poor who adhere to ways of life that directly contravene the belief that poverty can be anything like an ideal state. Thoreau's uncultured wealthy are "poor," yet at least they have the potential to change their lives, of becoming spiritually rich by adopting the voluntary poverty that *Walden* expounds. The uncultured poor, however, are destitute in a double sense because they lack even this potential for choice and regeneration, so absolute is their degraded lifestyle.[62]

Lawrence Buell is more sympathetic to Thoreau's claims about simplicity and voluntary poverty, viewing him as a significant contributor to an admirable tradition seeking "self-imposed moral and economic limits" against the mainstream of American liberalism.[63] Jones, however, expresses the frustration many readers have with what they take to be Thoreau's patronizing middle-class moralism and a significant lack of appreciation for the very real difficulties experienced by the "degraded poor," whom Thoreau contrasts in "Economy" to the "degraded rich."[64] One can easily imagine a reader of "Baker Farm" feeling deeply uneasy about the degree to which Thoreau's middle-class privilege allows for a tone-deaf (at best) response to the difficulties confronted by a poor Irish family.

Be this as it may—and I share with Jones a discomfort with the patronizing tone of this passage, which I consider to be the ugliest moment in *Walden*—this should not distract us from the main claims Thoreau wants to make. Even if he was unsure about how to approach the *involuntary* poor, there are two important points to remember. The first is that Thoreau was very critical of any social and economic order that produced the involuntary poor in the first place. When he observes that in our own society "the luxury of one class is counterbalanced by the indigence of another," he is clearly critical of the practices that have produced this inequality and the indigence of the "degraded poor." When considering the power and influence of the railroad, he admits that it is a "*comparatively*" good thing the poor Irish have accomplished with their labor in this country. By "comparatively," however, he only means, "that is, you might have done worse; but I wish, as you are brothers of mine, that you could have spent your time better than digging in this dirt."[65] He may not have a fully developed understanding of how best to counsel those made poor and degraded by the poverty created by our current social order. It is beyond a doubt, however, that Thoreau makes no apologies for the economy that produces this order. The second point is that he does in fact have a suggestion for how to approach this broader question of the social order as a whole: those in a position where they can meaningfully *choose* poverty, simplicity, and a turning away from the luxuries stimulated by the market economy should make this choice immediately and for their own sake. By working to become "worthies" of the world, individuals will be turning away from the luxury that generates inequality, injustice, and the "degraded poor" in the first place. Regardless of our judgment about how effective Thoreau's plan of voluntary poverty may be, it is obvious that he is much more interested in promoting a transformation of contemporary society than he is in only ameliorating or softening its current effects. Readers will disagree about whether or not Thoreau is promoting a useful radicalism, but, useful or not, his radical intentions are clear: voluntary poverty is a part of his program for challenging the inequalities and injustices, and the dissatisfactions, of contemporary American society.

THOREAU ONCE WROTE IN his *Journal*, "We live by exaggeration."[66] Years later, he wrote to a friend about his inclination to exaggerate: "I trust that you realize what an exaggerator I am,—that I lay myself out to exaggerate whenever I have an opportunity,—pile Pelion upon Ossa, to reach heaven so. Expect no trivial truth from me, unless I am on the witness-stand."[67] This rhetorical technique was helpful both for getting his audience's attention and for provoking them, allowing him to be, at times, outrageous while drawing stark and clear lines of moral demarcation. It was an artistic technique, the poet's license, to drive his point home by overdrawing it. So, for example, he writes, "With respect to luxuries and comforts, the wisest have ever lived a more simple and meagre life than the poor." Taken literally, this is a claim that could drive a poor person crazy; who is this middle-class man to suggest that the wise have lived more meager lives than that forced upon me! Understood as a provocative rhetorical tool used to address his (relatively) affluent audience, however, the claim is one that might well lead to some soul-searching about living a simpler, less materialistic, and less consumer-oriented life.

He self-consciously piles "Pelion upon Ossa, to reach heaven," but his more literal-minded readers, and all readers looking for exactly the kind of practical reforms Thoreau suggests we must seek, are left to sort out the details of exactly what this "voluntary poverty" would look like if we were to seek it. One fairly radical take on this can be found in the examples of those Mark Sundeen calls "unsettlers," individuals who seek to radically simplify their lives and live in the closest harmony with the natural world they can achieve. "Unsettlers" are tempted to submit to all the constraints of nature as a kind of liberation from what they view as the moral emptiness and violent hypocrisy of modern society. These individuals not only recognize but embrace to some significant degree the confining limits of nature. One such individual, Ethan Hughes, founded the Possibility Alliance and established a cooperative permaculture farm in Missouri, where members live simply and as lightly as possible on the land: they use no electricity or petroleum products, participate only minimally in the cash economy and at a level well under the poverty line, have no flush toilets, live in very small and simple homes, and will use automobiles and modern medicine only in emergencies. Hughes believes, "The greatest conspiracy on the planet is that we need to oppress, kill, and pollute in order to get our needs met."[68] Inspired in part by Thoreau, Hughes and other "unsettlers" hope to extricate themselves from participation in what is thought to be an unjust, unhappy, and unsustainable society; a basic goal is to "not depend on the [social] system anymore."[69] This withdrawal, in fact, is viewed as the greatest challenge the hated system can face: if people simply refuse to participate in these broader institutions, they will collapse under their own weight. Individuals such as Hughes believe they are both affirming a more humane life and significantly challenging the legitimacy of what they view as the inhumane and unjust world at large.[70]

It is easy to find ammunition to criticize "unsettlers" such as Hughes. The claim of hypocrisy, or, at least naïveté, will be raised by those who point to the experience of Hughes's wife, who became very ill after giving birth. She required nine months of hospitalization, which generated a bill of $17,000, paid for by Medicaid because the family was living a subsistence life and had no savings and no medical insurance. The extreme implications of the family's ideology might have been to let the woman die, and we can be grateful that they failed to have the courage of their convictions in this case, even if it forced them to depend both on modern technology and the significant wealth of their fellow citizens. This example is entirely predictable, but there were other losses in this particular family's choice to withdraw from the corruptions of modern life that are less obvious at first glance. The young mother had been trained as a classical singer in her youth and young adulthood. Living as a homesteader confined the family and their limited community of like-minded individuals—who refused to travel to cities to experience the arts found there, and who likewise rejected modern electronic access to the universe of recorded and broadcast music— to the folk arts they could produce for themselves. To fully reject modern society is not only to reject industrialism, technology, and administration: it is to reject much of the arts and learning that are all of a piece with the rest.[71]

Yet, for all the excesses, paradoxes, and suspected hypocrisies of those who wish to reject the modern control of nature, Sundeen is certainly right to find evidence among his unsettlers of a "stream that runs through our history—a stream that has not yet prevailed but refuses to die."[72] Although it is true that the extremity of Hughes's solution to the problem of voluntary poverty places it beyond what most American citizens would choose (and well beyond what many such citizens could survive with), Hughes and his cohort nonetheless share a kind of entrepreneurial courage and commitment often admired in other contexts. Probably the greatest weakness to their experiment is similar to a great weakness often identified in Thoreau's reform projects: a seeming unwillingness to fully admit or appreciate the degree to which we are all implicated in the broader society around us, from the technology and energy that produces the bicycles the Hughes's believe are acceptable technologies of transportation, to the safety net of modern medicine (and the universe of science and technology it draws upon) that is available if and when required, to say nothing of the roads traveled on to access medical services. What this suggests, however, isn't necessarily a failure of the unsettler project, unless we are being more scrupulously judgmental than is probably warranted. Complete submission to nature is obviously not possible this side of death. What the unsettlers provide is a particularly aggressive attempt to readjust and rebalance our relationship to the natural order. Even if they represent an extreme solution to this problem, they are still very much a part of this broader "stream that has not yet prevailed" and "refuses to die."

We can see elements of the same concern among much less marginal groups in American society. Andrew Bacevich, a widely respected historian and public intellectual, fears that freedom in the contemporary United States has been degraded to little more than a form of profligacy—a profligacy that has corrupted the state by demanding the satisfaction of our ever-expanding material wants.[73] Political theorist Patrick Deneen worries that our desire to master nature reflects a corruption of our moral sensibilities: "Nature comes to be viewed as a recalcitrant opponent of our ability to realize our diversity of faculties, requiring a massive project of overcoming its manifold limits, in the first instance by mastering the natural world in every possible respect . . . and ultimately our own natures, such as mere bodily limits of longevity, our genetic code, and of course, sexual identity and reproduction."[74] Environmentalist Bill McKibben argues that our endless consumerism promotes an isolating individualism, compromising our communities and producing a perverse form of wealthy unhappiness.[75] Legal scholar Jedediah Purdy argues that this rage of wants is also threatening our democratic possibilities: "Democratic failures are often failures to impose self-restraint, and self-restraint is exactly what environmental politics needs."[76] Novelist Ann Patchett publishes a widely discussed account of her experiment to avoid (unnecessary) shopping for a year.[77] This quick sampling of concerns could be multiplied significantly, and it doesn't even touch on the lively popular and advice literature about uncluttering our lives, getting our spending habits under control, and trying not to let consumerism distort our moral sensibilities.[78] Many of us suspect that our desires have become powerful and ungoverned, and that this threatens our environment, corrupts our politics, suppresses our communal life, and damages our happiness. The level of voluntary poverty sought by

Sundeen's unsettlers may be beyond the reach (or desire) of most Americans, but it is not at all unusual to hear laments about how subversive our wealth is to our most considered purposes.

The difference between Ethan Hughes and other critics of American wealth, consumerism, and materialism is one of degree and not of kind. It is obvious that there are elements of the modern world even Hughes will not abandon if he could (which, in any literal sense, would be impossible anyhow; we are simply too embedded in the world to imagine a life that disavows the entirety of this embeddedness), even though he aggressively renounces much more than most critics of American profligacy. This is just another way of saying, perhaps, that "voluntary poverty" is a relative, rather than an absolute, term. It is best understood as a form of moderation, rather than a radical rejection of the present world. Keep in mind that Thoreau believed the wise learn to use civilization properly, rather than reject it entirely.

The fear that wealth and luxury are tied to injustice is an ancient one. In *The Republic*, Glaucon accuses Socrates of constructing an imaginary city so barren of pleasure that the citizens, though moderate and just, would be unhappy. Socrates had imagined they could feast on bread made of wheat and barley, drink wine, and enjoy sex moderately enough to keep the population within their means to support. At Glaucon's prodding, however, delicacies such as olives, cheeses, and desserts are added to the imagined diet, and then even more is demanded: that the citizens should recline on couches, dine at tables, and enjoy the fancy foods known in contemporary Athens. Once these elements are incorporated, however, the imaginary city becomes luxurious and "feverish." Socrates suggests that once such pleasures are unleashed, there will be the need for more land to produce greater wealth. There will also be a need for larger armies to both protect this wealth and to make war on neighbor's resources. Wealth, in short, exacerbates powerful desires, which in turn produces unjust impulses and actions.[79] The biblical contrast between the luxuries ("flesh pots") of Egypt and the promised land of milk and honey provides a similar message about wealthy but unjust empires and moderate pastoral justice and simplicity.[80] In modern political theory, Rousseau provides perhaps the most famous and provocative example of a similar argument in the dedication of his *Discourse on the Origin of Inequality* to his native Geneva. The relatively simple and provincial city of his birth is imagined as the model of republican virtue, and contrasted to "the grandeur of palaces, the beauty of carriages, the sumptuous furnishings, the pomp of spectacles, and all the refinements of softness and luxury" found in cosmopolitan, sophisticated, and unjust Paris.[81]

In the American tradition, Aldo Leopold, one of the most thoughtful and influential environmental thinkers of the twentieth century, is concerned about this same problem. Leopold is best known for promoting a moral idea he calls the "land ethic." He argues for an expansion of our ethical perspectives, from a focus on the relations between human beings to a moral understanding of the human relationship with the rest of the natural world. Most famously, he argues for a new ethical understanding of the land as a whole, which "changes the role of *Homo sapiens* from conqueror of the land-community to plain member and citizen of it."[82] He believes that such an ethic can be informed by, indeed can grow from, our increasing ecological knowledge. Leopold's experience as a forester for the U.S. Forest Service, and then as a professor of game management at the University of Wisconsin, suggested to him that our scientific knowledge of ecology is great enough now to understand that people are best understood as members of the much broader biotic community. This is the idea that modern environmentalists have been most excited about developing and criticizing in the generations after Leopold's death in 1949.[83]

The broader thrust of Leopold's thought, however, is hinted at by his claim, in "The Land Ethic," about why it is we are reluctant to embrace this increasingly obvious need to expand our moral universe: the corruption of our moral vision by short-sighted and even vulgar economic self-interest.[84] Here we find the theme that stretches across the full range of his writings, an attack on the utilitarianism of modern (mainly economic) thinking, and an appeal to an older, broader, less materialistic set of values. While this theme obviously shares with "The Land Ethic" a concern about the current state of our ethical vision, the deeper stream of Leopold's thinking looks more to restoration of this vision than the invention of an altogether new one.[85] Here, rather than with his land ethic, we find Leopold most helpful for thinking about the program of voluntary poverty.

The problem Leopold identifies with modern utilitarianism is twofold. First, by reducing our values to economic considerations, our understanding of the world becomes narrowed to market relationships. In his beautiful *A Sand County Almanac*, he tells us that the two "spiritual dangers" of not owning a farm are "supposing that breakfast comes from the grocery" and thinking that "heat comes from the furnace."[86] Modern society makes us ignorant of the basic processes hidden by modern commerce and technology. We come to know the world through commercial transactions and technological processes that we don't begin to understand or place within any broader context. A great simplification of understanding takes place. A deeper knowledge of the world is replaced with an illusion that the grocery and the furnace are the sources of the goods that answer to our wants and needs. We develop a tunnel vision that sees only the built world, and fails to see, let alone appreciate, the natural objects and processes that underlay the modern economy. Second, this tunnel vision leads us to a specifically moral blindness: it promotes the "modern dogma" of "comfort at any cost."[87] What Leopold understands as the short-sighted economics of consumer satisfaction actually blinds us to deeper human goods, such as adventure and beauty.[88] Throughout his career Leopold was disgusted by the American preoccupation with material wealth and economic development. In 1923, he wrote, "In past and more outspoken days conservation was put in terms of decency rather than dollars."[89] A year later a similar criticism was sounded: "Do economists know about lupines?"[90] He criticizes the "Boosters" and "Babbitts" of the American economy, and argues that we are being overwhelmed by a false, and shallow, conception of progress.[91] Just as Thoreau believed the "expediency" of politicians and businessmen debased their moral evaluations, so Leopold contends that economic calculation threatened to blind us to all other moral commitments and values. If we are to value wilderness, for example, as a part of life with little or no economic utility, we will need to contain, limit, and control the economic impulse and perspective.[92]

So, what does he have in mind as an alternative to this modern sensibility? He wants to promote, instead, what he calls "split-rail Americanism," the attitudes and knowledge he believes to have been stimulated by the frontier and conventional rural life.[93] Like his neighbor in Madison, Frederick Jackson Turner, Leopold worries that the technology and comforts of contemporary life are leading to a corruption of the American character: "For three centuries the environment has determined the character of our development; it may, in fact, be said that, coupled with the character of our racial stocks, it is the very stuff America is made of. Shall we now exterminate this thing that made us American?"[94] The mechanized world undermines our "split-rail" values of self-sufficiency and self-restraint, replacing it with a utilitarianism that worships "comfort at any cost." His task as a conservationist and educator is to provide a strategy for American citizens to rediscover these earlier values by pushing back against the utilitarianism of modern society. As he tells us in the foreword to *A Sand County Almanac*, it is by spending time on his farm that he and his family "try to rebuild, with shovel and axe, what we are losing elsewhere. It is here that we seek—and still find—our meat from God."[95] His aim, in the *Almanac* and elsewhere, is to inspire others to resist "too much modernity."[96] Conservation is a practical end in itself, but it is more than this—it is also a means to a broader political project of encouraging Americans to temper their utilitarian desires and to discover other significant human goods, from beauty to adventure to modesty and humility before nature. Such a "shift in values," he believes, is best achieved by "reappraising things unnatural, tame, and confined in terms of things natural, wild, and free."[97] The careful means by which Leopold introduces the reader of the *Almanac* to the natural world around the sand farm is only his most artistic attempt to promote this broader sensibility as a counterweight to the world fashioned by the modern economy. As we will see in chapter 3, Wendell Berry argues that we need to return to a more modest, thrifty, and conserving economy if we are to significantly combat the violence we currently unleash both against the land and toward one another. Leopold is making a similar argument about the need to moderate our consumer wants for the sake of conservation and in order to live more satisfying lives. Moderation is the key to addressing our environmental and many of our human difficulties. In the *Almanac*, Leopold is not only teaching us where heat and food come from; he is also teaching us to see the beauty of, to feel awe before, and revel in the experience of the natural world.

When we think of the Thoreauvian promotion of "voluntary poverty," we probably do best to think of it in terms such as these: as a moderating and reorienting force, rather than as a radical break with the contemporary world. There is an obvious prudential reason for this: we are, without a doubt, much more likely to reorient than to reinvent society. To suggest this is by no means to underestimate the difficulty or even unlikelihood of such a reorientation. Nonetheless, to build on elements of our shared experiences and histories is a much more promising project than to overthrow these traditions altogether and begin the world anew. This prudential consideration also points to a moral issue: we can imagine moderating and reorienting our practices without setting in motion deep and violent social dislocations, but it is hard to see how any radical project of reinvention could prevent both excessive and unintended perverse outcomes.

For the intellectual historian Christopher Lasch, whom George Scialabba calls "our premier social critic,"[98] this reorientation would require a championing of what he identifies and defends as the "sensibility of the petty bourgeoisie."[99] Unlike Aldo Leopold and Wendell Berry, Lasch's populism is not grounded in an agrarian (or frontier) tradition, but it cuts more generally across the whole modern economy.[100] Lasch shares with Berry, however, the view that the spirit of science, even more than of capitalism, is the source of the desire to master nature and produce a world of universal abundance.[101] This is, however, a destructive and self-defeating fantasy, Lasch believes, both for ecological and political reasons. In light of what he assumes to be increasingly obvious environmental limits to economic growth, it is simply no longer realistic to pursue expanding economies; the "belated discovery that the earth's ecology will no longer sustain an indefinite expansion of productive forces deals the final blow to the belief in progress."[102] The belief in and unbounded commitment to economic progress and the mastery of nature has led American society to champion abundance over justice and equity. What Lasch identifies as the tradition of "progressive optimism," or what others would call the liberal mainstream of American social and political values, is built on "a denial of the natural limits on human power and freedom" and "cannot survive for very long in a world in which an awareness of these limits has become inescapable."[103] The tradition of progressive liberalism, however, gives us few resources for thinking about the natural resource and moral limits demanded by a serious commitment to equality, justice, and what would today be called "sustainability": "Equality now implies a more modest standard of living for all, not an extension of the lavish standards enjoyed by the favored classes in the industrial nations to the rest of the world. In the twenty-first century, equality implies a recognition of limits, both moral and material, that finds little support in the progressive tradition."[104]

Historian Jill Lepore once called the book in which Lasch made these arguments in greatest detail, *The True and Only Heaven*, his "grumpiest,"[105] but we would be hard pressed to describe his final book, *The Revolt of the Elites*, written during his final illness and appearing four years after *Heaven*, as any less grumpy. At the end of his life, Lasch was convinced that the elites in the United States were incapable of either understanding or accepting the "natural . . . moral and material" limits promoted in the earlier book. But although the elite classes have been utterly corrupted by luxury and power, the more modest values of the "lower middle class" continue to find a home in nonelite communities. Contemporary elites have essentially become cosmopolitan tourists in their own societies, which is not a perspective "likely to encourage a passionate devotion to democracy."[106] In contrast to the enclaves of privilege, it is "middle-class neighborhoods that sustained a vigorous civic culture."[107] These civic cultures reject the kind of individualism we find among elites, an individualism that encourages both consumerism and a preoccupation with personal professional achievement, and an indifference to inequality. The middle and working classes, in contrast, seek more modest and stable communities. Whereas elites value overcoming, mastery, continual progress, and personal gratification, nonelites are much more likely to "understand, as their betters do not, that there are inherent limits on human control over the course of social development, over nature and the body, over the tragic elements in human life and history."[108] They are more likely to embrace the communal goods of family, religion, sacrifice, and community. In short, for Lasch, the elite classes have lost the social virtues that are only preserved in the groups least associated with the power, prestige, and accomplishments publicly championed in the media, intellectual circles, and professional life: "In an age that fancies itself as disillusioned, this is the one illusion—the illusion of mastery—that remains as tenacious as ever."[109] Tenacious, that is, among the minority who shape the governing values of society. Lasch's populism imagines a natural home for alternative and more attractive values among common working people, even as these values are increasingly held in contempt by social, political, intellectual, and commercial elites.

Richard Rorty's critical review of *Revolt of the Elites* nicely illustrates what's at stake in the debate between the Thoreauvian tradition of moderation and the broader celebration of progress in American life. Lasch's populism, Rorty claims, was built on a "nostalgic romanticism in which he specialized."[110] In Rorty's view, the elites Lasch loathed were responsible, in the second half of the twentieth century, for making the United States "into a less self-righteous, more self-aware, and more just country," and Lasch's ideological blinders forced him to miss these positive developments.[111] It is true that Lasch's evaluation of our civic health was radically different than Rorty's. From the perspective of the first quarter of the twenty-first century, however, it would be difficult to know if Rorty's elites or Lasch's lower-middle-class populism were more to blame for stimulating a deeply polarized civic culture and increasingly perverse and undemocratic national politics: our political class has simply turned its back on the responsibilities of leadership, while the populist many are drawn toward demagogues and simmer with rage against what look to their eyes like the smug complacency of progressive elites. At the present moment there seem far too few heroes and glimmers of light in our public life for either those who place their faith in the moral virtues of the people or those who look to the wisdom and civic commitment of elites. For all of this, it is actually hard not to think that Rorty's trashing of Lasch's final public statements was less about the empirical state of affairs in the final decade of the twentieth century than it was about the moral sensibilities separating himself from Lasch. For Rorty, it is simple pap and cowardice to claim that limits are to be forced upon us, and that the path of wisdom is to embrace and respect the limits we experience. For Lasch, Rorty captures the arrogance of self-satisfied progressive intellectuals he believes are responsible for social inequality and ecological catastrophe, and for whom common citizens are, at best, to be educated away from their ignorance and bigotry, and, at worst, to be carefully managed and controlled. Twenty years after Rorty's review of *Revolt of the Elites*, it is all too easy to make the case against either thinker.

Even if Lasch is unpersuasive in locating the virtues of moderation and the acceptance of limits in the working and lower-middle classes, he may have been right, however, to believe that such virtues were required for a healthy and just democratic order. Here, in fact, is the most important source of his disagreement with a progressive liberal like Rorty. Like Thoreau and others in his tradition, Lasch believes that democratic society requires citizens capable of self-discipline and moderating their passions.[112] Rorty, in contrast, thinks democracy legitimately rebels against conventional and natural constraints. He demands that free men and women, constructing a democratic world together, be viewed as divine, that is, as potentially limitless, with no higher moral authority standing over them.[113] It is precisely this Enlightenment perspective that Lasch, with Leopold and Thoreau, believes is ultimately subversive to moral integrity. Only a voluntary simplicity and moderation can mitigate the excesses of that dominant tradition.

The desire to control the market economy's pull on our behavior, to moderate our wants and needs, to minimize utilitarian goods for the sake of maximizing other humane values, has clearly been very much alive in American culture since Thoreau called us to voluntary poverty. The general thrust of this desire attempts to embrace the best of our civilization while also challenging the corruption represented by crass materialism and a narrow utilitarianism. Thoreau valued voluntary poverty as a means to important moral ends; indeed, the verse he quotes at the end of "Economy" warns against the vanity of valuing poverty as an end in itself. The point is to free us for the most meaningful and important parts of life, to help us extricate ourselves from economically exploitative relationships, to allow for personal independence, and to prevent us from being alienated from our work and the economic elements of our lives. Personal satisfaction and justice toward others are the true goals of voluntary poverty, and these are the standards by which this economic simplicity is to be evaluated. There will always be seekers and ascetics who are drawn to extreme renunciation. The model for a democratic social order, however, must be something available to a broader majority, a life with potentially great satisfactions even within the humble context of perhaps significantly diminished consumption. Bill McKibben has written, in this vein, "I'm not suggesting an abrupt break with the present, but a patient rebalancing of the scales."[114] Such a position does not provide an exact or unchanging standard for evaluating consumption and technology at any given moment. The "rebalancing" act is in truth a never-ending project. This view, however, seems both humane and in keeping with the Thoreauvian tradition as a whole.

The following comments by Alan Mittleman are not specifically addressed to Thoreau's idea of voluntary poverty, but rather to the broad perspective of Jewish thinking about human nature. They speak to the point at hand, however, by honestly conveying the problem we have identified: How are we to appropriately assert ourselves in the world while also being respectful of the world we are acting within?

The ambivalence of the Jewish tradition toward human nature is an attitude well worth cultivating. We are holy—and capable of unimaginable evil. Judaism reminds us of both. We have the creativity and freedom to remake the world, and now, increasingly, to remake ourselves. Our own survival might well depend on cultivating anew a sense of limits. Adam and Eve were expelled from the Garden of Eden for transgressing a limit. Limits there will always be, many imposed by human nature. Our dignity inheres in knowing when and how to master them, and when and how to accept them with respect.[115]

Such a perspective, I am suggesting, is similar to that promoted by the Thoreauvian tradition when it counsels a cultivation of voluntary poverty. This is a hard teaching, requiring discipline and good judgment about our real needs. It calls us to rebel against the idea that the economy is an end in itself, and to remember the freedom that a proper economy serves. It also calls us to rebel against the idea that the economy is best conceived as a project of aggression against and mastery of the natural world. Respect both for nature and our most humane goods requires a moderation of our economic life.

HISTORIAN YUVAL HARARI HAS argued that the modern social contract requires giving up meaning for power: "On the practical level modern life consists of a constant pursuit of power within a universe devoid of meaning."[116] The world Harari describes (and embraces) promises comfort and pleasure, but even if it can deliver these goods (that is, even if the environmental consequences of this social contract aren't going to come home to roost in the near future), it is clear that such a world can also easily lead to the kind of "quiet desperation" Thoreau wrote about more than a century and a half ago—a society, we shouldn't be surprised to find, with high levels of suicide, addiction, depression, and the rest of the personal and social problems associated with the affluent world. Thoreau's call to voluntary poverty has significant attractions even beyond any role it may play in helping us address environmental emergencies and necessities. Perhaps it is true that turning away from the consumerism and materialism of the modern economy could help us cultivate other, higher, and more satisfying human goods, such as beauty and community. Possibly we might even discover the "meaning" that Harari so cavalierly dismisses as beyond the reach, or even the desire, of modern people. When Kristin Kimball writes of the farming life she and her husband have chosen (contrary to the expectations generally accompanying individuals with undergraduate degrees from Harvard and Swarthmore, respectively), she writes of this adopted "dirty life" with great affection and commitment. Far from meaningless, the work she embraces is hard, sometimes heartbreaking,[117] mysterious, and deeply satisfying: "I was in love with the work, too, despite its overabundance. The world had always seemed disturbingly chaotic to me, my choices too bewildering. I was fundamentally happier, I found, with my focus on the ground. For the first time, I could clearly see the connection between my actions and their consequences."[118] Although she and her generation of young organic farmers work much harder than Thoreau recommends in *Walden*—indeed, the work is unrelenting, and far from limited to six weeks of labor a year!—the work is driven by love and commitments that significantly transcend the logic of the market and the utilitarian calculation of consumption.

When we think of what voluntary poverty might reasonably mean today, the new agriculture represented by people such as Kimball is an illustration of some possibilities. The local food and organic farming movements are very much a part of the broader agrarianism that is an offspring of *Walden* today, and we'll return to this movement, best represented in the work of Wendell Berry, in chapter 3. This ideal obviously stands in the greatest contrast with the consumerism, expanding economy, mobility, and dynamism of the modern world. Instead, this "Thoreauvian" agrarianism emphasizes rootedness and localism, economic self-sufficiency and continuity from generation to generation. This project is clearly humane, attractive to many, and in significant ways unstable when confronted by the powerful economic forces of society at large. The popularity of writers in this tradition and even the ubiquity of modern marketing based on the appropriation of central ideas from this tradition (simplicity, back to nature, etc.) suggest the degree to which living more moderately and with greater respect for the natural world resonates as a desire, hope, or fantasy in contemporary society. Such ideas motivate utopian agrarian communities and less utopian local agriculture and farm-to-table movements. All such movements face the difficulty of knowing just how much of modern technology, social organization, science, and markets to draw on in developing a more modest and natural way of living, and how to maintain a consistent approach to these matters. The story told earlier about Ethan Hughes's wife being rescued by modern medical technology when she suffered complications during childbirth should not, I again suggest, be read as an illustration of hypocrisy. Rather, it is a poignant story about the difficult choices faced by those seeking a Thoreauvian independence in the contemporary world—such as, in this case, when we are forced to choose between independence, on the one hand, and respect for life and the mitigation of human suffering, on the other.

The most common critiques of this tradition reflect these difficulties. First, it will be claimed that Thoreauvians of various stripes fail to speak to the full array of economic needs in modern society. Rod Dreher, for example, is generally friendly to agrarians such as Kristin Kimball, yet he promotes industrial production over agrarian self-sufficiency as a more realistic and helpful economic strategy.[119] Quite simply, locally oriented agrarian and artisanal society, even if it could provide work for the vast majority of those who need it (which it can't), is not capable of generating much of the foundational technology (from steel, to internal combustion engines, to electronics, to chemotherapy drugs) that are increasingly assumed to be essential components for acceptable levels of human health and flourishing. Second, some of the most prescient criticisms suggest that a Thoreauvian economic program simply does not address the needs and interests of large constituencies in complex modern democracies, such as the urban poor, for example. Along these lines, Nora Hanagan suggests that the impersonal forces in modern society, from nation-states to world markets, will not disappear just because a group of citizens attempts to withdraw its support from them. On the contrary, these great world-organizing forces will continue to rule us, and the only real option available to democrats is to develop practices relevant to mass publics in an industrial society, as John Dewey suggested almost 100 years ago in *The Public and Its Problems*.[120] Addressing her comments to Wendell Berry, Hanagan writes:

> Berry's own political vision—indebted as it is to Jeffersonian republicanism—is rooted in an overly narrow set of experiences, namely, the experience of small family farmers in rural America. Essentially, Berry transforms a way of life that has contributed to human flourishing in particular times and places into a standard to which contemporary American society must conform. At the end of the day, both Jefferson's ward system and Berry's local economies are attempts to create institutions that conform to universal principles—in this case minimizing dependency— that will enable citizens to dictate their relationship to the outside world for the foreseeable future. These projects are destined to fail for precisely the reasons Dewey identifies.[121]

Criticisms such as these amount to a claim that the idea of voluntary poverty is little more than a private lifestyle choice with no broader significance, political or otherwise, to the problems of the "great society"[122] at large.

The strongest set of challenges to the contemporary versions of "voluntary poverty" suggests that this project could actually hinder our ability to responsibly address the crushing problems we face and will face more dramatically in the near to mid-range future. Agricultural scientist Louise Fresco, for example, criticizes organic farming, in part, because she believes it is significantly less efficient than other farming methods: "Organic farming is not an innocent option but an implicit decision to use land and resources inefficiently."[123] She is optimistic about the possibility of being able to feed a growing worldwide population,[124] but only if we are committed to more efficient farming methods. Put another way, she views organic farming as incompatible with sustainable farming.[125] From her perspective, self-sufficient agrarianism is a sideshow at best, a drain on valuable agricultural resources and focus at worst. Mark Denny is even more pessimistic, suggesting any agriculture that separates itself from the scientific tools and techniques of the "green revolution" may threaten our ability to address the needs of a growing population: "Returning to environmental sustainability may mean insufficient food for two billion of the people who will be born over the next few decades. Pick your poison—or rather, pick theirs."[126] In Denny's estimation, annual food production will need to increase up to 70 percent by 2050 in order to meet the needs of the projected population.[127] Were a project of Thoreauvian voluntary poverty to be taken seriously in the affluent regions of North America, we might fear that such a development could prevent us from both recognizing and addressing what is in fact a food emergency facing the global community over the next generation or two. Critics such as Hanagan fear that agrarianism is insufficiently attentive to the demands of democratic society at large, but scientists such as Fresco and Denny give us reason to fear the economic implications of an inward-looking movement for personal and local self-sufficiency.[128] We will return to political matters in chapter 2. For now, the economic concerns are enough to give pause.

ANSWERING THESE CRITICS RETURNS us to our original observations about what we would properly mean by "voluntary poverty." If it includes a radical renunciation of science and technology, and a complete return to premodern technologies, methods, and beliefs about the way the natural world works and is constituted, we are right to fear that voluntary poverty would promote inhumane and morally irresponsible behavior and choices. In private life, it could mean subjecting innocent children, for example, to greater risks of illness and death than could be easily justified in the world in which we now live. In public life, it could inhibit reasonable public policy from addressing the kind of problems we have been discussing. In both cases, a willful refusal to participate in the modern world could inflict unnecessary and unjustifiable suffering on constituencies large and small.

There is no reason to think, however, that voluntary poverty, properly understood, should require such renunciation. Thoreau and Leopold were both sophisticated natural scientists; what they were proposing was not an abandonment of "civilization," but rather a taming and control of it. In Thoreau's language, the problem is to figure out how to ride on the railroad, rather than have the railroad ride on us; in Leopold's terms, how to educate ourselves to live more respectfully with the land; in Lasch's language, how to accept the limits of nature with grace and dignity. Each of these projects requires moderation and simplification of economic life, but none, as formulated in these authors' writings, requires the renunciation of human knowledge or the project of mitigating and, to the reasonable degree possible eliminating, human suffering. On the contrary, the project of voluntary poverty is conceived, persuasively or not, as a humane project of living more reasonable, free, and satisfying lives. The point is to cultivate the most rewarding aspects of modern society and abandon the alienating elements.[129]

Three points need to be recalled about this position. First, voluntary poverty is only convincingly approached from the perspective of affluence. As Amartya Sen observes, "To be able to fast, Mohandas Gandhi had to have the option of eating (precisely to be able to reject it); a famine victim could not have made a similar political point."[130] The project being defended is a project for the wealthy, or at least not the indigent and deprived. This is a choice for a society that generates too much, that has become so successful at satisfying the necessities of life that the unnecessary begins to loom large enough to become a power unto itself. This power paradoxically robs the affluent of control over their own lives. The point here is not significantly different from that made by Marx about the degree to which even the bourgeoisie are unable to control the world they appear to dominate.[131] To be voluntary, the choice must be real, and this can only come from a position of affluence and relative privilege. Whatever confusions or condescension we find in *Walden* concerning the *involuntary* poor, these are not of great moment to the broader point. What is being proposed in this tradition concerns a choice by the privileged, more than an escape hatch for those already "degraded" by involuntary poverty. Those in desperate conditions around the world need more equitable social systems to eliminate the extreme poverty and inequality they suffer, not copies of *Walden* as a program for teaching them to solve their own problems.

The second point to recall is that voluntary poverty, just like claims about "privilege," "affluence," and "wealth," is a relative idea—it makes sense only in relation to the existing conditions of the moment. This makes a term that sounds like a kind of absolute much more difficult to get a responsible handle on. Yet, despite how difficult and slippery the concept is, it is nonetheless essential to try to approximate it. Bill McKibben observes, "What makes us [as people] unique is that we can restrain ourselves."[132] This capacity does not explain the degree to which this restraint is required, or the forms restraint will appropriately take. Such evaluations require judgment, which is a practical art in never-ending and continual need of adjustment and reevaluation. There is no reason to believe that the specific conditions of voluntary poverty can be identified with precision or in a way that will be broadly accepted by multiple individuals or with consistency over a significant period of time. On the contrary, even if it were widely adopted in a free society, it is likely to have a flavor akin to something like religious observance. Despite the inevitable variation in how free individuals have chosen to practice religious traditions, the traditions can be meaningful across a wide variety of observances. Perhaps the pursuit of voluntary poverty could function in a similar way.

A third point to keep in mind is that voluntary poverty, in this Thoreauvian tradition, is a practice aimed first and foremost at personal satisfaction. With the development of environmental crises, we recognize that simpler and less materialistic ways of living may be required by the environmental facts of life. However, the most important points made by Thoreau, and later Thoreauvians such as Leopold and Kimball, concern the relationship of simplicity to a conception of human thriving more than to the demands of emergency management. It is inevitable that we sense both of these needs in the twenty-first century. To reduce voluntary poverty to survival calculations, however, is to subvert the joy, beauty, and human satisfaction promised by the tradition. Put another way, to bear its fruit, voluntary poverty must be an act of human choice; to be forced to embrace poverty from necessity is to lose one's freedom and submit, in new form, to an alienating reality.

There are a number of challenges facing any advocate of voluntary poverty or moderation. First, it is certainly common enough to feel as though the forces of commerce are simply too vast and powerful for individual choices to have a significant effect on the general thrust of social and economic developments for the great majority of citizens. Modern market society feeds a seemingly infinite (and always to be rediscovered and recultivated) consumer demand. The seductions of comfort, power, and pleasure appear much greater than the discipline of choice and moderation. There looks to be a kind of inevitability at work here, with forces so powerful that even those who think they are driving them are, in fact, as much the playthings of them as everyone else. This is a deeply fatalistic attitude, and McKibben is at least partly right to suggest that the "idea of inevitability is a ruse, an attempt to preempt democratic debate."[133] Yes, those who find voluntary poverty foolish or threatening will simply claim that its advocates are "unrealistic," or that they refuse to face the facts of modern life. Even those who champion moderation, however, may fear that the forces of excess are simply too great to resist. A strong few can resist the temptations of the market and turn to other than commercial goods, but perhaps it is beyond hope that a significant element in modern society can in fact be persuaded to make such a choice. The evidence of the powerful seduction of cell phones alone gives reason to be pessimistic on this score.

Second, it may not be true that we are in a position to be selective about which elements of the modern economy and technology to embrace and which to resist or reject. Just as it may be the case that the attractions and seductions of modern market society overwhelm even the most compelling concerns about it, so it may be that a society that gives us desirable technologies (say, antibiotics) will also give us both trivial (say, video games) and vicious (say, in-humane, crass, and nasty social media) technologies. It may be that the freedom required to produce one is also the freedom that as-sures at least some of the other. A modern commercial society is both vibrant and crass, and it isn't clear that making it less crass is possible without also making it less vibrant. All these elements may be parts of a single package. To think that we can maintain a moder-ate version of our society without damaging the functioning of the whole is a sobering idea. Some variant of this claim is what drives a preoccupation with economic growth and the GNP. Transition to a more moderate, yet free, society might be much more economically unstable than an advocate of voluntary poverty expects.

Probably the greatest challenge raised by voluntary poverty concerns questions of coordination for thinking about how to ad-dress larger environmental and political problems. Market societies provide massive incentives for innovation and the stimulation of consumer demand. One needn't be a free market fundamentalist to recognize the power of these incentives and the degree to which they have played a huge role in stimulating entrepreneurial cre-ativity for both better and worse. The question is this: If we can imagine a society of individuals committed to some significant un-derstanding of voluntary poverty, can we imagine that society being aggressively innovative? Thoreauvians are lukewarm consumers at best, and quite conservative about the technologies required to meet daily needs (or, perhaps, it would be best to say they would be rela-tively indifferent to these technologies once a modest level of tech-nological proficiency is reached). Could a society of Thoreauvians, should some miracle bring one about, generate either the reserves of wealth or the scientific and entrepreneurial creativity to address the worldwide problems we face? It may fairly be asked if modern striving isn't implicated in the creation of these problems. Indeed, it is. But it may equally be true that this striving is required for suc-cessfully addressing them. That, at least, is a danger that advocates of voluntary poverty must honestly consider.

Even in light of these concerns, there is good reason to think that some reasonable understanding of voluntary poverty (or

moderation, or simplification) is attractive for the reasons Thoreau provides us in *Walden*. It is a commonplace, and the popularity of contemporary self-help literature suggests it is probably
a commonplace reflecting no small measure of truth, that affluent
Americans are often plagued by having too much rather than too
little. In fact, most of what Thoreau is suggesting can sound plati-
tudinous and self-evident. Of course, we might think, we should
spend less time frantically earning and consuming and more time
pursuing pleasures of family and friends, art and beauty, play and
recreation. As we watch affluent and privileged children and young
adults suffering increasing levels of anxiety and mental illness,[134] it
is impossible not to reflect on the paradox that, especially in this
past generation, America's wealth has failed to produce a sense of
personal well-being, to say nothing of the degree to which it has
undermined rough equality, social solidarity, and political comity (to
put it politely). Who would deny that our contemporary "railroad"—
perhaps the best example is our electronic devices—seems to ride
on us rather than we riding on it? Is it unreasonable to think that a
more modest understanding of our economic needs might help us
live less indebted and more independent lives? There is very little
evidence to suggest that America's wealth has produced increasingly
happy and socially well-integrated individuals over time.[135] In fact,
there is significant reason to suspect the opposite.

Thoreau's motivations for living a simpler, more modest life
were at times more heroic and morally ambitious than those that
drive most of us in our daily lives of "quiet desperation." Salvation
is not what voluntary poverty can promise most of us, and although
a few may find great personal inspiration in Thoreau's quest for the
eternal, the vast majority of us seek something more modest and
mundane. We hope for meaning in our lives, for the deep satisfactions that come from significant relationships and useful work, and
for moral integrity in our personal and public lives. Immortality
may not be in the offing, but an improved human experience, not
just for individuals but perhaps for society more generally, may be
reasonably expected. The choice of voluntary poverty, perhaps best
described as a kind of modesty and moderation, may very well be a

necessary step in addressing the human damage to the environment. It may also help us think about the exploitative nature of many contemporary economic relationships and offer at least a partial remedy. Both of these points will need to be kept in mind as we consider, in the next chapters, the political implications of Thoreau's views. The most basic Thoreauvian claim about voluntary poverty is that this modesty must be thought of as a first step in the direction of a freer and more satisfying individual life—and must, at the end of the day, be chosen and evaluated on these grounds. As we will see in chapter 2, there are meaningful political implications for making this personal choice, but in Thoreau's opinion this choice is first to be made for the sake of private enjoyment.

TWO

DIFFERENT DRUMMERS

If a man does not keep pace with his companions, perhaps it is because he hears a different drummer. Let him step to the music which he hears, however measured or far away.

—Thoreau, *Walden*

Pursuing a simplified economic life opens up new possibilities for Thoreau, both in his private, interior life and in his relationships with others. We noted in chapter 1 that he viewed voluntary poverty not as an end in itself, but as a means for achieving greater goods and satisfactions. A "higher and more ethereal life,"[1] he believed, could emerge to the degree that we succeed in extricating ourselves from alienating, distracting, and unjust economic relationships and institutions. This leads us to Thoreau's famous comment about marching to a different drummer, which is probably the most recognizable moment in *Walden* after the appeal to simplicity.

Thoreau's intention is to encourage us to follow our own conscience, to break with the conventions and opinions of our society that can lead us away from moral integrity and toward a hopeless conformism. The image, however, can be misleading. It would seem to suggest that whatever drummer you hear is fine, that there is, perhaps, a different drummer for each of us. At the nonmoral level that is clearly true for Thoreau; he admired people who made their own lives, who were truly independent in this sense. At the moral level, however, the "different drummer" imagery might make us think that there are as many moral realities and perspectives as there are lifestyles and ways to be independent and free. This, however, is not Thoreau's view. On the contrary, he believed that free and independent individuals would discover the same moral truths and realities that underlie the world we all share, and that we are all equally bound to these truths. We all may have different paths of moral discovery, but the content of what is to be discovered is eternal and unchanging for Thoreau. This is why he believes we can profit from studying the wisdom from ancient Greece, from classical Chinese and Indian sources, and from poets and philosophers closer to our own time and place. It is conventional opinion that is most likely to blind us to moral knowledge, and finding our own drummer is less about discovering our own truths than breaking the shackles of our conventions to open up the broader moral reality to us.

When we investigate Thoreau's commitment to moral integrity, there is much to admire—for example, his courage and his optimism about the possibility for moral transformation, and his belief that a satisfying and admirable moral life is possible for all of us. There is also a significant danger that his moral commitments can lead to self-righteousness, inflexibility, and intolerance, especially when they are transferred directly into public life. This is no small concern, given Thoreau's reputation as a political thinker and his influence among political activists. Thoreau's moral project, however, never actually aimed at the pursuit or exercise of political power. On the contrary, he fastidiously avoided participating in political affairs his whole life. His concern as a moralist was focused, instead, on the prepolitical cultivation of character and dispositions he thought of as essential for any decent social and political order. Rather than seeking political power and authority, he confined himself to his role as a writer, using words and persuasion as his only tools.[2] We do well to remember exactly what it is he thought he had to share with us. As we'll see, although he (helpfully) focuses some attention on local political life, his primary attention is directed at the cultivation of the kind of moral character that will help us maintain clear moral vision, the courage of our convictions, and a recognition of our neighborly duties. Thoreau has little to teach us about direct participation in political affairs, and he can mislead us if we work too hard to make him speak directly to these concerns, but he has much to say about the preconditions for a decent and democratic social order and a satisfying personal life of integrity. These lessons may, in fact, be helpful, and even necessary, as we imagine the need to reconstruct the foundations of a democratic order in our own time.

IT IS OBVIOUS THAT the project of *Walden* is a thoroughly and unremittingly moral one. As Thoreau observes, "Our whole life is startlingly moral," and "There is never an instant's truce between virtue and vice."[3] We noticed in chapter 1 that Thoreau's conception of moral life draws no distinction between the right and the good, that for him what is ethical is also what leads to happiness and a fully human life. Indeed, his moral perspective draws on ancient conceptions of moral life in which ethics is thought of as less of a restraint on our desires (as it is in more modern conceptions) than as a guide to training and shaping these desires for the sake of the deepest human satisfactions. Thoreau's moral vision is radical, transformative, and, he believes, within reach for every normal individual.

The radical nature of this vision is demonstrated by the degree to which it presents itself as a profound break with the lives most of us live. Thoreau, in *Walden*, is a character who struggles for purity, cleanliness, and chastity in a corrupted, dirty, and profane world; consider, as just a particularly striking example, his comment about eating, in "Higher Laws": "The wonder is how they, how you and I, can live this slimy beastly life, eating and drinking."[4] We have seen how he desired to live in "the present always,"[5] and to leave the past and the future alone. In order to maintain the simplicity he promotes, he refuses to accept a gift of a doormat for his new home at Walden

Pond on the grounds that this object is an unnecessary luxury; he even suggests that by refusing the gift he is "avoiding the beginnings of evil."[6] Thoreau is delivering this comment with characteristic dry humor, but it is nonetheless striking to note that, humorously or not, his conception of luxury could question the moral propriety of something as useful, modest, and mundane as a doormat. Even this humorous exaggeration illustrates how radical the moral project is that Thoreau has in mind. The "waking up" *Walden* promotes is not just an improvement, a clarification, a gradual advancement, a program for moral progress. It is a radical challenge to, indeed it is the opposite of, the slumber Thoreau hopes we will join him in disrupting.

To live this wakeful moral life is to be transformed; the imagery of spring suggests resurrection: "In a pleasant spring morning all men's sins are forgiven," and what we witness is the recreation of the world.[7] We have seen his claim that if all would learn to live simply, crime would disappear.[8] Without inequality, injustice would also become just a bad memory, and men's "dirty institutions"[9]— the state, and the unjust institutions (such as slavery) it exists to protect—would likewise cease to have a purpose and would simply wither and die. The imagery of *Walden* has a strongly religious quality, beckoning rebirth and forgiveness, of moving beyond our sins and grief. The promise of *Walden* is that we can leave our guilt and sorrow behind and live a new life of the saved. Thoreau's beautiful language is best read at length here:

> Such a [spring] day is a truce to vice. While such a sun holds out to burn, the vilest sinner may return. Through our own recovered innocence we discern the innocence of our neighbors. You may have known your neighbor yesterday for a thief, a drunkard, or a sensualist, and merely pitied or despised him, and despaired of the world; but the sun shines bright and warm this first spring morning, recreating the world, and you meet him at some serene work, and see how his exhausted and debauched veins expand with still joy and bless the new day, feel the spring influence with the innocence of infancy, and all his faults are

forgotten. There is not only an atmosphere of good will about him, but even a savor of holiness groping for expression.[10]

The radical nature of Thoreau's moral vision reflects a correspondingly transformative potential for those who adopt it. This salvation may be earthy, but salvation is not too strong a word for what Thoreau has in mind.

Such a radical transformation, Thoreau suggests, is available to all, but it requires individuals to take full responsibility for themselves. This helps to explain his hostility toward philanthropy, or "Doing-good," which he describes as a fool's errand.[11] Most importantly, Thoreau believes philanthropic "reform" is in truth no reform at all. It is actually a form of "goodness tainted"[12] since it reinforces unequal relationships and dependencies. He polemically (and comically) writes: "If I knew for a certainty that a man was coming to my house with the conscious design of doing me good, I should run for my life, as from that dry and parching wind of the African deserts called the simoon, which fills the mouth and nose and ears and eyes with dust till you are suffocated, for fear that I should get some of his good done to me,—some of its virus mingled with my blood."[13] Thoreau suggests that the good one does must be unintentional, that it must grow from the example of being one of the world's worthies, rather than from patronizing (literally becoming the patron of) others. He is as opposed to welfare functions of the government as he is to philanthropy, referring to the state as a "desperate odd-fellow society."[14] As he writes in *Civil Disobedience*, he believes that turning government into a mutual aid and insurance society (like the fraternal Independent Order of Odd Fellows, first established in the United States in 1819) strips individuals of their independence: "The American has dwindled into an Odd Fellow,—one who may be known by the development of his organ of gregariousness, and a manifest lack of intellect and cheerful self-reliance."[15] Thoreau praises his friend Bronson Alcott, a "true friend of man; almost the only friend of human progress," for being "pledged to no institution" in society, for being a morally virtuous and independent man.[16] Indeed, in Thoreau's view virtue is built on such independence.

This idea of moral independence reflects Thoreau's commitment to self-invention, his belief that in meaningful ways individuals must be sufficient unto themselves when it comes to building moral lives: "I am not aware that any man has ever built on the spot which I occupy. Deliver me from a city built on the site of a more ancient city, whose materials are ruins, whose gardens cemeteries."[17] Thoreau, of course, draws liberally on the ideas of the ancients—both Eastern and Western—to guide his own investigations, and as far as the metaphor of ancient building materials is concerned, he has, in the chapter prior to that in which this comment is found, noted that he used old (recycled) bricks to construct his chimney.[18] But despite the fact that his purpose is the renewal rather than the invention of moral life, the process must grow from our independence and individuality. Only individuality allows us to cut through the "mere smoke of opinion"[19] to find the truth that apparently escapes the many. One must be self-reliant to achieve Thoreau's moral goals, and he believes that such self-reliance is possible for us all even if most of us are too caught up in the conventions of contemporary society to exercise this moral potential.

These elements of Thoreau's moral perspective in *Walden* are consistent with what we find throughout his writings. Consider, for example, his early (1843) review of a book by the technological utopian J. A. Etzler. Thoreau heaped contempt on the author of *The Paradise within the Reach of all Men, without Labor, by Powers of Nature and Machinery: An Address to all intelligent men, in two parts*, and all those who sought the improvement of the human condition through engineering and the mastery of nature. What is striking about this underappreciated essay, "Paradise (To Be) Regained," is that Thoreau's critique is based less on what modern environmentalists might expect or seek—that is, a concern about the unintended environmental consequences of the attempt to master nature—than on a belief that technological optimists aim way too low in their aspirations for human improvement, ignoring our deeper spiritual needs. In addition, the emphasis on control of the material world requires that we approach reform collectively; the heroic engineering projects imagined by Etzler require vast cooperation and coordination throughout the society as a whole. Thoreau attacks both of these emphases. Capturing a millennial spirit not uncommon in his day, he suggests that if we focus on the "paradise within," we will be able to dispense with the need for a "paradise without."[20] The sun, whose power will drive Etzler's machines, is "but the shadow of love,"[21] the true and higher aim of human development. Redemption of the inner personal life is as much a preoccupation for the young as for the mature Thoreau. His consistent view of moral life emphasizes the independent responsibility of individuals apart from their social or collective identities. As he writes in "Slavery in Massachusetts," "I would remind my countrymen, that they are to be men first, and Americans only at a late and convenient hour."[22] Being "men" requires less a shared identity and social cooperation than a personal relationship with nature and an understanding of the general principles of right and good.

The most obvious, and least surprising, element of Thoreau's moral theory is its individualism. This quality of Thoreau's thinking can be (and often is) exaggerated, but Thoreau, after all, praises solitude in *Walden*,[23] and in the year he published *Walden* he wrote to a friend about how he finds it "very unprofitable to have much to do with men."[24] We need to be careful not to exaggerate this matter for Thoreau; the chapter in *Walden* following "Solitude" is "Visitors," which is full of society and includes Thoreau's observation that he believes he enjoys the company of others as much as anyone else: "I think that I love society as much as most, and am ready enough to fasten myself like a bloodsucker for the time to any full-blooded man that comes in my way."[25] Nonetheless, the moral life is for Thoreau in the first instance a private concern. The move to Walden Pond was motivated primarily by the need to transact what Thoreau refers to as some private business.[26] So, as we would expect, moral life, in Thoreau's portrayal, is first and foremost personal and private. As he suggests in "Life without Principle," our moral well-being is focused "inward and private."[27] Or, as he says in the very first volume of his *Journal*, "How alone must our life be lived!"[28]

It is also unsurprising that this conception of the moral life is deeply idealistic and antimaterialist. Again, in "Life without

Principle," Thoreau demands that "a man had better starve at once than lose his innocence in the process of getting his bread."[29] We have already discussed Thoreau's contempt for utilitarianism, which he believed was both an unprincipled form of opportunism and a conflation of lower with higher moral goods. Thoreau's defense of John Brown dramatically illustrated his lack of respect for utilitarian calculation; the popular view of Brown's act as a fool's errand drove him to fury: "Many, no doubt, are well disposed, but sluggish by constitution and by habit, and they cannot conceive of a man who is actuated by higher motives than they are. Accordingly they pronounce this man insane, for they know that *they* could never act as he does, as long as they are themselves."[30] It is the widespread consequentialist habit of weighing possible outcomes that leads Thoreau, in "Slavery in Massachusetts," to suggest that the "majority of the men of the North, and of the South, and East, and West, are not men of principle."[31] When it comes to moral life, "expediency" is all too often, in his view, an unprincipled moral charade, a compromise, even a negation, of morality itself.[32] Material interests always threaten to produce moral corruption, and the good or ideal always transcends material interests. This is why Thoreau believes wealth is such a threat to our moral well-being; when we have wealth, it simply weighs too heavily in our moral calculations for us to maintain our integrity.

Less obviously, and perhaps more importantly, Thoreau's perspective is deeply uninterested in, even antagonistic to, politics as a moral project as most of us think about it. I am not claiming that Thoreau didn't have political opinions; he obviously did, and both lectured and published about them. One need look no further than the abolitionist writings, from *Civil Disobedience* to "Slavery in Massachusetts" to the John Brown essays, to understand this; he was also influential in bringing abolitionist speakers, such as Wendell Phillips, to the Concord Lyceum. In addition, Thoreau was aware that his private concerns at Walden (and throughout his life) had political implications for helping to understand and shape the kind of citizens we become.[33] Clearly, Thoreau's ideas are a significant presence in the tradition of American political thought, because he influenced, primarily but not only through *Civil Disobedience*, so many political actors and activists, especially during and since the civil rights movement. My claim, therefore, is not that there are no significant political implications contained within, or significant political influences of, Thoreau's writings. Neither claim would be persuasive. Indeed, my concern in this chapter is to think honestly about these implications and influences. So, what do I mean by suggesting that Thoreau's moral perspective is fundamentally apolitical? Quite simply that Thoreau sees little of moral value, and much to be morally appalled by, not only in the public life of his moment but in political affairs more generally.

The evidence for this is overwhelming and found throughout his works. In *Walden*, he only briefly discusses the arrest that would lead, eventually, to his writing *Civil Disobedience*. But even in this brief discussion, he refers to the government and the unjust practices in society protected by the state (such as slavery) as "dirty institutions," and part of a "desperate odd-fellow society." He makes it clear that he "was never molested by any person but those who represented the state."[34] Comparable contempt for public life is found as early as his "Natural History of Massachusetts" (1842), where he suggests that "men are degraded when considered as members of a political organization."[35] This attitude persists in his late "A Plea for Captain John Brown" (1859) when he contrasts Brown's heroic attack with the "trivialness and dust of politics." In one of his most powerful political passages, he defends defiance of the Fugitive Slave Law, in "Slavery in Massachusetts," by suggesting that one can't be held responsible for trampling a law in the dirt when it was, in fact, born in the dirt already (overseen by Webster, "like the dirt-bug with its ball").[36] In this, as in many cases, Thoreau's disgust is with the contemporary politics of slavery and imperial war with Mexico. But there is also an underlying contempt in much of his writing for political life in general. It is true that he imagines that a good government makes life more valuable, while bad government degrades it; he claims that were he to find a "free state, and a court truly of justice . . . I will fight for them, if need be."[37] In "A Yankee in Canada," arguably his most patriotic work, he finds the politics of the United States superior to those of our neighbor to the north, since our politics is, overall, "much less . . . with us."[38] Despite these few more positive comments, he is, in truth, skeptical about the very possibility of such free states and just courts, and his faint praise for American politics is simply that there isn't as much of it as there is in other societies. Little is to be expected from public affairs aside from the enforcement of injustice and the limiting of personal freedom.

The most developed of Thoreau's political comments are found in *Civil Disobedience*, in which he declares, at the end of the essay, "It is not many moments that I live under a government, even in this world."[39] Government has contributions to make to human well-being, he concedes, but these concern mainly the nonmoral administration of affairs. "Government is at best but an expedient; but most governments are usually, and all governments are sometimes, inexpedient."[40] We know from his critique of Paley's utilitarianism that he believes "expediency" cannot be the proper foundation of moral life; good government, it seems, for Thoreau, would pursue responsible and competent management, but would refrain from meddling in the moral lives of citizens. His contempt for the current U.S. government, with its protection of slave power and its waging of unjust war in Mexico, knows no bounds: "How does it become a man to behave toward this American government to-day? I answer, that he cannot without disgrace be associated with it."[41] But even a less corrupt government, even a purely "expedient" government, could claim no moral command over an individual of conscience. "Must the citizen ever for a moment, or in the least degree, resign his conscience to the legislator? Why has every man a conscience then? . . . The only obligation which I have a right to assume, is to do at any time what I think right."[42] Although he does seek to speak, in the opening passage of the essay, as a citizen, as the text develops the status of citizenship is dropped in favor of the (morally unacceptable yet what he takes to be descriptively accurate) category of "subject." He makes it clear that his moral obligations to others are defined more by his relationship as a neighbor than by being subject to a common political authority.[43] It is not just to his state, but to any state, that Thoreau's moral self-conception makes him wish "to withdraw and stand aloof from it effectually."[44] Even aside from his critique of democratic decision-making—which he equates with (immoral) gaming or gambling[45]—it is clear that Thoreau's moral subject is an individual standing outside and independent of the state, any state, and that he draws his moral knowledge and integrity from higher law.[46]

This understanding leads Thoreau to propose a form of "resistance to civil government" (the original title of the essay we now know as *Civil Disobedience*) quite different from that expected by many readers today. We may look for advice about political organizing, civic engagement, protest politics, and so forth, but we find complete silence on these conventional political tools and strategies. Instead, his advice to abolitionists is that they should immediately withdraw their support, "in person and property," from the government of Massachusetts.[47] Withhold one's taxes, refuse the protections of the government, live a life independent of political authority and obligations. Simply refuse to recognize the government and withdraw from the reach of its institutions as much as possible. In "Slavery in Massachusetts," Thoreau's rage against the state is amplified even above that found in *Civil Disobedience* ("My thoughts are murder to the State, and involuntarily go plotting against her"[48]), mainly because he is beginning to see, in light of the Fugitive Slave Law, how difficult it will be to truly extricate ourselves from the injustices of the state.[49] But even at this later date, Thoreau's activism counsels withdrawal more than engagement. "Let each inhabitant of the State dissolve his union with her, as long as she delays to do her duty."[50] In both of these great abolition essays, Thoreau's proposal is for conscientious individuals to withdraw from public life. He knows this is hard, especially for those with property and therefore in need of protection (which is in part why, as we saw in the previous chapter, he counsels the cultivation of voluntary poverty). His radicalism is aimed at delegitimizing the state by withdrawing all material and moral support from it. The integrity of moral life requires such withdrawal. To directly engage the state on its own terms is hopelessly corrupting.

Finally, both the radical and seemingly apolitical character of Thoreau's moral ideas reflect what can only be honestly described as moments of contempt for much in his society at large. Again, it is important not to misunderstand the claim that is being made here. It is a bit of an old saw to describe Thoreau as misanthropic, and we've seen plenty of comments in the course of this discussion that could lead one to think of him in this way. It is also true, however, that Thoreau was deeply loyal, responsible, and loving to his family, with whom he lived most of his life (excepting the college and Walden years, a brief and unhappy stay on Staten Island as a tutor to Emerson's nephews, and two periods of residence in the Emerson household). He was fond of, and loved by, children (Emerson notes, in his eulogy for Thoreau, that despite being a "hermit and stoic," he was very fond of children and young people).[51] He was active in the Concord Lyceum, serving as an officer for the organization and supporting its projects as a sponsor and a speaker (more on this below). He was a village man who, while eccentric and prickly, was also well integrated into the life of his community. He was known for throwing neighborhood parties when his impressive annual watermelon harvest was ready. Thoreau's biography clearly suggests that the character, Henry David Thoreau, crafted by the author of *Walden*, was more solitary and independent than the author himself. Nonetheless, Thoreau's writings suggest at times a deep alienation from both his fellows and his nation. The question here doesn't concern the legitimacy of this alienation; we can certainly sympathize with the anger over slavery and imperial war, and the more this anger burns the more unsurprising it is that Thoreau was increasingly alienated by what he viewed as the moral compromises and complacency, if not the outright moral complicity with these crimes, of so many of his fellows in Concord and throughout the United States. We can certainly understand this contempt, but it is also important to understand that it both separated him from others and made it increasingly difficult to imagine ways in which these relationships could be repaired. The radical intensity of his views, the transformative hope for what these views could promote, is in part the consequence of both anger and separation. In an early *Journal* entry, Thoreau writes, "My countrymen are to me foreigners."[52] In a late *Journal* entry he suggests, "There is nothing to redeem the bigotry and moral cowardice of New-England in my eyes."[53] Perhaps the most moving description of Thoreau's alienation from his fellows is found in *Civil Disobedience* when he describes his release after his night in jail:

> When I came out of prison,—for some one interfered, and paid that tax,—I did not perceive that great changes had taken place on the common, such as he observed who went in a youth, and emerged a tottering and gray-headed man; and yet a change had to my eyes come over the scene,—the town, and State, and country,—greater than any that mere time could effect. I saw yet more distinctly the State in which I lived. I saw to what extent the people among whom I lived could be trusted as good neighbors and friends; that their friendship was for summer weather only; and that they did not greatly propose to do right; that they were a distinct race from me by their prejudices and superstitions, as the Chinamen and Malays are; that, in their sacrifices to humanity, they ran no risks, not even to their property; that, after all, they were not so noble but they treated the thief as he had treated them, and hoped, by a certain outward observance and a few prayers, and by walking in a particular straight though useless path from time to time, to save their souls. This may be to judge my neighbors harshly; for I believe that many of them are not aware that they have such an institution as the jail in their village.[54]

Thoreau could not feel at this moment, or at least professed to not be able to feel, moral kinship with many of those around him. Their views, in his opinion, were too morally contemptable for him to even imagine that he and they were of the same "race." What Thoreau is feeling is not the agony of deep and serious disagreement with his brothers and sisters; it is a concern—or at least a fear—about whether there is even a brotherhood or sisterhood here to build on.

In his eulogy for Thoreau, Emerson writes, "But Thoreau never faltered. He was a born protestant."[55] Emerson also notes the stoic—and martial[56]—elements of Thoreau's moral character. For all this complexity, Emerson is certainly right to stress Thoreau's tendency to embody a kind of radical Protestantism, despite his self-conscious attempt to distance himself from the orthodoxy and outward practices of organized Christianity in New England.[57] At the end of the day, he simply couldn't escape certain strains of this inheritance: a radical sense of personal responsibility; an appeal to the authority of individual conscience; a moral seriousness prone to contempt for those less morally serious, austere, or disciplined, or whose sense of conscience leads them in different directions; and an unsurprising alienation from others that grows from the profoundly demanding nature of his own moral commitments. Emerson, again, is a helpful authority, given his centrality to Thoreau's personal life and his contribution to Thoreau's intellectual development. He notes that Thoreau's "virtues, of course, sometimes ran into extremes," and wonders if this "severity of his ideal interfered to deprive him of a healthy sufficiency of human society."[58] There was an undeniable moral heroism to Thoreau, but the very extremity of this heroism contains within it potential vices, such as inflexibility, a lack of generosity for others, and self-righteousness—all matters Thoreau's critics have loudly hammered away at for the more than a century and a half since the publication of *Walden*.[59] The question for us is what, for better and possibly for worse, we learn from these qualities.

THE ELEMENT OF TRUTH informing these criticisms, even if exaggerated, is enough to make us take stock of the problems we may face if we ask Thoreau's ideas to do work that he himself was reluctant to ask of them. Before we turn to the helpful lessons Thoreau *does* offer for considering our social and political lives, it is probably best to clarify the ways in which Thoreau's ideas could mislead us when thinking about political obligations and strategies. Once these are fully appreciated, however, we will see that Thoreau still supplies significant ideas about some of the connections between private moral considerations and a rejuvenated social and political ethics.

What Thoreau's moral sensibilities will not give us, it seems, is a clear, consistent, coherent, complete, or fully responsible politics.

Martin Luther King Jr. generously suggested that he had learned a significant lesson from Thoreau, a lesson, as the title of his brief essay suggests, in the "legacy of creative protest":

> During my early college days I read Thoreau's essay on civil dis-obedience for the first time. Fascinated by the idea of refusing to cooperate with an evil system, I was so deeply moved that I re-read it several times. I became convinced then that non-cooperation with evil is as much a moral obligation as is cooperation with good. No other person has been more eloquent and passionate in getting this idea across than Henry David Thoreau.[60]

In earlier generations, Mohandas Gandhi, Emma Goldman, Leo Tolstoy, and a few other radicals and visionaries had claimed inspi-ration from Thoreau's work and example. Since King gave his ap-proval to Thoreau in the 1960s, it has become commonplace among political activists of many stripes to draw on Thoreau for both in-spiration and legitimacy. It is certainly true that one can easily draw from Thoreau a sense of irreverence toward the status quo, a skep-ticism about social and political authority, an appeal to moral prin-ciples beyond conventional political norms, and a strong sense of personal responsibility to resist immoral political acts and authority. All of these can help inform one's political impulses, but they are insufficient in and of themselves to suggest an obvious political pro-gram or strategy. This was so obvious to Hannah Arendt that she was incredulous that anyone thought Thoreau had anything at all to teach us about politics, given his preoccupation with individual conscience:

> Here, as elsewhere, conscience is unpolitical. It is not primarily interested in the world where the wrong is committed or in the consequences that the wrong will have for the future course of the world. It does not say, with Jefferson, "I tremble *for my country* when I reflect that God is just; that His justice cannot sleep forever," because it trembles for the individual self and its integrity.[61]

For those, like Gandhi and King, who are interested in civil disobedience, Arendt thought that Thoreau, like Socrates, was actually profoundly unhelpful: "The trouble is that the situation of the civil disobedient bears no analogy to either for the simple reason that he never exists as a single individual; he can function and survive only as a member of a group."[62] Thoreau's concerns are primarily private, and fail to provide us, in Arendt's view, with any moral resources for thinking about the basic reality of all politics—that is, the requirement of debating with, working with, coordinating with, and compromising with other people. Even if Arendt underestimates the degree to which Thoreau offers some moral insight for King and other political actors engaged in resisting injustice and illegitimate institutions, her observation about Thoreau's lack of interest in coordinated action with others is not without power.

We find these difficulties illuminated in a recent book by climate change activist Wen Stephenson, who writes about the need to organize and struggle against the fossil fuel industry and its political enablers. Stephenson explicitly draws on Thoreau to build his case. The Thoreau he draws on is not an anachronistic environmentalist but rather an abolitionist who believes that "to live in harmony with nature is to act in solidarity with one's fellow human beings."[63] He is clear that what draws him to Thoreau's abolitionist writings is, in part, the "bracing moral clarity and uncompromising urgency of the abolitionist cause."[64] Although it isn't obvious that "solidarity" is a word that fully captures Thoreau's attitudes toward others, it is obvious that Thoreau's moral certainty and commitment draws Stephenson to him, as does Thoreau's sense that this moral commitment grows from a personal transformation. Stephenson's preface clearly connects his project of personal renewal to the overarching symbolism of *Walden*: "This is a book about waking up," not just for himself, he suggests, but for everyone.[65] Stephenson's book weaves together the story of his own recovery from alcoholism with his embrace of the climate movement. He admits at the outset that his political activism reflects his own need to be saved.[66] He ties his personal journey to the "*spiritual crisis*, or struggle, at the heart of the climate crisis and the climate struggle."[67] He does worry a bit about "self-absorption," but he suggests he has discovered a path "out of self-absorption to engagement."[68] Much of the book is confessional, in order to underscore the struggle he has engaged in to discover and maintain his own moral integrity.[69] He admits that he and his political heroes in the movement have no plans or "workable solution" for climate change, but suggests that such plans and solutions aren't really their responsibility.[70] Instead, their task is to help alter the conversation around climate politics: "The movements that change the world are moral struggles—and spiritual ones."[71] Stephenson's book, in short, is about moral transformations rather than anything resembling the promotion of a particular political program. There are vague comments about the need for "community," the usefulness of a constitutional convention to "form a new government in this country," and the promotion of "climate democracy,"[72] but the sensibility conveyed is decidedly *hostile* to promoting specific policy proposals and initiatives. Describing young activists, he suggests, "More important than any particular action and its outcome is to understand what led these young people to it—not their media talking points, but how they understood, as individuals, what they were doing and why."[73] If personal moral salvation is achieved, the hard details of a political program will, presumably, fall into place.

Stephenson thus provides us with the paradoxical example of a political activist primarily concerned with personal moral transformation. The result is, unsurprisingly, a remarkably unfocused political program. There is great human concern here, but little to help understand the practical connections between "fighting for . . . each other" and the immediate steps to be taken to combat climate change. Stephenson's book brings us closer to *Pilgrim's Progress* than it does to any concrete environmentalist political plan or strategy. Stephenson can be criticized for significantly exaggerating Thoreau's political activism. Yet he captures clearly and accurately the Thoreauvian preoccupation with individual moral integrity. In light of the degree to which he shares with Thoreau an overwhelming concern with personal redemption, the lack of focus on the politics being promoted is no more surprising for Stephenson than it is for Thoreau.

But the concerns we may have about the relation between Thoreau's morality and the politics it can generate are greater than a worry about its lack of political focus and sophistication. That is, there are reasons to fear that its dangers are not confined to the consequences of political incompetence. The classic text to consult here is Max Weber's "Politics as a Vocation," delivered as a lecture to German university students in 1919. Weber distinguishes between two ethical perspectives, an "ethics of ultimate ends" and an "ethic of responsibility." The first of these is concerned only with the intentions of the actor, independent of possible consequences or outcomes to be expected from acting on these intentions: "The believer in an ethic of ultimate ends feels 'responsible' only for seeing to it that the flame of pure intentions is not squelched: for example, the flame of protesting against the injustice of the social order."[74] Thoreau obviously represents a particularly pure form of Weber's moral type; we have discussed his consistency, energy, and bitterness in attacking consequentialist ethics.[75] The problem with this perspective, for Weber, is that it is naïve about the nature of politics, and thus about the nature of morality in relation to politics. What makes the modern nation-state distinctive from all other social institutions is less its function(s) (different states assume different responsibilities relating, for example, to education or health care) than the means at its disposal for enforcing its will. Unlike all other social institutions—be they economic, religious, cultural, educational, fraternal, or whatever—the "decisive means for politics is violence."[76] In the final analysis, the state's power grows from its ability to enforce its will by violent means. These are awesome powers, and perverse ones, where good outcomes can grow from terrible means, and poor outcomes may very well result from refusing to use such means. Weber calls these powers "diabolical," and he suggests that "he who lets himself in for politics, that is, for power and force as means, contracts with diabolical powers and for his action it is *not* true that good can follow only from good and evil only from evil, but that often the opposite is true. Anyone who fails to see this is, indeed, a political infant."[77]

An advocate of an ethic of absolute ends is therefore guilty of misunderstanding the core realities of politics, and the degree to

he may lead us to believe. The contest between liberal tolerance and
the conscientious believer has never, in truth, been decided once
and for all. Philip Gura argues that "romantic activists" (such as
Thoreau) in the nineteenth-century United States rejected the kind
of liberal pragmatism Fasolt defends—the pragmatism that grows
from agreeing to keep "first principles," and thus conscience, out
of the political realm—as a matter of moral integrity. These romantics' core commitment to moral individualism, Gura believes, promoted a politics of self-righteousness that made compromise and
conciliation simply look immoral: "Inspirational as the ideal was,
it foundered on the rock of self-righteousness and shattered under
the weight of the [Civil War's] hundreds of thousands dead."[85] Andrew Delbanco caused a stir a few years ago when he published
an essay, "The Abolitionist Imagination," in which he explains his
fears that the "sacred rage of abolitionism," its "moral urgency and
uncompromising fervor," contains a view of politics as a holy war
and "bespeak[s] a zeal for combatting sin, not tomorrow, not in due
time . . . but *now*."[86] He never doubts the righteousness of the abolitionist cause, but Delbanco nonetheless worries that the style of
politics abolitionists cultivated becomes open to all dissenters across
the political spectrum, including those without such stable or persuasive moral grounds to stand on: "It seems to me to be a mistake
to underestimate the persistence of abolitionist sentiment as an element of American life."[87] Delbanco's defense of a more doubting
liberalism, a "many-mindedness" rather than an "ardent simplicity"
of moral commitment,[88] enraged critics who felt he was unable to
distinguish between substantively just (and therefore justifiable)
political movements (such as abolitionism) and other unjustifiable
(because unjust) forms of moral absolutism.[89] Delbanco represents
a case of the liberal desire to privatize conscience, and perhaps even
to weaken its hold on us, which looks to the righteous like a failure
of moral character.[90]

Regardless of how you view the debates generated by Delbanco's
thesis, it is hard to deny that moral certainty and absolutism has become a depressingly common element in the dysfunctional politics
of our own moment in the United States (and elsewhere in the liberal

world). In his Nobel acceptance speech, Barack Obama worried, for good reason, about the "satisfying purity of indignation."[91] Such indignation has become most obvious today on the right (first in the Tea Party movement, then culminating in the "populist revolt" of the Trump election in 2016), but it can be found playing a significant role on the Left (as seen in Occupy Wall Street and the rise of Bernie Sanders as a morally outraged outsider crashing the Democratic Party). Significant fears have arisen, in fact, about the stability and future of the liberal world in light of the growing illiberal impulses of moral intolerance and absolutism. There is talk about divisions in the citizenry becoming so great as to be irreconcilable, and even if this is (we hope) an exaggeration, ideological polarization has become alarmingly great—reinforced by gerrymandering, seemingly limitless private funding sources to influence candidates, the narcissism of social media, and an apparently omnipresent army of Russian-sponsored social media bots—and looks unlikely to decline anytime soon. The problem we face does not grow from a lack of moral commitment. Rather, we are threatened by the visceral, intractable, and militantly incompatible commitments found across the political spectrum. Constantin Fasolt's suggestion that conscience means war, at least to the degree conscience is mobilized in the political world, hits close enough to home to suggest we have reason to be alarmed.

There appear to be good reasons to distrust any politics built on an "ethic of absolute ends," as Weber suggests, and we may fear, in light of the catastrophes of the twentieth century, that we in the twenty-first century have not learned this lesson as sufficiently as we should.[92] True as this may be, however, there is also, as Thoreau and many others have made clear, good reason to resist any liberal moderation that is complacent about injustice, especially if the injustices under consideration are radical, severe, and central to the normal functioning of the society claiming the need for moderation and compromise—an injustice, say, such as that of slavery in the antebellum United States. Ta-Nehisi Coates has suggested that "banditry was not incidental to America, it was essential to it."[93] The democratic regime that was expanding during Thoreau's lifetime was built on a racist social order committed to enslaving the African and murdering or expelling the indigenous native, according to Coates. In light of this plain reality, to plead for compromise and moderation, as did Daniel Webster for example, looks a good deal like not facing up to the moral facts confronting the new nation. Delbanco may be right to suggest that "abolitionism still compels us to ask what is, alas, a perennial question: How much blood for how much good?"[94] We are also surely justified to ask with Thoreau, however, if there may be injustices that make a mockery of such liberal pragmatism and "expediency." Fearsome as the politics of absolute ends may be, the alternative sense of responsibility may end up promoting significant complicity with injustice.

Weber was, in fact, sensitive to this problem and explained that a fully responsible politics must find a way to accommodate both ethical sensibilities. At the end of "Politics as a Vocation," he writes, "Politics is a strong and slow boring of hard boards. It takes both passion and perspective."[95] Without passion (a commitment to broad moral principles and ideals) one's perspective will likely suffer from the narrowness, even the moral blindness or incompetence, critics such as Thoreau worry about. Likewise, without a conception of the real options available at a particular political moment, broad general commitments can lead to either destabilizing (and thus counterproductive) demands or the self-righteous washing of one's hands of political responsibility. Despite his legitimate concerns about an ethic of ultimate ends, Weber admits in the final analysis that a fully responsible moral perspective in public life combines a concern for ultimate ends with a feel for particularity and practical options, of better and worse in a specific context. Remember how moved Weber was by the sight of an individual who is mature, committed, responsible, and takes his stand. Weber completes his observation, noting that "every one of us who is not spiritually dead must realize the possibility of finding himself at some time in that position. In so far as this is true, an ethic of ultimate ends and an ethic of responsibility are not absolute contrasts but rather supplements, which only in unison constitute a genuine man—a man who *can* have a 'calling for politics.'"[96] Political responsibility requires we find a way to serve both ethics.

Weber's lectures were delivered to students preparing for careers in public service and were thus aimed at future political professionals. The principles he discusses are as relevant to responsible democratic citizenship, however, as they are to responsible civil servants. It is not enough, Weber is suggesting, to have deep commitments, nor is it enough to be clear about the particular conditions, interests, and possibilities found in a specific political moment. Weber leans more toward the specific and the particular, but he is also sensitive to what is lacking in this kind of knowledge alone. To be responsible in the political world, he believes, is a remarkably difficult task, in which one is confronted by great uncertainty. One might conclude, in fact, that there will be greater uncertainty as the problems confronting the political community grow more intense. But Weber is clear: political responsibility requires both judgment and moderation. There is no determinative science or certainty in political life; we are forced to judge, and our judgment must account for moral concerns pulling us toward different ends of the moral spectrum. Weber believes there is no evading this truth. This is why the political vocation is haunted by tragedy, and it is thereby only suited to responsible, moderate, and politically mature individuals.

It is also, we might suggest, what makes being a responsible democratic citizen so difficult, particularly in moments of crisis or in the face of significant injustice. The most satisfactory analysis of contemporary threats to American democracy is probably that offered by Steven Levitsky and Daniel Ziblatt in their recent book *How Democracies Die*.[97] Despite the obvious value of formal constitutional and legal structures, Levitsky and Ziblatt explain the critical role of democratic norms for bringing order, stability, and cohesiveness to democratic political institutions. The key for successful democracies is for political actors to tolerate the existence of opponents and show restraint in the exercise of power; democrats must refuse to use the full extent of their formal power to silence or eliminate opposition, even when this is within their reach.[98] Political polarization in the United States has led to the breakdown of these democratic norms in the relationship between the major political parties and their partisan bases. Profound distrust of political elites clearly reflects a polarization deep within the electorate, with the gap in understanding and trust growing ever greater between "red" and "blue" America. President Trump has spoken openly and often of wishing to jail political opponents. He has also routinely railed against the free press, suggesting it is an enemy of the people that needs to be restrained, if not actually abolished.

Levitsky and Ziblatt trace the attack on democratic norms primarily to the Republican Party in the post–civil rights era; the postwar norms between the parties had been built on an agreement to enforce racial exclusion of (especially) African Americans, and the Democratic Party's embrace of the civil rights movement destroyed the trust that had existed in the critical truce between the parties.[99] They believe it is clear that the "Republican Party has been the main driver of the chasm between the parties,"[100] and that the main sources of the chasm are fundamentally opposed and strongly held views about race and religion.[101] Even if the Republican Party and its base shoulders most of the blame for the increasing threat to democratic norms, however, the only way to prevent the complete deterioration of democratic institutions is to find ways to reestablish commitments to a more moderate politics. Democrats and independents, that is, will have to find ways to keep from falling into the same style of antidemocratic politics as the Republicans have succumbed to, even as the pressures to respond in kind to the Republicans grow exponentially. (In honesty, of course, these pressures have not always been resisted.) In the context of increasingly extreme politics of "absolute ends," large sectors of American society are called upon to develop a more moderate balance between "absolute ends" and "responsibility" for the sake of democratic principle and in the hope of reviving more democratic practices.

This commitment to moral balance is by no means the dominant sensibility in Thoreau's moral vision. This makes the direct application of his moral ideals to politics potentially dangerous. He can encourage within us, if we are not careful, an impulse to refuse the options that are actually available in our historical moment, a temptation to wish a plague upon the houses of all political actors, and a longing to retreat into a morally self-satisfied private life. The contrast between Thoreau and Lincoln, which has been made before, comes to mind in this context.[102] We certainly see in Lincoln the kind of mixed moral evaluation Weber has in mind, and one less congenial to Thoreau. Lincoln was obviously a shrewd political calculator, drawn less to the language of right and wrong than to that of better and worse. In a speech on the Kansas-Nebraska Act, for example, he famously proclaimed, "Much as I hate slavery, I would consent to the extension of it rather than see the Union dissolved, just as I would consent to any GREAT evil, to avoid a GREATER one."[103] He also, however, thought a great deal about the principles that give the relative terms "great" and "greater" meaning. In an 1859 letter, for example, he wrote:

> All honor to Jefferson—to the man who, in the concrete pressure of a struggle for national independence by a single people, had the coolness, forecast, and capacity to introduce into a merely revolutionary document, an abstract truth, applicable to all men and all times, and so to embalm it there, that to-day, and in all coming days, it shall be a rebuke and a stumbling-block to the very harbingers of re-appearing tyranny and oppression.[104]

David Bromwich notes that abolitionists such as Thoreau "had been right" about the moral horror of slavery, and we may very well believe, with scholars such as Manisha Sinha, that these abolitionists were the most far-reaching visionaries of their generation when they imagined a just and racially integrated democratic America.[105] Yet for Bromwich, "none of their number could have done what Lincoln did, and not only because of their severity and the incapacity for common feeling that went with it. Hatred took them so far that it prevented their loving their country for what it might become."[106] The claim is that the view of morality defended by Thoreau, and others like him, led to an alienation from American society so great that planning the actual events leading to slavery's abolition became, for them, an increasingly remote possibility. It is not necessary, for our purposes, to pass judgment on the abolition movement as a whole, as Bromwich does, for us to see the tendencies in Thoreau's thinking that can lead in directions Bromwich criticizes.

It is not a unique finding to suggest that Thoreau's moral perspective is less than adequate for developing a complete approach to politics, or for thinking about the full range of obligations facing democratic citizens. Indeed, there is a well-known literature criticizing Thoreau precisely for his lack of political sophistication, and even the potential dangers of his perspective.[107] It is also true that there has been a revival of interest in recent years in the political implications of his thinking.[108] My intention at the moment is simply to suggest that the conception of moral responsibility we find in *Walden* and the rest of Thoreau's writings, including his most political essays, is not by itself likely to generate a fully satisfactory understanding of how we might fulfill our obligations as citizens. This is certainly true when addressing routine democratic decisions and processes; overheated moralism is not helpful or appropriate in the routine give-and-take of deliberations of this kind. It is also true, however, in moments of more significant conflict and when facing significant injustices. These more extreme contexts certainly call for greater moral passion, but they also require, in Weber's language, a commitment to "responsibility" that is, at best, not fully developed in Thoreau's moral thinking.[109]

OBSERVATIONS SUCH AS THE above might make us believe that Thoreau has little to teach us about our social and public lives, but such a conclusion would be premature and, I believe, a mistake. His moral perspective turns out to be quite helpful for thinking about some critical elements of any rejuvenated democratic political culture. As long as we are careful not to ask more of Thoreau concerning political matters than he is able to bear, there are democratic lessons to be gleaned from his moral theory.

When teasing out these lessons, we mustn't lose sight of the fact that Thoreau himself never focused on developing a full political morality or philosophy. His concerns lay elsewhere, with private life and civil society. He never sought political power or public authority with which to impose his views on others. He hoped to influence the character of American individuals and in this way the commitments of local American communities. His aim was mainly to encourage moral self-reliance and courage, for the good of individuals themselves but also to develop the preconditions for a more just and equitable public life. The tools he worked with were never more than those available to a writer and lecturer. Those who have sought a full set of political instructions from Thoreau are as unrealistic as are those who accuse him of promoting an undemocratic or even tyrannical politics of the individual will. Thoreau's moral hope lay not in politics but elsewhere.

When Thoreau famously brags "as lustily as chanticleer in the morning, standing on his roost, if only to wake my neighbors up,"[110] he is not speaking as a citizen, and he certainly is not claiming to be a leader or an authority of any kind. He speaks as a neighbor. This is a democratic relationship, but not a political one (at least in Thoreau's sense). He is assuming a common lot, an equality of status and concerns, that makes reaching out to those around him a natural impulse, a sharing of experience with those he wishes well. In Nancy Rosenblum's reading, "When identity as a citizen or 'officer of the government' is not something we can accept for ourselves, then Thoreau speaks as a 'well-disposed man' and a neighbor. He retains association, common ground, reciprocity. He acknowledges all the 'duties' of neighbors. Neighbor is for him the foundational, residual democratic status."[111] Neighborliness is the foundation upon which moral relationships in civil society grow. We have seen the quite intense alienation Thoreau experienced in his relationship to his society. Despite this, there is a live impulse toward neighborliness in *Walden* and other works.

For Thoreau, politics is derivative rather than sovereign. That is, along with Emerson (and most liberals) he believes our politics is shaped by prepolitical moral dispositions rather than the institutions and activities of politics. Indeed, to look to the political world to set the moral terms for citizenship is, from Thoreau's perspective, to overestimate the power of politics and its moral authority.

When he writes in "Life without Principle" that the "chief want" of every state is a "high and earnest purpose in its inhabitants,"[112] his assumption is that this "high and earnest purpose" is found in the moral life prior to, and beyond the reach of, the political. This is why he can speak, in *Civil Disobedience*, of the higher principles directly accessible to the conscientious individual, principles that provide whatever integrity may be found in either our constitutional order or our Bible.[113] This is why Emerson believed that "in dealing with the State, we ought to remember that its institutions are not aboriginal, though they existed before we were born: that they are not superior to the citizen: that every one of them was once the act of a single man."[114] Or, as he put it in a late essay, "Politics is an after-work, a poor patching. We are always a little late. . . . What we call root-and-branch reforms of slavery, war, gambling, intemperance, is only medicating the symptoms."[115] Moral reform begins, as the example of *Walden* illustrates, at the private level. Only with these beginnings are we in a position to influence broader social, and then political, relationships and institutions.

Emerson and Thoreau both offer optimistic assessments of the potential political effect of moral reform. Emerson writes, "The antidote to this abuse of formal Government, is the influence of private character, the growth of the Individual; the appearance of the principle to supersede the proxy; the appearance of the wise man, of whom the existing government, is, it must be owned, but a shabby imitation."[116] The dream is that with the development of such principled individuals, the need for government declines. We must not, Emerson writes, "doubt that roads can be built, letters carried, and the fruit of labor secured, when the government of force is at an end. Are our methods now so excellent that all competition is hopeless? Could not a nation of friends even devise better ways?"[117] Emerson's view, in short, is that purely voluntary relationships among "friends" could eliminate the political category of "citizen" altogether. His emotional heat is impressive: "A man has a right to be employed, to be trusted, to be loved, to be revered. The power of love, as the basis of a State, has never been tried."[118] A few years later, in *Civil Disobedience*, Thoreau's more restrained appeal to neighborliness captures a similar idea: there are nonpolitical principles for living together, above and beyond our roles as citizens, which need to be attended to. In the final sentences of *Civil Disobedience*, the language of neighborliness is ascendant even in Thoreau's speculations about a future, fully just political regime:

> Is a democracy, such as we know it, the last improvement possible in government? Is it not possible to take a step further towards recognizing and organizing the rights of man? There will never be a really free and enlightened State, until the State comes to recognize the individual as a higher and independent power, from which all its own power and authority are derived, and treats him accordingly. I please myself with imagining a State at last which can afford to be just to all men, and to treat the individual with respect as a neighbor; which even would not think it inconsistent with its own repose, if a few were to live aloof from it, not meddling with it, nor embraced by it, who fulfilled all the duties of neighbors and fellow-men. A State which bore this kind of fruit, and suffered it to drop off as fast as it ripened, would prepare the way for a still more perfect and glorious State, which also I have imagined, but not yet anywhere seen.[119]

Thoreau's individualism in no way prevents him from recognizing his responsibilities as a neighbor. In the opening passage of *Civil Disobedience* he declares that he intends to speak as a citizen, rather than as a "no-government man,"[120] but he is unable to maintain this posture throughout the essay; he soon assumes that all governments treat individuals as subjects rather than as citizens, and his rebelliousness emerges accordingly.[121] Even in an unjust polity, however, it appears that the social duties of neighborliness make their rightful claims upon us.

The view Thoreau and Emerson defend blends pessimism with optimism concerning differing contexts for moral life. They share a pessimism about political life. For Thoreau especially, citizenship, at least in its common understanding, is likely to be corrupting: "I cannot for an instant recognize that political organization as *my* government which is the *slave's* government also."[122] He tells us that the "mass of men serve the state thus, not as men mainly, but as machines, with their bodies," and for these citizens Thoreau has the most terrible contempt: "Such command no more respect than men of straw or a lump of dirt." The few who try to serve as complete men—that is, with their consciences and their bodies—must, given the injustice of most states, usually resist the state, and are thus "commonly treated as enemies by it."[123] The state behaves like a half-wit, like a "lone woman with her silver spoons," and doesn't know its friends from its enemies.[124] Thoreau is certainly right to insist that the state demands loyalty even to its injustices, and he is equally right to emphasize the enormity of the injustices in the United States during his lifetime. He was writing in the aftermath of the expansion of white male suffrage during the Jacksonian period, but as Coates forcefully reminds us, white male citizenship and black slavery (to say nothing of the killing and forced migration of Native American populations) were elements of a single order. This is just to say that the antebellum United States was a deeply illiberal and undemocratic polity overall, and Thoreau was by no means unjustified in his skepticism about the moral integrity of citizenship in such a context. "How does it become a man to behave toward this American government to-day?" The answer is that "he cannot without disgrace be associated with it." We may think Thoreau lacks the moral subtlety in his analysis that we find in the complexity of Lincoln's teleological vision of the future potential of American democracy. It is also true, however, that the American polity he lived in had a terrible rot built into its foundations, and this rot implicated all those enjoying the benefits of citizenship. The citizen of the United States was citizen to the same government that governed slavery. Ignoring this or wishing it was otherwise didn't make it so.

We have found in Thoreau's thinking a remarkable optimism that individuals could cultivate and maintain moral integrity in the private and social spheres—in opposition to the political world, if need be—despite his pessimism about political life and the degree to which he believed politics represented a threat to moral integrity.[125] Such integrity is difficult, of course, but the point of *Walden*, and also *Civil Disobedience* and so much of Thoreau's work, is that we should believe in and pursue personal moral transformation. The entire purpose of these texts is to persuade us to seek moral integrity and the satisfactions it brings. The Thoreau of *Walden* is nothing if not optimistic about the possibility for self-improvement and the power such self-improvement can have not just for one's private affairs but also for the world at large.

The moral context of our lives as citizens in twenty-first century America has obviously changed considerably from the world Thoreau faced. The Civil War put an end to slavery, but the failure of Reconstruction was assured by the tacit agreement between the major political parties to respect democratic norms only on the condition that African Americans be excluded from meaningful citizenship. When this agreement began to disintegrate under the stress of the civil rights movement in the last half of the twentieth century—with Democrats accepting (at least in principle) and Republicans resisting (at least to some significant degree) the full integration of African Americans (and other nonwhites) as equal citizens—two consequences resulted: first, we now at least formally aspire to being a (domestically) just democratic order; second, as Levitsky and Ziblatt have demonstrated, the appearance of this aspiration marks the beginning of the gradual eroding of democratic norms among political elites that appears to be climaxing as these words are written. Although the full promise of a heterogeneous democracy has never been achieved, and is currently under significant and sustained attack, the case can be made that at least there continues to be an aspiration to create, in Danielle Allen's words, "a multiethnic democracy in which no particular ethnic group is in the majority and where political equality, social equality and economies that empower all have been achieved."[126] In Allen's view, such a democracy is the highest aspiration and promise of the United States looking to the future. To accept the challenge of her vision is to suggest that we live at a time with great threats to the justice of our political order, but also with great possibilities for an expanded and more inclusive democracy. It is true, as Manisha Sinha points out, that abolitionists during Thoreau's lifetime envisioned and had hopes for a multiethnic democracy.[127] Yet American democracy looks much more possible today, in a morally meaningful sense, than it did during Thoreau's lifetime. There is certainly nothing inevitable about this, as the current attacks on democratic norms make clear. Even with skepticism concerning the present health of democratic politics, however, there is a much stronger case to be made about the possibility of cultivating just relationships in today's political life than there was in the antebellum. By Thoreau's own standards there is a case to be made that participation in our contemporary civic life is not as obviously corrupting as it was at earlier stages in our nation's history. In fact, to the degree that a truly democratic, open, and heterogeneous society is within practical reach, politics may offer significantly greater moral uplift—again, on Thoreau's own terms—than antebellum politics could be reasonably thought to have offered.

Today we have a different reason to be skeptical about public life, at least those of us who are "merely" citizens rather than members of the tiny elite of professional politicians and political professionals in control of our public affairs. This is not a moral consideration so much as it is simply a practical recognition of political realities in the modern age, and it runs in the opposite direction from the optimism of the previous paragraph. A character in one of J. M. Coetzee's novels observes, "It is hardly in our power to change the form of the state and impossible to abolish it because, vis-à-vis the state, we are, precisely, powerless."[128] This impotence applies not only to any desire we might have to change or abolish the state; for most of us, significant political influence is simply beyond any reasonable expectation. Even with extensive opportunities to vote, speak or write our minds, support lobby organizations, campaign, and otherwise involve ourselves with public affairs, the fact is that political power has become, over the course of our political history, increasingly remote. We currently live under a national security state that monitors with almost zero transparency the lives of every resident; we live in a world with nuclear weapons, in which a single individual—the president of the United States—has virtually unchecked power over the life and death of untold millions;[129] we live under the authority of a state in which plutocratic power buys access and influence to political power with almost unchecked arrogance and irresponsibility; we share whatever democratic power we have (assuming we are not political elites or plutocrats) with a huge number of other citizens (200 million people were registered to vote in the United States in 2016);[130] if these numbers aren't imposing enough, many of us live in congressional districts gerrymandered to such a degree that political party competition is all but meaningless. In all these respects, the power and potential influence of our citizens has shrunk enormously in the years since Thoreau was writing.[131] Even if there had been reasons for a citizen during Thoreau's lifetime to be skeptical about his ability to significantly influence political events, these reasons have grown exponentially in the intervening century and a half since Thoreau's death. It is simply implausible to believe that any one of us has much potential democratic efficacy, especially at the national level. It is true that organizations mobilizing like-minded individuals can gain power and influence to greater or lesser degrees. Even then, powerful organizations tend to grow into enormous and impersonal institutions with little concern for, or responsibility to, a given individual within its ranks. In truth, the gap between my political interests and my political efficacy is so great as to suggest that Coetzee's character seems to have it just about right. The state cares nothing for me, except to the degree that I represent a potential threat. My ability to influence the state is minuscule even if I am a responsible, well-informed, voting, and meeting-attending citizen. The state is, for all practical purposes, a power outside my control.[132] No amount of democratic propaganda about government by and for the people can erase this fact. Is there any reason why a conscientious and responsible citizen in the United States today shouldn't feel a deep sense of powerlessness in the face of our political problems, conflicts, and the threats to democratic norms and institutions, to say nothing of the prospects for war and peace? Isn't this feeling of powerlessness exactly what has exacerbated our contemporary political turmoil?[133]

There are at least two observable responses to this sense of powerlessness. The first is an upsurge of populism, an angry attack on social and political elites and the routine politics of power-sharing, negotiation, and compromise. This populism, in John Judis's phrase, functions "as warning signs of a political crisis":[134] large clusters of citizens feel abandoned by the globalized economy, disrespected by the cosmopolitanism and secularism of liberal culture, threatened by feminism and multiculturalism, and enraged by what they consider their betrayal at the hands of the governing class. This sector of society is mobilized by grievances of this kind and flock to demagogues who promise to crush the snobby, the successful, and the powerful, who promise, in President Trump's phrase, to "drain the swamp." We may differ about the dangers of such movements,[135] the legitimacy of the grievances that drive them,[136] and the degree to which democratic institutions will contain them. The point here is simply that such populism, growing from rage and hatred, and aiming to capture and (in Steve Bannon's use of Leninist imagery) smash the state, has little to recommend itself in Thoreau's perspective. Thoreau shares a deep contempt for the politics of his age, and he also has an occasional populist comment scattered throughout his writings—the most famous is his appeal to rural citizens against urban political elites in "Slavery in Massachusetts."[137] Overall, Thoreau's recommendation isn't to mobilize political grievance, but rather to withdraw support from the state. It is turning away, rather than "draining the swamp" or dismantling the state, that Thoreau teaches.

A second response to contemporary political frustration and alienation is closer to Thoreau's moral sensibilities insofar as it proposes disengagement with the broader political and social environment. This is the "Benedict option" popularized by Christian conservative and public intellectual Rod Dreher, who has concluded that from the perspective of those who share his faith, the "public square has been lost."[138] In light of the liberalism of the Obama years, followed by what he takes to be the fraudulent demagoguery of Trumpism, Dreher concludes, "We faithful orthodox Christians didn't ask for internal exile from a country we thought was our own, but that's where we find ourselves."[139] His proposal is to turn from political engagement and instead establish islands of orthodoxy within the broader liberal culture: "We should stop trying to meet the world on its own terms and focus on building up fidelity in distinct community."[140] Like St. Benedict, Dreher recommends a retreat of the committed into enclaves apart from the broader society. There they will be able to protect and nurture their values—to preserve them for the future in a way that seems impossible when living submersed in the "poison of secular culture."[141] One needn't be an "orthodox Christian," of course, to feel sympathy with Dreher's recommendation. Any disaffected community, be it built around religion, politics, or lifestyle, finding itself alienated from the values and practices of the broader U.S. economy and society, could be tempted to establish separatist enclaves to prevent dilution of their own values within liberal society as a whole.

Yet even here we find noticeable tension with Thoreau's recommendation. To see this, consider what Thoreau tells us in *Walden* and *Civil Disobedience* about his arrest and the hours following his release. He devotes less than one paragraph of *Walden*, at the end of "The Villages," to a discussion of this event from the summer of 1846. He tells us about walking to town to pick up a shoe at the cobbler, about being "seized and put into jail" for not paying his poll tax, and thereby failing to recognize the legitimacy of the state that demanded the tax. Thoreau inveighs against the "dirty institutions" and "desperate odd-fellow society" of the state, but notes that "I might have resisted forcibly with more or less effect, might have run 'amok' against society; but I preferred that society should run 'amok' against me, it being the desperate party." He was released the next day, picked up his mended shoe, "and returned to the woods in season to get my dinner of huckleberries on Fair-Haven Hill."[142] In *Civil Disobedience* he tells us a bit more about the incident. For our purposes it is helpful to reflect on his expanded discussion of retreating to Fair-Haven Hill after his release: "When I was let out . . . , I proceeded to finish my errand, and having put on my mended shoe, joined a huckleberry party, who were impatient to put themselves under my conduct; and in half an hour,—for the horse was soon tackled,—was in the midst of a huckleberry field, on one of the highest hills, two miles off, and then the State was nowhere to be seen."[143] In this generally neglected comment, Thoreau makes clear that his trip to the huckleberry field was in the company of others, that he was, on account of his expertise as a naturalist, understood to be a leader of the group, and that when in nature with this small society, there was nothing to tie them, during those hours, to the politics that had recently led to his arrest. He is not desperate, like angry populists, to attack the government, but is, instead, pleased to join others in enjoying the bounty and beauty of nature wholly beyond the sight of the state. Thoreau here hints at a "natural" community, voluntary and without coercion or formal law, that he enjoys and feels at home with.

This might seem to suggest that Thoreauvian sensibilities could lead us in the direction of Dreher's recommendations. Yet, despite their shared desire to disengage from the state and elements of the broader society at large, we also find a noticeable tension between Dreher's and Thoreau's views. Thoreau's conception of neighborliness differs from the idea of a "Benedict option" (of any doctrinal persuasion) in that it does not appear to require doctrinal homogeneity. From a Thoreauvian perspective we might be concerned that in fact we are actually already much closer to Dreher's position than Dreher suspects. Marc Dunkelman points out that American society has become in many ways increasingly segregated in the past generation: "The social character that has developed in the last several decades has had the counterintuitive effect of driving us into isolated corners of society full of people just like us. Our desire to 'be who we are' has morphed into a desire to 'be among people just like us.'"[144] Many other observers have noticed this same process, with the growth of income-based neighborhoods, gated communities, age-segregated retirement communities, and so forth, and the way these developments have led to a significant diminution of heterogeneous neighborhoods. To the degree that we already *have* segregated ourselves, Dreher's proposal may be more indicative of our problem than a solution to it. In Dunkelman's view, these demographic developments have contributed to our political polarization: "Those on the other side of any given issue now are not only wrong, they're almost alien."[145] Intensity of partisanship reflects more than residential patterns, of course—racial politics since the civil rights movements of the 1950s and 1960s is largely to blame for the breakdown of respect for political norms between the major political parties. But Dunkelman (and others) are surely right to think that our residential patterns (and the increasingly privatized schooling of our children) *do* likely help to make those living under dissimilar conditions stranger and more alien than they would be under more integrated circumstances. Michael Sandel observes that democracy "does not require perfect equality, but it does require that citizens share in a common life."[146] That common life is threatened by residential and social segregation of all sorts.[147] The Benedict option self-consciously embraces, out of despair and desperation, an attack on common experiences; only by setting the homogenous group apart, can its distinctive commitments be cultivated in an otherwise hostile environment. The Benedict option is not a strategy for a future democratic revival. It is an abandonment of the democratic vision for any beyond a small group of like-minded individuals.

Neighborliness is significantly different from this separatist impulse. Thoreau did believe that Massachusetts had reason to separate from the slaveholding South, and individuals likewise had an interest in separating from all (mainly economic, but also religious and other) institutions implicated in slavery and its perpetuation, but he nonetheless promoted a general neighborliness toward those among whom he lived. Our present-day experience, confirmed by social scientists such as Dunkelman, is that "neighborhood" has become a relatively homogenous environment, but the village life Thoreau is referring to is a world in which farmers, artisans, laborers, professionals, and entrepreneurs were much more likely to live in proximity to one another than they are today. George Scialabba has suggested that the "beginning of political decency and rationality is to recognize others' similarity in important respects to oneself; that is, to identify imaginatively."[148] This is much less likely to happen with people who live apart, who do not, in Sandel's words, "share a common life." How much less frequent will such recognition be if we purposefully separate into doctrinally opposed enclaves?

Proximity is not itself sufficient to produce egalitarian recognition between people, or, to put it another way, to produce neighborliness.

The slave plantation, the feudal manor, and the industrial town provide plenty of evidence that unequal, undemocratic proximity is historically more common than democratic neighborliness; the rich and powerful have always required their workers and servants, and there's overwhelming evidence that they have generally been perfectly capable of both living closely with and believing in their own special superiority to common people. A social order with significant democratic equality is a precondition for neighborliness,[149] as is a commitment to egalitarian respect and recognition. The point here is simply this: Thoreau points to neighborliness as an essential component of moral life. If we are to take his moral lessons seriously, we must take seriously the suggestion that we cultivate neighborliness. This would imply bringing together people from different walks of life within a shared (proximate) community of egalitarian respect. This is not a claim about political democracy writ-large, but it is a claim about democracy's building blocks, about the elements of prepolitical democratic civil society.

The duties of neighborliness, for Thoreau, are not confined to maintaining good fences, occasional acts of mutual aid in moments of need, and a general leaving of one another alone the rest of the time. Although Thoreau obviously values solitude and personal independence, these goods do not, to his mind, exclude all collective acts of self-improvement. The critical passage in *Walden* concerning this point is found at the end of "Reading." Unsurprisingly, Thoreau criticizes collective action aimed only at pursuing our material well-being. The twist in his comment is that he suggests, instead, that we should be focusing on our collective intellectual and moral well-being: "We spend more on almost any article of bodily aliment or ailment than on our mental aliment."[150] Addressing his neighbors as his "townsmen," he proposes spending more on the Lyceum and public library, on imagining how to turn villages into universities, into "uncommon schools" that do not "leave off our education when we begin to be men and women." The village should be the "patron of the fine arts," should "hire some Abelard to lecture to us," should spend money on intellectual goods of greater value than trade and agriculture. "The one hundred and twenty-five dollars annually subscribed for a Lyceum in the winter is better spent than any other equal sum raised in the town." If we had our priorities in order, we would have sufficient wealth to cultivate our highest capacities. It is worth returning to these comments in detail:

> To act collectively is according to the spirit of our institutions; and I am confident that, as our circumstances are more flourishing, our means are greater than the nobleman's. New England can hire all the wise men in the world to come and teach her, and board them round the while, and not be provincial at all. That is the *uncommon* school we want. Instead of noblemen, let us have noble villages of men. If it is necessary, omit one bridge over the river, go round a little there, and throw one arch at least over the darker gulf of ignorance which surrounds us.[151]

Two points are worth noting here. First, we see the degree to which Thoreau is advocating a reformed public life at the local, neighborly, level. He doesn't use the words "politics" or "citizen" in this paragraph, but instead refers to a shared collective life at the level of the village or town. His goal is clearly a reformed common world, aimed less at wealth and power than philosophical cultivation. Second, education is central, for Thoreau, to pursuing and nurturing this reformed collective life.[152] His hostility to Massachusetts's and the nation's politics (these together constitute Thoreau's understanding of "the state") is matched by his optimism about the potential for moral and intellectual reform not only at the individual level, but also at the local level. This includes what I referred to earlier as the "social sphere," or what we might think of as civil society combined with local democratic self-governance.

Thoreau can imagine a renewed neighborliness that would set the stage for a democratic cultivation of moral and intellectual goods shared among neighbors. Neighborliness, in short, would ideally lead to shared educational commitments. Remember that in "Life without Principle," Thoreau suggests that we must learn to "Read not the Times," but instead, to "Read the Eternities."[153] The key to developing a "high and earnest purpose" is to step back from the noise and distraction of contemporary affairs and think more philosophically, more about general principles and less about the crises of the moment. We will never cultivate an "elevation of purpose," as he writes in *Walden*,[154] or challenge the want of a "high and earnest purpose" among our citizens, as he comments in "Life without Principle," without such reflection. In addition (or as a compliment) to neighborliness, Thoreau is placing his moral hope, in good American fashion, in the power of education. The education he has in mind is of a particular kind; it is a liberal education rather than an education in immediate affairs. The distinction here is not between vocational and liberal learning, since, as Thoreau insists, liberal learning is deeply implicated in how we choose to live at the most practical levels: "To be a philosopher is not merely to have subtle thoughts, nor even to found a school, but so to love wisdom as to live according to its dictates, a life of simplicity, independence, magnanimity, and trust. It is to solve some of the problems of life, not only theoretically, but practically."[155] Instead, his contrast is between an education that can discover and cultivate elevated purposes, and one which merely represents an ad hoc response to conditions as they randomly or accidently present themselves in the world around us.

The education Thoreau is promoting, both for the sake of private satisfaction and as the project of a rejuvenated community life, is parallel to his promotion of nature as an educator, which we will discuss in chapter 3. The argument is that our moral life has been overwhelmed by "expediency," that is, the preoccupation with immediate costs and benefits, and we have lost our anchor in moral principles deeper than consequentialist calculation. Liberal learning serves, from Thoreau's perspective, to allow us to step back from the parade of contemporary issues, events, and personalities, and to think more seriously and deeply about our obligations to ourselves and others. To do this is quite literally, for Thoreau, to learn to consult the philosophical and poetic traditions of world culture (we mustn't forget Thoreau's proficiency in the Western Greek and Latin traditions, his deep interest in classical Indian and Chinese philosophical traditions, and his familiarity with numerous modern languages, all of which opened up a universe of ideas well beyond his own New England inheritance). Neighborliness and liberal education are tied together by his (punning) insistence that the neighborly village or locality become the "*uncommon* school we want" (public schools were called "common schools" at this time).

It is striking that the kind of reflection and learning Thoreau is promoting is precisely the kind attacked on at least two significant fronts in our own time. Most obviously, the glut of information provided by the Internet continues to fuel a condition David Foster Wallace refers to as "total noise."[156] One recent critic has suggested that "tech companies are destroying something precious, which is the possibility of contemplation."[157] David Brooks points out that despite its usefulness "for the tasks and pleasures that require shallower forms of consciousness," these technologies "often crowd out and destroy the deeper forms of consciousness people need to thrive."[158] Much ink is spilled attacking the echo chambers of the Internet, the narcissism and blinkered vision it promotes, the paradox that as the information available to us approaches infinity our critical capacities for sorting and evaluating this information seem to atrophy proportionally. This problem has grown so pervasive that the U.S. presidency was captured in 2016 by a candidate who routinely distributed false or misleading information, and just as routinely denied the reality of true information and responsible reporting, a candidate described by one journalist as "postliterate—total television."[159] Significant elements of the U.S. electorate were unable to distinguish between professional journalism and the work of malicious Russian Internet bots spreading anti-Clinton and politically divisive propaganda. As our attention span shrinks to take in only the briefest moment, the twenty-four-hour news cycle plays to our desire for continual stimulation, public discourse shrinks to bumper-sticker and headline phrases and slogans, and our ability to evaluate our condition within broader and more stable contexts is significantly compromised.[160] "The Times" that Thoreau referred to, the newspapers during his lifetime, have been replaced in our own by fake news, Fox News, and the rest of the cable news channels, drowning out the idea of "the eternities" altogether. In our context, such eternities look either fraudulent or irrelevant to the conditions of our frenetic public life. Even intellectuals have become deeply skeptical about the reality of the "eternities," the stable moral principles Thoreau believed we should individually and collectively seek.

The second significant threat to Thoreau's position in our own time is found, paradoxically, in our educational system. It isn't news that liberal education is in retreat today. Even liberal Democrats such as Barack Obama, himself the product of an excellent liberal education, seem only able to evaluate American education from the perspective of economic development. Once wealth and commerce become the overriding (perhaps the only) standards, the kind of education Thoreau is promoting doesn't stand much of a chance. Consider, for example, economist Bryan Caplan's recent book, *The Case against Education.* When evaluated from the perspective of economic efficiency, Caplan assures us that "the humanistic benefits of education are mostly wishful thinking."[161] He would shut down all "impractical" departments in public schools and universities and cut all public funds to them in private institutions.[162] By "impractical" he means pretty much exactly the kind of ideas and disciplines Thoreau is promoting—philosophy, the arts, literature generally, everything we might call the humanities: "Making kids study irrelevant [i.e., not vocational] material for a decade-plus is timelessly dysfunctional."[163] The Internet, which seems so dysfunctional from the perspective of thoughtful and responsible evaluation, seems like a godsend to Caplan (he calls it a "Merit Machine"[164]), who views education as nothing more than skills acquisition. Caplan knows he's making an extreme argument, and his libertarian sensibilities enjoy the provocation. Those who want to defend liberal education entirely on practical grounds—something of a cottage industry in an age of reverence for the practical and applied arts[165]—will find the purely utilitarian calculations in Caplan's analysis strongly threatening to their project.[166] This would not surprise Thoreau in the least; we have already seen how strongly he objected to utilitarianism as a moral guide, and he would certainly scold those who defend "the eternities" on utilitarian grounds. It is also clear that the market-efficient education Caplan promotes (which would require the government to stop being involved in education altogether)[167] may provide vocational efficiencies. There is no conception here, however, of any public goods beyond these vocational efficiencies. Caplan's workers could not be expected to know anything beyond the more or less narrow set of skills required by their vocations. For the economist, this is not a concern; Caplan conveys no belief that individuals, or society at large, require more. Marilynne Robinson addresses the point like this:

> The argument everywhere now is that the purpose of education should be the training of workers for the future economy. So the variety of learning offered should be curtailed and the richness of any student's education should be depleted, to produce globally a Benthamite uniformity of aspiration and competence, and a subservience to uses not of his or her choosing. Max Weber's iron cage is slamming shut.[168]

Patrick Deneen is persuaded that our liberal society inevitably destroys liberal education, since liberalism "begins with the assumption that we are born free, rather than that we must learn to become free."[169] As Deneen understands it, liberal education begins with the assumption that freedom must be learned by studying what is known about appropriate limits, forms, and possibilities for human life. Liberal education, thus, seeks a philosophical understanding of the human condition. It is a fundamentally moral project, aiming to teach not skills alone but the art of living more broadly, the goods of a humane, appropriate, and satisfying life. Caplan's libertarian hostility to both state-supported and liberal education for children and young adults captures, in exaggerated but recognizable form, the liberal idea that "nature" gives us the appropriate impulses, wants, and desires that can then be effectively channeled by a market economy. No education in freedom is required; what we want is the protection of freedom for naturally self-aware and desirous individuals.

Despite Deneen's skepticism about liberal society's openness to liberal education, the democratic impulse in U.S. history has witnessed the steady expansion of liberal education for larger and larger sectors of our society over time. The opening of American colleges and universities to a broad democratic constituency, beginning in the nineteenth century and continuing over the course of the twentieth, aimed well beyond the goal of providing higher levels of vocational expertise. In many cases, such expert training was reserved for graduate study, while undergraduates were to be exposed to a general education less for the sake of their vocational development than to encourage their civic and humane growth. Even though it had long been recognized that elites insist on such learning for their children, Americans demanded that such was also the right of citizens from all walks of life. Robinson observes that it seems an odd perversion of contemporary society that we should reserve broad, humane thinking for specialists in the academy alone: "Surely it was never intended that the universities should do the thinking, or the knowing, for the rest of us. Yet this seems to be the view that prevails now, inside and outside the academy."[170]

Perhaps Deneen is right that liberalism, broadly conceived and experienced, tends to encourage a crass evaluation of all learning by the standards of economic utility. Nonetheless, there is a significant countercurrent in the American tradition, of which Thoreau is representative. Here, education is conceived as something to be widely distributed precisely *because* it should not focus on economic and vocational development alone.[171] The abolitionists, among whom Thoreau was a fellow traveler, were committed, in Robinson's words, to the "liberating force of education,"[172] and were part of a Protestant democratic reform movement committed to providing excellent public libraries, schools, and museums (she neglects to mention the profoundly important Lyceum movement, to which Thoreau was deeply committed).[173] Perhaps it takes one of our great contemporary novelists to expose the degree to which the economic and vocational assumptions in our current educational debates have debased our own educational inheritance. "I have felt for a long time," Robinson writes, "that our idea of what a human being is has grown oppressively small and dull."[174] Instead of being committed to education as an introduction of all students to the wide range of what is known and has been thought as a way of preparing them for the possibility of deeply satisfying and responsible adulthoods, we more and more think that all we can, or perhaps even should, supply them with is the narrow set of skills with which to pursue their economic livelihood.[175] The aim of a broad education is partly to allow democratic citizens to develop the knowledge and sensibilities required to prevent the powerful and interested from running roughshod over them.[176] There is even more to this liberal educational project, however. Yes, there has been the hope that broad general learning would promote democratic accountability, a widely equitable prosperity, and civic responsibility. It has also been believed that it would allow individuals their best opportunity for living interesting, self-aware lives. Robinson's comment about her childhood teachers in Idaho illustrates this value: "We were positively encouraged to create for ourselves minds we would want to live with. I had teachers articulate that to me: 'You have to live with your mind your whole life.' You build your mind, so make it into something you want to live with. Nobody has ever said anything more valuable to me."[177] All advocates of liberal education believe, as do Thoreau and Robinson, that there are both public and private benefits to learning broadly about the world as it has been and as we have inherited it. To focus our attention only on the contemporary moment, let alone only on economic matters, is to significantly shrink our ambitions. It is also to cripple our ability to think seriously and responsibly about our immediate concerns. In Thoreau's terms, to study "the eternities" is essential to our moral development. Anything less will compromise our moral capabilities, and such compromise will inevitably harm both our public and private lives.

THOREAU HAS BEEN SOMETIMES portrayed as the "hermit of Walden Pond," but he was far from advocating withdrawal or support for Descartes's motto "He lives well who is well hidden." The project of developing and maintaining moral integrity includes a significantly private component, but it also includes both neighborliness and a commitment to broad humane learning for a constituency as deep and wide as the democratic social order as a whole. Thoreau's pursuit of moral purity does not give us a fully developed democratic politics, nor in truth did it aim to produce one. We can be misled if we look to Thoreau for this, but even so, he does supply us with significant resources for helpfully thinking about the preliminary conditions for such a politics. Wendell Berry suggests, "We have no right to hope for a better world unless we make ourselves better men."[178] Berry captures a Thoreauvian sensibility in his comment, and Thoreau himself has provided some significant recommendations for how we might approach this project. To look for a more developed politics in Thoreau's moral thinking is to attempt to take Thoreau where he himself did not care to go. His insistence on neighborliness and liberal learning, however, may very well supply some democratic fortification against the threats to democracy we face today. I'll have more to say about these matters in my conclusion, but for now it is enough to recognize that Thoreau's moral project has much greater significance for thinking about the problems of democracy than we might be led to believe by his preoccupation with private life and personal moral awakening.

THREE

LEARNING FROM NATURE

Before we can adorn our houses with beautiful objects the walls must be stripped, and our lives must be stripped, and beautiful housekeeping and beautiful living be laid for a foundation; now, a taste for the beautiful is most cultivated out of doors, where there is no house and no housekeeper.

—Thoreau, *Walden*

Thoreau tells us that he "went to the woods because I wished to live deliberately, to front only the essential facts of life, and see if I could not learn what it had to teach, and not, when I came to die, discover that I had not lived." His goal was to "rout all that was not life."[1] The assumption was that he—and we—are too commonly distracted by cares, concerns, beliefs, and commitments that are, in reality, superfluous, unnecessary, superficial, and threats to our best interests and well-being. Life in the woods had the advantage of placing Thoreau outside the main hustle and bustle of Concord's daily life and allowing the noise of the village to be replaced by the sights, sounds, and feel of nature. This did not require that Thoreau retreat to unpeopled wilderness—an option he never seriously entertained in the fashion of, say, John Muir in Yosemite. Rather, the nature Thoreau seeks is on the border of human settlement; he speaks in "Walking" of the "border life" he has cultivated,[2] and Walden Pond is itself on the border of Concord Village and is commonly frequented by walkers, wood choppers, ice harvesters, fishermen, and other visitors, to speak nothing of the railroad running along the west side of the pond. Nonetheless, it is far enough from the town to dampen the noise of daily business and gossip, thus allowing Thoreau a more independent vantage point from which to consider his own life. Late in *Walden* he observes "how deep the ruts of tradition and conformity" run,[3] and his plan is to allow nature to offer more basic, essential lessons. He went to Walden to learn from nature, to attend to whatever instruction he could extract from her.

He in no way implies that this is an easy or simple task. When he suggests that "Nature has no human inhabitant who appreciates her,"[4] he is assuring us that learning to listen to nature requires effort and commitment. He writes a number of years later, "There is just as much beauty visible in the landscape as we are prepared to appreciate,—not a grain more," since "Nature does not cast pearls before swine."[5] So we need to prepare ourselves and open ourselves to nature's teaching, which requires at least a psychic distancing from our conventional social world—a couple of years at a neighboring pond, to say nothing of daily walks in the woods, fields, and meadows, are helpful in cultivating this psychic distancing. There is another essential element of this distancing that is important to recognize: for Thoreau, it must be freely and willfully chosen. It takes an act of decision. Emergency will not thrust these truths upon you or force you to learn what nature has to offer. Emergencies may force us to "rescue the drowning,"[6] but this is an obligation we have no (moral) choice but to respond to; we shouldn't expect moral illumination from this obligation—what needs to be done is clear enough as it is. The problem Thoreau is concerned with is a deeper one, how to deliberately choose a freer life. The lessons of nature must be freely sought to be learned. This, we will see, is an important point and will become relevant when we consider environmental thinking from our own time.

Once we begin to listen to nature, Thoreau believes we can expect a number of developments. One is that we become increasingly receptive to beauty. A taste for the beautiful, he believes (in good romantic fashion), is best cultivated "out of doors"; this is where we learn "beautiful living."[7] In addition to offering us beauty, nature presents us with symbols and images that reflect our conditions or concerns. Thoreau hoes beans "for the sake of tropes and expression, to serve a parable-maker one day."[8] He is "thankful that this pond was made deep and pure for a symbol."[9] The animals around us, he suggests "are all beasts of burden, in a sense, made to carry some portion of our thoughts."[10] His is a writer's, an artist's point: there is imaginative potential in nature capable of provoking us to think about ourselves and our condition in new ways, of shaking us out of the "ruts of tradition and conformity." This is not a simple-minded claim about a literal correspondence between natural objects and elements of human nature. It is a claim about the power of nature to provide imaginative grist for the mill, for our ability to be consoled, in our own desperation, by the "bravery of minks and muskrats."[11] When we look sympathetically and imaginatively toward nature we will find both beauty and the symbols that make moral inspiration possible. To change our lives, we need to be both attracted and inspired by alternative possibilities, and nature can suggest these to us. As Thoreau notes in a poem, only the practiced ear can hear what Walden Pond has to teach.[12]

Thoreau thus appears to believe that living in closer proximity to and sympathy with nature helps to cut away the superfluity in our lives so that we can "front only the essential facts of life." To do this is to recognize that nature is "our common dwelling,"[13] that the "essential facts of life" are really of the same sort for all of us. When he suggests, "Be it life or death, we crave only reality,"[14] the reality we find in nature reflects universal qualities. Indeed, this reality contrasts with the superficiality and transience of the world of human affairs. In nature, we are able to penetrate the surface of things, to find the changeless, the timeless, the eternal: "God himself culminates in the present moment, and will never be more divine in the lapse of all the ages."[15] In nature we are able to experience the moment, to live in the moment, which is what it means to be blessed, to be most alive.[16] Living close to nature, just like studying the world traditions of philosophy and literature, can teach us to "read the Eternities" rather than finding ourselves sidetracked by "the Times."[17] When we forget our affairs and focus our experience on the living world around us, we are able to simply live, to experience life in its most immediate and satisfying incarnations. These qualities are all related, for Thoreau: the cutting away of the superfluous; the awakening into the moment; and recognition of the timeless and universal. These qualities allow us the chance to be fully alive, which is also to share in understandings and experiences that are universal to people in all times and places. To capture these personal and human truths requires, for Thoreau, simplicity and a deep willingness to live "life near the bone where it is sweetest."[18] It requires that we turn to nature and become receptive to its most basic lessons. If we can do this, we, like the pond, can awaken to a new, robust, and even "timeless" or "eternal" life.

There is obviously a lot at stake, in Thoreau's mind, when he encourages us to "grow wild according to thy nature";[19] we can understand why he will famously claim, in "Walking," "In wildness is the preservation of the world."[20] We can also understand why it is that he will encourage us to preserve natural lands around our towns and villages: "Our village life would stagnate if it were not for the unexplored forests and meadows which surround it."[21] He is keen to remind us of the need to treat the natural world with respect.[22] We obviously must work with and enjoy the fruits of nature, but we must never forget that the highest goods are moral, rather than utilitarian or material.[23] He tells us, in light of his own bean-hoeing, that we need to be focusing more on the cultivation of a new generation of men than on beans.[24] Thoreau had written to his friend Blake (after the terrible death of Margaret Fuller in a shipwreck off Fire Island) that "our thoughts are the epochs in our lives, all else is but as a journal of the winds that blew while we were here."[25] Our thoughts partake in the universal and unchanging; this is the fundamentally idealist lesson of both philosophy and nature, most of what they have to teach. It is our intellectual, moral, and spiritual needs and potential to which nature ultimately speaks, beyond the utilitarian desires and requirements of our bodies.[26] Thoreau would later write, "All of our improvements, so called, tend to convert the country into the town. . . . Thus we behave like oxen in a flower garden."[27] If we think of the town as catering to our material needs, we degrade ourselves to the degree to which we fail to preserve the true resources of "the country," or nature, around our towns.

This point is important for helping alert us to a common misunderstanding about Thoreau's project. There are well-mined passages in Thoreau's writings that capture a biocentric ethos, such as in *Walden* when he warns his readers (actually, it is "mothers" he explicitly addresses) "that my sympathies do not always make the usual phil-anthropic distinctions,"[28] or in *The Maine Woods* when he writes about the value of all creatures and the spiritual nature of pine trees.[29] It is certainly true that he encourages us to respect the intrinsic value of all the elements of the natural world. But at the end of the day his project and perspective is overwhelmingly humanist. Consider his comment, in *A Week on the Concord and Merrimack Rivers*, "The sun is not so central as a man,"[30] and one of his last public pronouncements, in "The Last Days of John Brown," "For my own part, I commonly attend more to nature than to man, but any affecting human event may blind our eyes to natural objects."[31] In his *Journal*, Thoreau writes that "man is all in all, Nature nothing, but as she draws him out and reflects him."[32] None of these remarks should surprise us, given the general concerns of *Walden*.[33] Thoreau does not provide a systematic environmental ethic to fully explain the relationship between human and nonhuman value. What is clear is that he loved and respected nature deeply,[34] while also caring, above all, about the moral reform of human beings and the role nature might play in this reform. For our purposes, it is sufficient to note that Thoreau believed that for people to live both satisfying and morally compelling lives (which, as we have seen, constitute one and the same project for him) requires an inclination to learn, and talent for learning, from nature. Such learning is not simply looking in a mirror; nature, for Thoreau, has independent status and value. His project as a writer and artist, however, is primarily to use the natural world as a force for moral awakening or reform, and it is this project that makes him so significant in our American ethical traditions of thinking about nature.

There are important elements of Thoreau's discussion of nature that appear less settled or coherent than those we have mentioned so far. The "Higher Laws" chapter appears, at best, uncertain or ambivalent about the relation of nature and the wild to moral principle. He tells us, on the one hand, that he values the wild no less than the spiritual, and illustrates the point with his famous description of having the impulse to devour a live woodchuck. He also moves from discussing this wildness to explaining his repugnance toward animal food in any form and, then, to his claim that "Chastity is the flowering of man" and that "Nature is hard to be overcome, but she must be overcome."[35] Thoreau appears to be moving in two different directions in these passages: on the one hand, he seems to long for the transcendence of the body and material life altogether (recall his comment, "The wonder is how they, how you and I, can live this slimy beastly life, eating and drinking"[36]); on the other hand, he appears to be promoting the transformation and sacralization of the body through moral reform (here he draws on Indian and Chinese religious traditions). The evidence in this chapter alone would suggest that Thoreau was himself unsettled in his relationship to sensual life. Even if this is so, however, it should not distract us from the overall thrust of his perspective on the moral power of nature. As conveyed in *Walden* (and elsewhere), nature is a moral teacher of the greatest power. When we learn to attend to nature, we learn to live in the present, to focus on what is essential rather than ephemeral, and we experience what is timeless and eternal. In this way, nature helps us learn to live as fully, responsibly, and meaningfully as possible. Even if Thoreau himself hasn't been able to successfully untangle all of nature's lessons, he nevertheless points us, powerfully, in these directions.

THE NATURAL LANDSCAPE WAS the first great resource of liberation for Europeans migrating to North America. Whether it represented a haven for purified religious practice in Massachusetts Bay or Pennsylvania, or, in other colonies, a context within which to exploit natural resources for the sake of riches, the land was the site for the colonists to pursue their dreams, to free themselves from the constraints in their homeland. This, of course, was not the case for all who were new to this continent. For those who came to the Americas in chains, the land was a prison and, as Kimberly Smith notes, was viewed "not as pristine and innocent wilderness but as a corrupted land in need of redemption."[37] The African American tradition of environmental thinking, in Smith's analysis, has portrayed the natural environment as scarred and distorted; only free people can have a "healthy relationship to nature"; nature's potential is in a freer future, rather than the experience of the Founding.[38] For those who had freely chosen their new homes in what would become the United States, however, the natural environment, for all the suffering and difficulty it presented, provided the basic ingredients and preconditions for their deepest hopes and desires. As the nineteenth-century poet would put it, the landscape represented a "sweet land of liberty." The colonial world was not a liberal world, of course; it was not committed to individual autonomy or to what we would come to think of as the forms of modern freedom. That would come later, especially after the Revolution and, in the nineteenth century, with the growth of market society. Nonetheless, even the preliberal European forebears experienced the natural world in North America as the context within which they could enjoy a liberation from the constraints of European politics and society.

To liberate was by no means to assure the virtue of the people, however. Samuel Danforth preached a famous election day sermon in Boston in 1670, in which he reminded his audience of their special

"Errand into the Wilderness," their plan to establish a purified Christian community. Their decision to colonize "this waste and howling Wilderness" grew from their "Liberty to walk in the Faith of the Gospel with all good Conscience according to the Order of the Gospel, and your enjoyment of the pure Worship of God according to his Institution, without humane Mixtures and Impositions."[39] Danforth's audience had strayed from its mission and needed to be called to resist the "Pride, Contention, Worldliness, Covetousness, Luxury, Drunkenness and Uncleanness" that "break in like a flood upon us."[40] His reminder was needed to bring the congregation back to the realization that the liberty they gained in New England was to be used to strive for a religious practice no longer viable in England.

> To what purpose then we came into the Wilderness, and what expectation drew us hither? Was it not the expectation of the pure and faithful Dispensation of the Gospel and Kingdom of God? The times were such that we could not enjoy it in our own Land: and therefore having obtained Liberty and a gracious Patent from our Soveraign, we left our Country, Kindred and Fathers houses, and came into these wilde Woods and Deserts; where the Lord hath planted us, and made us dwell in a place of our own, that we might move no more, and that the children of wickedness might afflict not us any more.[41]

The liberty granted by this "New-England," which distinguished it from "other Colonies and Plantations in America" was precisely this "Ministry of Gods faithful Prophets, and the fruition of his holy Ordinances."[42] The natural environment was the context for a new beginning, fraught with religious and moral significance. But the people themselves required constant moral vigilance in this new land if their mission was to retain its moral purpose and preserve any possibility for success. Indeed, both the challenges and the bounty of the land threatened to generate behaviors and attitudes contrary to this mission—behaviors and attitudes that "break in like a flood" upon the people in this new world. Only continual reminders and chastisement, such as Danforth's sermon, could help keep the community firmly fixed on the goals their liberation was originally motivated by. The land could liberate, but could not of itself purify.

Early in the life of the new nation, however, there was significantly greater optimism about this issue than what is found in Danforth's Puritanism. The land itself came to appear to promote the kind of virtues required by free peoples. When Thomas Paine wrote in *Common Sense* that the colonists had it in their "power to begin the world over again," and that the "birth-day of a new world is at hand,"[43] his idea was that the Europeans in America were freed from Old World corruptions and decadence. It was possible for them to now live natural lives, that is, lives in direct contact with nature and inspired directly by nature's lessons. Perry Miller argues that Paine's tremendous success in capturing the moral imagination of the Revolutionary generation "consisted not so much" in the claim "that independence from England made common sense as in its implication that only America was close enough to nature, only these simple people were sufficiently uncorrupted by the vices of civilizations to permit common sense to operate at all."[44] The appeal of this claim was not limited to Paine's generation. Two generations later, Ralph Waldo Emerson argued, "The perpetual admonition of nature to us, is, 'the world is new, untried. Do not believe the past. I give you the universe a virgin today.'"[45] Nature, that is, erases the burdens of history and allows us a radically fresh start in the world (indeed, Emerson had ended *Nature*, his first book, with the charge to American individuals, "Build, therefore, your own world").[46] Two hundred years after Paine wrote *Common Sense*, President Reagan endorsed Paine's claims on the night he accepted the Republican nomination for the presidency in 1980.[47] A cornerstone of the American claim to be an exceptional nation has been this idea that our natural environment has allowed us to be forthright, direct, honest, natural people, uncorrupted by the artificiality and viciousness of undemocratic cultures or the burdens of ignoble histories. Common sense, rather than a dissembling sophistication, has been thought, in the United States, to be a gift of nature.

Thomas Jefferson expressed what has been perhaps the strongest version of this understanding when he suggested that farmers were the "chosen people of God,"[48] and that the "cultivators of the earth are the most valuable citizens."[49] The promise of America included the prospect of widely available and (relatively) equitably distributed land. Most Americans could become independent farmers. The immense landscape conquered from the native peoples, home to no ancient (European) families to claim control and ownership, allowed political democracy to grow from the wide access to natural resources. A huge percentage of Americans could be independent producers, and this independence would encourage virtues of self-discipline, foresight, public spiritedness, and concern for local affairs, and economic and moral independence. Wealth would be widely distributed, as would a particular kind of personality—proud, responsible, intelligent, industrious, neighborly. Under these conditions, nature would conspire with liberty to produce virtuous citizens. Put another way, liberty and virtue would be mutually supporting, given an appropriate relationship with the natural world.

A contemporary meditation on this Jeffersonian legacy is found in Charles Fish's beautiful memoir of a modern family farm. Writing at the end of the twentieth century, Fish recognizes that he was "born into the thinnest shadows of the vanishing era."[50] He grew up in town, but he spent summers on the family farm outside Rutland, Vermont, worked by his grandmother and uncles. As an adult who chose a life far removed from the farm, Fish provides no simple romantic portrait of this agrarian life. Nonetheless, he recognizes the virtues produced by the stern discipline the farm imposes upon the farmer: "I came to recognize a spirited nature which had been tamed and civilized by good upbringing and which had the good fortune to be engaged in work that demanded responsibility, decisiveness, action and vigor. In the heat of the forge, his native force was not weakened but was brought to a fine edge and applied where it was useful; he was well tempered."[51] Because the farmer lives in close proximity to—indeed, in participation with—nature, the cycles of birth and death are always immediately present, and Fish notes the irony that scatological vulgarity in thought and language increase to the degree one is removed from agrarian realities of waste and blood; the suburban or urban dweller is more likely to cultivate vulgarity, perhaps even as a virtue, than the farmer who lives daily among these elemental forces.[52] The discipline and moderation of the farmer contrasts dramatically with the excesses of consumer culture. Fish is clear that the farm does not promote philosophical virtues; indeed, he personally turned away from the agrarian world for precisely this reason. But it does tame, shape, and channel the human spirit, he believes, in an admirable and increasingly rare manner. This close contact with nature allows the farm to be a mechanism for training men and women in virtues that can never be comparably cultivated in more individualistic, urban, or market-oriented environments—environments further removed from the constraints and lessons of nature.

The good news is that Fish thinks there is reason to believe that an agrarian life can, in important and morally compelling ways, stimulate values Jeffersonians had in mind. The bad news is that the agrarian context he admires is disappearing from American society and has been disappearing for a very long time. And there is reason to believe that at least in part it is disappearing because of the values brought to agrarian life by American farmers themselves. Wendell Berry, in an early and important book, argued that the European migrants to North America had generally never been satisfied with where they found themselves: "As a people, wherever we have been, we have never really intended to be."[53] Berry suggests that the North American fur trade was much closer to being the model for European American relationships with the natural world than was Jefferson's agrarianism.[54] What this means is that the overall approach to the land among these farmers was much closer to industrial exploitation than republican agrarianism.[55] The wide availability of land, combined with a radically self-interested industriousness, attracted and reinforced the worst instincts of a restless people with an aggressive attitude toward the natural world. The struggle with nature can cultivate virtues and also vices, in some contexts promoting stewardship and humility, in others encouraging us to view nature as a medium upon which to display our power and mastery.

In a remarkable essay published by historian Carl Becker in 1910, "Kansas," we find a powerful argument about how the frontier selected for, and reinforced, a complex of behaviors and attitudes much closer to Berry's than Fish's (and Jefferson's) portrait. Following in the footsteps of his famous teacher, Frederick Jackson Turner, Becker elaborates on the effects of the frontier on those who settled there. His thesis is that a strong individualism was encouraged by the self-reliance and personal initiative demanded by frontier conditions; settlers simply could not survive and prosper in such a harsh environment without a good measure of these qualities. But the individualism nurtured under these harsh conditions has two distinctive qualities that may surprise us and even appear to contradict what we expect from individualists. First, Becker observes, the frontier conditions under which such individualism is nourished are quite similar for all those who experience them. Thus, "the frontier develops strong individuals, but it develops individuals of a particular type, all being after much the same pattern."[56] The result is less a society of diverse individuals than, paradoxically, a society marked by conformity and similarity. Because the frontier encourages the same qualities in individuals, they are likely to become, through independent means, quite similar in outlook and habit. In this way, "the individualism that is characteristic of America is one of achievement, not of eccentricity."[57] This helps to explain how it could be that an individualistic society could also be remarkably intolerant of difference and dissent: "It is an individualism of conformity, not of revolt."[58] What appear to be contradictory qualities grow, in Becker's analysis, from the same experience.

The second element of Becker's analysis suggests that the pragmatic character of Americas has often been misunderstood by observers. Yes, the energy and concentrated effort required by frontier living has the bluntly practical end of carving livelihood and civilization out of the raw materials of nature. The pragmatic, materialistic, and profoundly practical elements of the American character are justly famous. But this mustn't blind us, Becker suggests, to the tremendous idealism driving this entire frontier experience. Without an underlying faith and trust in human potential, people would never flock to the frontier in the first place, "for the frontier . . . offers little hope to those who see things as they are."[59] Realists would have little hope when sizing up the practical realities of the frontier.

The people who settled Kansas, in contrast, were driven by a faith approaching religious dimensions in their mission to use, tame, and shape the materials of the frontier into an environment both friendly to human life and as a monument to honor human achievement. "By some odd mental alchemy it thus happens that the concrete and the practical have taken on the dignity of the absolute, and the pursuit of convenience assumes the character of a crusade."[60]

The natural environment, for Becker, provides a fundamental set of facts helping to shape the American character, but the response to this environment was also deeply influenced by the type of individuals attracted to it in the first place. The Europeans in North America were, over time, less likely to be similar to Fish's farming relatives. Instead, they exhibited a noticeably more striving ambition and restless aggressiveness toward nature than we would expect from Jeffersonian yeomen. There is certainly a tradition of settled conservation of the landscape in America, but this tradition has been largely overshadowed, as Berry's earlier comments suggest, by a more industrial (if not rapacious) posture toward nature.

In *Democracy in America*, Alexis de Tocqueville quips, "Democratic peoples can amuse themselves well for a moment in considering nature; but they only become really animated at the sight of themselves."[61] This caustic observation correctly suggests that when Americans have thought about nature, it has almost always been in such a way as to think about themselves; perhaps the most obvious illustration of this tendency is Mount Rushmore, where the likenesses of four political heroes are literally carved into a South Dakota badlands landscape deserving of respect and awe in its own right. Nevertheless, even though it is true that the American relationship with nature is overwhelmingly colored by concern with human affairs, the critical edge of Tocqueville's observation is not fully deserved. In fact, the crucial split in the American conception of nature is precisely over the issue of whether nature provides appropriate limits for a morally admirable human life, or rather, in contrast, the context within which striving individuals prove their power and virtue by making nature conform to their will. If the former view informs Jefferson's (and Fish's) agrarianism, the latter is clearly dominant in the American tradition—even in its influence on much contemporary environmentalism. Both of these attitudes understand nature to be intimately involved with the moral development of Americans. They have significantly different perspectives, however, on precisely what this involvement properly amounts to. Tocqueville may be right, but the substance of his claim is significantly more complex than he implies.

Although the distinction between these two approaches to nature is significant, it hasn't always been as obvious as we might expect. We have noted that Emerson, in *Nature*, believed that Americans were in a position to begin the world anew, to escape the limitations, prejudices and habits of history and become, in contrast to Europeans, natural, free, and virtuous. In this book he also argues that without human contact, nature has no moral status or significance: "All the facts of natural history taken by themselves, have no value, but are barren, like a single sex. But marry it to human history, and it is full of life."[62] Emerson suggests that nature is "made to serve,"[63] that it "is so pervaded with human life, that there is something of humanity in all, and in every particular."[64] In perhaps the most famous passage in *Nature* he claims that if we approach nature with appropriate openness and vision, we will experience our own divinity: "Standing on the bare ground,—my head bathed by the blithe air, and uplifted into infinite space,—all mean egotism vanishes. I become a transparent eye-ball; I am nothing; I see all; the currents of the Universal Being circulate through me; I am part or particle of God."[65] It is striking that Emerson's consideration of nature seemingly leads to the disrespect of (or, at best, disinterest in) nature apart from human beings. Nature appears to exist for the sake of promoting and glorifying human potential. When we look at nature, we discover ourselves and our extraordinary, even godlike possibilities.

A less solipsistic reading of Emerson's message is also possible, however: rather than an anthropocentric ode to human greatness, *Nature*'s message may be more about how the natural world allows us to step outside ourselves, to gain a vantage point to challenge our temptation toward "mean egoism" and self-preoccupation. It provides a perspective to see beyond this more limited, individualistic scope of vision. Nature, that is, provides us with resources to understand ourselves in the deepest ways, to help us discover our greatest possibilities and character. In order to do this, it may need to chasten our common impulses and self-interest. Something like this could be what Emerson's friend Henry Thoreau meant when he claimed that "in wildness is the preservation of the world." Moral insight requires release from convention and the habits of society. The direct experience of nature provides this liberating and even humbling moral vantage point. Although we may find the muscular anthropocentrism of the first interpretation more explicit in Emerson's prose than the chastened moral education of the second, we can at least sense Emerson's own ambivalence on the issue.

IF EMERSON WAS HIMSELF unsure of which way to go, American society as a whole has not shared his ambivalence. We know from the vociferousness of Thoreau's protests that the general thrust of American economic life was leading, at best, toward a view of nature as resources for human exploitation and mastery. A popularized version of Paine or Emerson, suggesting that our passions and impulses were uncorrupted by history and thus reflected a kind of natural purity, was widely shared and, in Perry Miller's words, led to the conviction that "America, beyond all nations, is in perpetual touch with Nature," so we "need not fear the debauchery of the artificial, the urban, the civilized."[66] As delusional as this was, it encouraged a faith that unleashing economic energies across the continent provided the opportunity for democratic citizens to display their virtue through their vigor and industriousness.

This is not to suggest that there weren't dissenters, other than Thoreau, with significant concerns about this attitude. Two years after Thoreau's death, a brilliant book, *Man and Nature*, was published by George Perkins Marsh. Well before such observations became commonplace, Marsh warned about the pillaging of the natural landscape. "Man pursues his victims with reckless destructiveness," he observes.[67] The exploitation of the earth proceeds thoughtlessly and dramatically, and wherever man "plants his foot, the harmonies of nature are turned to discords."[68] These discords threaten not only the environment, but also the future welfare of the people who depend absolutely on the stability and prospering of that environment. Marsh was clearly alarmed:

> The earth is fast becoming an unfit home for its noblest inhabitant, and another era of equal human crime and human improvidence, and of like duration with that through which traces of that crime and that improvidence extended, would reduce it to such a condition of impoverished productiveness, of shattered surface, of climatic excess, as to threaten the depravation, the barbarism, and perhaps even the extinction of the species.[69]

Marsh sounded the alarm and suggested that a much wiser and farsighted approach to the natural world was required for the future well-being both of human society and the natural environment it depends on.

Such concern about the waste and destruction of natural resources informed the conservation movement during the Progressive era a few years after the publication of Marsh's book. Gifford Pinchot— friend to Theodore Roosevelt, the first professionally trained forester in the United States, the first chief of the U.S. Forest Service, and governor of Pennsylvania—referred to Marsh's *Man and Nature* as an "epoch-making book,"[70] and used his position of influence, authority, and professional expertise to help shape the Progressive agenda of conserving natural resources: "The conservation of natural resources is the key to the future."[71] This conservation requires the scientific management of resources, and an understanding of their importance in industrial terms; a forest, for example, is "strictly a factory of wood."[72] Pinchot was not, himself, without sympathy for those who loved forests in more aesthetic and noninstrumental ways, and who were disgusted by the role of the profit motive in promoting aggressive and destructive deforestation. Unlike the "denudatics" (those who aimed at a simple and uncompromising preservation), however, he had (in his view) the courage and the intelligence to admit that one could not simply outlaw the activities of the lumbermen. The powers at play were far too great for this: "The job was not to stop the ax, but to regulate its use."[73] Regulation would be accomplished by transforming the forests into sites for modern, scientific, industrial production, regulated and directed by state oversight. Pinchot and his contemporaries understood the obvious truth that unprecedented use of natural resources was necessary in modern society. Marsh had made clear, however, that unregulated and wasteful use would ultimately be self-defeating; it would destroy the goose that laid the golden egg. The task is not to restrict use, but to instruct and guide it, to make it wise and sustainable (our contemporary word, but the conservationists' idea): "The planned and orderly development of the earth and all it contains is indispensable to the permanent prosperity of the human race."[74] There is no question, from this perspective, that all the earth is available for humans to use as we please: "The earth and its resources belong of right to its people."[75] The only significant question is, how are these resources best used to assure that they will be available in the future for continued human growth and development. Scientific management and government regulation were not designed to inhibit the exploitation of the environment for human purposes; they were designed to make such exploitation intelligent and infinitely reproducible. In a message to Congress, Roosevelt (in words provided to him by Pinchot) made these points clearly: "The fundamental idea of forestry is the perpetuation of the forest by use. Forest protection is not an end in itself; it is a means to increase and sustain the resources of our country and the industries that depend upon them. The preservation of our forests is an imperative business necessity."[76] Marsh's alarm alerted Roosevelt and his comrades to the need for more directed and coordinated approaches to managing the natural environment than those promoted by an unregulated market.

Conservation was thus conceived as a support for the American project of using and subduing nature, rather than as a challenge to that project. Indeed, the aim was a greater and more effective mastery than what could possibly be achieved without scientific direction and administration. As Samuel P. Hays, the great historian of this movement, writes:

Conservation, above all, was a scientific movement, and its role in history arises from the implications of science and technology in modern society. . . . Its essence was rational planning to promote efficient development and use of all natural resources. . . . It is from the vantage point of applied science, rather than of democratic protest, that one must understand the historic role of the conservation movement.[77]

This was neither a populist nor an anticapitalist movement, and Hays is clear that corporations were as likely to support conservation measures as these measures were to produce popular resistance. Far from a grassroots democratic uprising, conservation grew from elite recognition of the need to take greater care in managing our resources. The general perspective was technocratic, in support of the growing modern democratic society and economy. As Roosevelt stated in 1908: "Let us remember that the conservation of natural resources . . . is yet but part of another and greater problem . . . the problem of national efficiency, the patriotic duty of ensuring the safety and continuance of the Nation."[78] The prudence of farsighted leaders would conserve the resources needed by this dynamic, evolving, and aggressive society.

The passion of Thoreau's protests alerts us to the fact that the general thrust of American economic life was already clearly moving in this direction by the middle of the nineteenth century, if not well before then. A view not unlike a simplified Emersonianism, that our passions and impulses are uncorrupted by history and thus reflect a kind of natural purity, was widely shared and, recall Miller's words, led to the conviction that "America, beyond all nations, is in perpetual touch with Nature," so we "need not fear the debauchery of the artificial, the urban, the civilized."[79] Such a view was also built on a profound unwillingness to admit or face the brute violence, horror, and injustice that accompanied the European peopling of North America; it encouraged a self-congratulatory faith that unleashing economic energies across the continent provided the opportunity for the display of democratic virtue. Aside from the toll on the native peoples and those brought and held in servitude (or, post-Reconstruction, in peonage enforced by fraud and terror), by the beginning of the twentieth century it became increasingly clear that these energies were significantly threatening the stock of natural resources even on the vast scale of the North American continent. Progressive conservationists understood that scientific management of these resources would be required to assure their perpetual availability to American society. Such a recognition, however, in no way challenged the dominant attitude of this society: that the landscape, with all its natural resources, provided the appropriate materials for democratic society to use as it saw fit in order to continue to grow, develop, increasingly flourish, and come into its own. The scientific management of these resources was itself an element in the proper mastery of nature for democratic ends. Though there would be dissenters to this view, the natural world increasingly appeared as the backdrop upon which democratic society would paint its portrait, rather than the educative context that would chasten and restrain our desires and impulses. If thinkers such as John Muir and Aldo Leopold would appeal to a less aggressive and more modest strain of American thinking about nature, these voices were faint and far between as the nation was transformed from a rural, agricultural society to an urban, industrial one. As shrewd as any observer of these developments, Perry Miller, in the 1960s, criticized Thoreau by suggesting that he was irrelevant in his own day and that he (and other like-minded writers) "provide us today with no usable programs of resistance."[80] In fact, for Miller, Thoreau's writings are an example of a "refusal to accept what I would hopefully term adult status."[81] Regardless of whether we agree with Miller's harsh assessment,[82] the point for the moment is simply that the Thoreauvian view of nature has been a minority one, contrasting with a more widespread desire to aggressively control and shape the natural world to conform to human will.

Just as this attitude informed the conservation movement of the Progressive era, so would it inform, to a significant degree, the mainstream of the environmental movement of the late twentieth and early twenty-first centuries. Accepting "adult status" has meant, for the vast majority of Americans, endorsing the project of mastering nature, as both the humane requirement for addressing human problems and suffering and for demonstrating our talents, skills, and virtue—even our "exceptionalism." The modern environmental movement is often dated from the first Earth Day in 1970, along with the establishment of the federal Environmental Protection Agency (EPA) by President Nixon in the same year. In many ways, the growth of the environmental regulatory regime in the last third of the twentieth century represents merely an extension of the conservation legacy from the Progressive era. It is true that there were nonutilitarian elements of this regime—most noticeably the Endangered Species Act—but the vast majority of environmental legislation, concerning clean air and water, for example, and the administrative oversight of natural resource extraction, was designed to mitigate externalities that escaped market discipline and to otherwise correct market irrationalities for the sake of public health and the intelligent exploitation of our landscape into the future. Progressive-era conservationists aimed at "wise use," while environmentalists today aim at "sustainability"; both movements are best understood by their focus on the rational use of natural resources. The mainstream of neither movement aims to radically reorganize society or challenge our deepest values.

Environmentalists and environmental regulators insist, of course, that we must moderate our demands on nature in order to limit our exploitation of the land and its resources to the degree necessary to assure their ongoing health and availability. This insistence does not necessarily challenge the view, however, that nature exists first and foremost to serve human purposes. The dispute with those who feel oppressed by environmental regulation is more often over the facts of the case—that is, about the need for such regulation to maintain our health and lifestyle into the future—than it is about principles concerning the relationship of humans to the natural world. Environmentalists are more often worried about what they take to be foolish behavior (regarding, say, our approach to climate change) than they are with attacking the foundations of mainstream public values as a whole. It is significant that the profound conflicts between environmentalists and the Republican Party in the twenty-first century have focused on empirical facts. The fights have become so strident and ideological—like the rest of our contemporary politics—that this fundamental truth is hard to see at present. In the final analysis, however, conservative Republicans—this includes President Trump, his secretaries of the interior and EPA, and the leadership of the Republican Party as a whole, and the active base of the party—are persuaded not that the facts are against them, but that the facts are being distorted by self-interested, ideologically liberal, and dishonest members of the scientific community (to say nothing of the Democratic Party as a whole). Neither camp wishes to fundamentally alter the basic modern project or the structure and values of contemporary society, despite their profound distrust of one another and their competing views about how to pursue this goal. Disagreement often takes the form of a fight between libertarians and those who believe state power is required to correct for damages caused by inequality and externalities in civil society.[83] For contemporary conservatives, environmentalists are insidious and potentially tyrannical liars; for environmentalists, these conservatives are fools. Such political differences are real enough and are extremely destabilizing, but they are differences within the overall (increasingly dysfunctional) family of the modern liberal world.

SOME OF THE MOST extreme, yet influential, elements of contemporary environmentalism bring these values into sharp focus. In 2004, Ted Nordhaus and Michael Shellenberger, two professionals in the environmental movement, published *The Death of Environmentalism*. The authors' worry was that the methods of the environmental movement, developed in the battles of the 1960s and 1970s, had proven ineffective in the conservative political climate of the new century. Despite declining effectiveness, the movement was mired in its routines, especially regarding climate change. Arguing that environmentalists need to "rethink everything,"[84] they sketched a strategy that could bring environmental concerns out of their "special interest" bunkers and integrate them into a broader progressive political program. The narrow focus on technocratic public policy and environmental regulations needs to be replaced, they believed, by a broader political vision focused "around core American values."[85] The narrow and negative focus of contemporary environmentalism must be replaced by "something inspiring,"[86] a more comprehensive political movement that integrates environmental concerns with the labor movement and other conventionally liberal constituencies.

This declaration was followed three years later by a book, *Break Through*, in which Nordhaus and Shellenberger tease out the full implications of their argument. As much as anything else, they argue, environmentalism has become handicapped by its negativity, its demands that we regulate and limit our activities: "Few things have hampered environmentalism more than its longstanding position that limits to growth are the remedy for ecological crisis."[87] A progressive politics, and the Democratic Party, must focus "more on aspiration than complaint, on assets than on deficits, and on possibility than on limits."[88] Inspiration should be taken from the "new high-tech businesses and the new creative class" that drives them,[89] for it is entrepreneurial energy and intelligence, not regulatory restraint, that will invent the technologies that will be both green and productive. "We must choose between a politics of limits and a politics of possibility. . . . And, most of all, we must choose between a resentful narrative of tragedy and a grateful narrative of overcoming."[90] Environmental thinking must be turned to the cause of producing, rather than limiting, prosperity. Only when environmental thinking is tied to economic growth and technological innovation will the movement be able to win allies and enter into the full life of American democracy.

One can read *Break Through* as very much a Silicon Valley manifesto, riding the wave of confidence in the potential of the postindustrial economy; there is a very techno-geek, California feel to the book. But it is not only technological optimism driving this vision, although there is that in plenty. Another critical claim that must not be overlooked is that a basic presumption driving the environmental movement—that people and nature are radically separate, that nature requires our protection and preservation, and that this requires certain sacrifice on our part for the sake of the nonhuman world—must be rejected. The claim, in short, is that the very category of "natural" is meaningless and unhelpful. Humans are a part of the natural world, just as much as anything else we find in the earthly environment, and it is our nature to build our world in such a way as to assure our prosperity. Indeed, the appeal to nature as something apart, as something with independent intrinsic value, they contend, has undemocratic implications: "What use is there in referring to what Nature wants, other than as a strategy to short-circuit democratic politics by asserting authority for a higher power?"[91] The appeal to nature apart from human interests is a tool in the politics of resentment, in which liberal "revenge fantasies" are spun out of hostility toward the ascendant political conservatism.[92] Instead of indulging in such fantasies, however, environmentalists should learn from their more successful political opponents. Such lessons suggest that environmentalists and those on the Left in general need to learn to tell stories of overcoming and triumph, instead of stories of danger and defeat. Shellenberger and Nordhaus fly to rather impressive rhetorical heights on this matter: "We will not put the world back the way it was, nor will we renounce our desire to control nature. We have risen, not fallen. In the words of one founding father of environmentalism, who long ago broke from the politics of limits, 'We are as gods and might as well get good at it.'"[93] Like Emerson, they believe "the only sin is limitation."[94]

Nordhaus and Shellenberger are certainly breaking with significant elements of the contemporary environmental movement, but their position is much less surprising or unique than we may think when viewed in the broad sweep of American history. Their appeal is simply to the revival, in the environmental movement itself, of a form of thinking that has long driven the moral perspective of American democracy toward nature. It is not only that nature exists for man's purposes. It is that nature serves a particularly ennobling function for human beings: both virtuous individual and democratic achievement are encouraged by our struggle to control the natural environment. Bringing themselves back in line with what they see as the core American values referred to in *Death of Environmentalism*, they celebrate opportunity and prosperity, and the creativity and self-fulfillment these encourage. This vision is the same as that which inspired the Progressive generation's conservationism, with its optimism about creating meritocratic and democratic possibilities for all. In a flourish of rhetorical flamboyance, they approve of Nietzsche's critique of resentment, and embrace his promotion of power, assertion, and willfulness, presumably without his pessimism about the pathetic weakness of the democratic many.[95] A more conventional environmentalism, they believe, is the true threat to democratic values: "The politics of limits will be anti-immigration, anti-globalization, and anti-growth. It will be zero-sum, fiscally conservative, and deficit-oriented. It will combine Malthusian environmentalism with Hobbesian conservatism."[96] Rhetorical excess aside, what the authors have done is precisely what they promised in 2004: to bring their environmental program to a liberal progressivism, a respect for political partisanship and the demands of democratic mobilization, and a commitment to an expanding economy. For Nordhaus and Shellenberger, nature dissolves as an independent entity and becomes a mere extension or expression of human will. There is no independent nature to admire, respect, or try to leave alone to some degree.

It is important to recognize that the character of the disagreement between these rebels and others in the environmental movement (Bill McKibben called Shellenberger and Nordhaus the "bad boys" of the movement after the publication of *Death of Environmentalism*[97]) is primarily political and pragmatic. Their concern is that environmentalists have become too pessimistic about limited resources, technological innovation, and a growing economy. Although it is true that many environmentalists do not share their optimism about technology and the market, and fear that a growing economy is unsustainable given the facts of resource scarcity, this is a significant yet pragmatic disagreement, rather than a disagreement over deeper moral principles and commitments. Even pessimists in this conversation are generally arguing for the best possible management of our environmental resources for the sake of the greatest possible human flourishing. Limits are obstacles to be managed and overcome rather than embraced as morally ennobling.

An emphasis on "sustainability" is, in the final analysis, an emphasis on the expected limits of human self-assertion, not as a morally educative reality but rather as a simple pragmatic fact of life, as a requirement of survival. Mainstream environmental organizations are more pessimistic about resource scarcity and human foolishness than are Nordhaus and Shellenberger, and more trusting of government regulation and less trusting of the market, but these are still arguments within a shared tradition. Human mastery of the natural environment is still the goal for both, even though there is deep disagreement about the degree to which this is possible and the best way to approach this utilitarian project. What is being proposed by Nordhaus and Shellenberger is a different political strategy and environmental rhetoric, but not a fundamental reorienting of the general thrust of contemporary society. This is more an argument about what is possible than about what is desirable.

Around the turn of the twenty-first century—that is, around the time that Nordhaus and Shellenberger were beginning to work out the ideas for their call to transform the environmental movement—scientists and others were beginning to introduce a new term, the Anthropocene, into the environmental conversation. The idea is that we have entered a new geological era, one fundamentally influenced by human activities, so there is no longer any meaningful component of the biosphere that hasn't been noticeably altered by the presence of human beings; in fact, human behavior has become the single greatest influence on the environment in which we live. The climate and environment no longer stand apart from people, to be managed and contended with to the best of our abilities. Instead, the whole of the natural world is itself increasingly a human creation. Observers from George Perkins Marsh[98] to Bill McKibben[99] have been deeply concerned about the effect of human industriousness on the environment, but the idea of the Anthropocene views this transformative activity as the basic reality to be negotiated in human affairs.

This reality indeed terrifies many environmentalists, who fear we are insufficiently wise or disciplined to manage such responsibility, but Bruno Latour has probably offered the most persuasive evaluation of the moral significance of the Anthropocene:

> It is impossible to appeal to the "equilibrium of nature," or to the "wisdom of Gaia," or even to its relatively stable past as a force that was capable of restoring order every time politics divided these scattered peoples excessively. In the epoch of the Anthropocene, all the dreams entertained by the deep ecologists of seeing humans cured of their political quarrels solely through the conversion of their care for Nature have flown away. For better or for worse, we have entered into a *postnatural* period.[100]

If the Anthropocene really does describe the contemporary human condition, Latour seems absolutely right that this would challenge any respect we may have for nature outside of human choice and action. In the more blunt and optimistic formulation of Stewart Brand (referred to approvingly above by Nordhaus and Shellenberger, but about which Latour would be deeply skeptical), "We are as gods and have to get good at it."[101]

This is precisely the clarion call that has rallied a group of influential environmentalist scholars, scientists, advocates, and activists around the label "ecomodernists," who issued an "Ecomodernist Manifesto" in early 2015.[102] From the perspective of this manifesto, the trick to becoming increasingly responsible stewards of the natural world is our ability to successfully remove ourselves from nature: "Cities occupy just one to three percent of the Earth's surface and yet are home to nearly four billion people. As such, cities both drive and symbolize the decoupling of humanity from nature, performing far better than rural economies in providing efficiently for material needs while reducing environmental impacts."[103] Engineering and technology are the keys to both human flourishing and environmental protection. The task isn't to integrate human beings more appropriately and lightly into natural environments, but rather to separate the human from the natural as much as possible. "Urbanization, agricultural intensification, nuclear power, aquaculture, and desalination are all processes with a demonstrated potential to reduce human demands on the environment, allowing more room for non-human species." In contrast, "Suburbanization, low-yield farming, and many forms of renewable energy production . . .

generally require more land and resources and leave less room for nature."[104] It is our liberation from nature that will best serve both ourselves and the natural world.

From this perspective, there is no reason to question contemporary understandings of human well-being—emphasizing ever increasing wealth, comfort, safety, health, and longevity—in order to manage and minimize our environmental effects. On the contrary, we must embrace, rather than mitigate, the logic of technological innovation and economic growth in order to properly embrace a respect and enjoyment of the natural world. Indeed, the protection and conservation of wild nature requires the separation of the bulk of economic and social life from as much of the wild landscape as possible. "An Ecomodernist Manifesto" professes a love for the rich diversity of nature, suggesting that although wild nature is unnecessary for human material prosperity, it *is* essential for human spiritual and aesthetic well-being: "The case for a more active, conscious, and accelerated decoupling to spare nature draws more on spiritual or aesthetic than on material or utilitarian arguments. Current and future generations could survive and prosper materially on a planet with much less biodiversity and wild nature. But this is not a world we want nor, if humans embrace decoupling processes, need to accept."[105] The modern values of material prosperity, personal freedom, and responsible liberal democracy are all, in this view, mutually reinforcing: "We offer this statement in the belief that both human prosperity and an ecologically vibrant planet are not only possible but also inseparable. . . . We value the liberal principles of democracy, tolerance, and pluralism in themselves, even as we affirm them as keys to achieving a *great* Anthropocene."[106] The ecomodernist project, built very much in the spirit of Nordhaus and Shellenberger's call for the transformation of the environmental movement, is nothing if not optimistic about our ability to continue to reap the promise of the Enlightenment well into the future.

To note the anthropocentrism of this vision is to recognize that this radical wing of the environmental movement has two components, one essential and the other optional (almost vestigial from an earlier, more romantic era). The essential element is to protect human life within a cocoon of artificial inventions and comforts. This project is progressive and never-ending, since the dangers we face and the desires we have and develop are also never-ending. It embraces liberal political administration and also the vigorous stimulation of technological innovation.[107] The optional element is the protection of biodiversity and wilderness systems. The ecomodernist position suggests that our spiritual and aesthetic needs demand such conservation efforts; a world without these natural goods "is not a world we want" nor "need to accept." But this is in truth a matter of choice rather than need, and it is not at all obvious that the technologically advanced civilization they champion will continue to be interested in such values at all—indeed, these look like lifestyle choices of the authors of the "Ecomodernist Manifesto," which they invite us to share, but which a liberal, free, and prosperous human civilization may or may not choose to embrace, depending on the uncertainties of whim and desire. There is nothing in the "Ecomodernist Manifesto" to persuade us that these values are essential to the human experience, even if certain individuals are drawn to them. Other individuals, surely, are not. Presumably in the kind of society they have in mind, this second environmental project—nature stewardship and wilderness preservation—would be selected, or not, by the market or by fair and democratic political processes, or perhaps by some combination of the two. The essential point is that the commitment to wild and diverse nature is supererogatory rather than foundational or essential to their vision.[108]

Even environmentalist critics of the ecomodernist position find themselves hard-pressed to avoid this position as long as they share the underlying utilitarian humanism informing it. Clive Hamilton observes the ecomodernist commitment to "secular humanism," which grants to humans "the authority to take control of nature" as first vigorously formulated in Enlightenment philosophy.[109] He is skeptical of the technological optimism fueling the ecomodernist perspective, but doesn't see any alternative other than to embrace the task of engineering nature.[110] Regardless of any sympathy he may feel for a stewardship perspective, such as that defended by Pope Francis in his widely discussed encyclical on climate change and inequality,[111] this is no longer an option as we enter the Anthropocene and leave the Holocene[112] behind: "Now, when Mother Earth opens her arms it is not to embrace but to crush us. Our goal can no longer be to 'save nature' but to save ourselves, from ourselves and from nature."[113] In the final analysis, it is hard to see how much distance there really is between his view and, say, that of Nordhaus and Shellenberger:

> In fact, my argument is not anti-technological but the reverse. Creativity—including, but by no means confined to, its expression as technological invention—is the defining quality of human beings, the world-making creatures. Our task on Earth is to use that creativity to transform the world around us in ways that allow humans *and* the natural world to flourish and strive to reach their boundless potential.[114]

There does not appear to be as much disagreement between Hamilton's moral hierarchy and the values informing the ecomodernist position he is so critical of. Technological mastery comes first (to the best of our ability), and then, to the degree possible, we should respect and leave the natural world alone. The latter is always contingent on our satisfaction concerning the former. And though ecomodernists are more optimistic about the technological ability to overcome resource constraints and mitigate negative ecological impacts than more mainstream environmentalists, and less enthusiastic about administrative technology, these are practical disagreements more than disagreements about the heart of a moral vision.[115]

The ecomodernist perspective is clearly tied to the familiar Progressive legacy of environmental conservation in the service of liberal democracy. It is also obviously related to a powerful technological utopianism. A number of years before the publication of the "Ecomodernist Manifesto," physicist David Deutsch published *The Beginning of Infinity*, which captured this optimism in a most extreme form.[116] Human beings, for Deutsch, are best understood as "factories for transforming *anything into anything* that the laws of nature allow." That is, people are "universal constructors."[117] Our evolutionary survival grows from this basic quality, which exploits the "intimate connection between *explaining* the world and *controlling*" it.[118] Claiming the legacy of the Enlightenment, Deutsch enthuses about our potential as problem-solvers, suggesting that the laws of nature "cannot possibly impose any bound on progress."[119] On the contrary, it is these laws, combined with our capacities to understand and use them to manipulate and transform nature, that is our great legacy from the past and hope for the future—a future that, in fact, allows for "infinite possibility" if we only embrace our essential human potential. Nature in and of itself is our enemy: the "biosphere is a grim place"[120] that "no more provides humans with a life-support system than it provides us with radio telescopes."[121] Anything we can do to transform the natural world in the service of human utility and power is for the good. It is our nature to transform the world, and our mastery is appropriately to be pursued without constraint.

In what is perhaps the best illustration of Deutsch's deepest commitments, he suggests that death itself will be overcome by human ingenuity. It is "absurdly parochial," he argues, to believe there is some "deep significance" in the fact that our bodies decay and die over time. On the contrary, rightly understood, the "problem of aging is of the same general type as that of disease."[122] The infinity Deutsch imagines includes overcoming all forms of danger and harm, including death. This idea has captured increasing numbers of technophiles in recent years, from historian Yuval Noah Harari ("for modern people death is a technical problem that we can and should solve"),[123] to young scientists in the transhumanist movement ("I do believe that death from aging is the biggest problem facing humanity"[124]), to protesters outside Google's headquarters with signs demanding "Immortality Now" and requests that the tech giant "Please Solve Death."[125] Journalist Mark O'Connell, writing about the transhumanist movement, quotes one individual hoping for a "liberation from the human form," and another suggesting that "flesh is a dead format."[126] As fringe as these attitudes are, they nonetheless represent at least a fantasy or dream informing the project of mastery. A character in a Don DeLillo novel suggests, much to this point, "At some point in the future, death will become unacceptable even as the life of the planet becomes more fragile."[127]

The ecomodernists say they value wild nature, but only from the perspective of urban society, with the protections this society provides so individuals may safely choose to enjoy the aesthetic and spiritual goods provided by nature without experiencing its discipline. Being integrated into the natural is not desirable; at the end of the day, nature is to be overcome, and the built world is to be embraced as self-validating. Transhumanists may be more optimistic than most (perhaps even delusionally so), but they do capture an Enlightenment dream. Max More, a prophet of this movement, writes in "A Letter to Mother Nature" that we will "take charge over our genetic programming and achieve mastery over our biological, and neurological process" and "seek complete choice of our bodily form and function."[128] All that should remain of us are our reasoning and willing capacities, as we are liberated from the confines and limitations of nature. The vision of the future is denatured, even disembodied, as the singularity replaces the longing for the resurrection of the body.[129]

A more sober account of our technological prowess is offered by Jennifer Doudna, a UC Berkeley scientist and pioneer in the field of gene editing. She is clearly uncomfortable with the ease by which her own CRISPR technology allows for the possibility of shaping, managing, and restructuring our genetic makeup. In her view, however, there is no reasonable distinction to be made between "natural" and "unnatural," so the only guiding moral principle for the use of such revolutionary and potentially transformative technologies is human utility. If her technology can alleviate human suffering, "the stakes are simply too high to exclude the possibility of eventually using germline editing [i.e., the editing of individuals' genetic code such that these changes will be passed to future generations]."[130] Despite working with a much less flamboyant rhetorical style than Deutsch, Doudna agrees that "one of the defining characteristics of our species is its drive to discover, to constantly push the boundaries of what is known and what is possible."[131] Paradoxically, human nature is appealed to as the moral rationale for why we needn't take nature seriously as a moral order. Our species's nature (that is, the qualities these scientists find within themselves and their professional colleagues, generalized to the species as a whole) is to strive to master the natural conditions required for our own well-being. The denial of a natural moral teleology is defended by an anthropocentric moral teleology. At the end of the day, despite her moral discomfort and occasional uncertainty, "it's important to let a desire to understand nature dictate the path forward."[132]

In response to attempts by bioethicists to regulate and control these types of scientific developments, Steven Pinker claims that the "primary goal for today's bioethics can be summarized in a single sentence. Get out of the way."[133] Scientists, in short, should be left to do their work. Doudna at least recognizes, in a way that Pinker's cavalier comment does not, the need for serious moral deliberation: "Essentially, we wanted the scientific community to hit the pause button until the societal, ethical, and philosophical implications of germline editing could be properly and thoroughly discussed— ideally at a global level."[134] But note two key implications of her comment: first, that the appropriate community for such a discussion is technologically expert; second, that this community is global and detached from any meaningful political responsibility. She observes that scientific knowledge can neither be unlearned nor confined to one nation: "Once a game-changing technology is unleashed on the world, it is impossible to contain it."[135] If nature is to be mastered, it is the scientific masters who will make the decisions about how to govern this process. Even they, however, appear driven more by events than by choice. There is certainly no local, or even national, democratic power to legitimately (or even imaginably) oversee this process, at least in the long run.[136] And again, we see an assumed teleology driving a perspective that claims to eschew all such naturalistic teleologies.

The point is not that ecomodernists or transhumanists represent the vast majority of environmentalists or scientists, let alone the population at large. On the contrary, they are minorities, in some cases a fringe (to many, comic or pathetic) minority, especially in the case of transhumanism. Yet they capture and exaggerate tendencies

in the dominant understanding of nature. In this way they help us
see the ideals underwriting many of our current modern attitudes.
It may be true that colonists and early Americans had hoped the
natural environment would encourage human virtue, would bring
out their most disciplined, restrained, yet independent and thoughtful qualities. It did not take many generations, however, to transform this hope, in the main, to the idea that we display our virtues
by conquering, rather than submitting to or reflecting, the natural order—calling into question the very idea of a natural order as
something demanding our moral respect and awe.[137] As our virtues
have come to be thought of as the virtues of mastery, so has nature become only alien and threatening, a set of raw materials to
be shaped as we see fit, or, at best, an aesthetic lifestyle choice for
well-outfitted and protected urban visitors. If nature exists primarily as the medium upon which we imprint our creative power
and ingenuity, moral life will grow from and reflect our power and
will alone. The initial dream that nature's nation would be a restrained and disciplined democracy has given way to a restless and
striving democracy, full of desire and conflict. The more we hope
to master the natural world, the less we seem able to enjoy a shared
vision of what is, in fact, good, just, and appropriate. We certainly
seem a long way from even the socially enforced conformity, growing out of shared experiences on the frontier that Becker identifies
in earlier generations. The American political community in the age
of Donald Trump looks to be devolving into angry and warring
tribes rather than reflecting an intuitive or unthinking conformism;
any more optimistic and admirable vision of shared public values
seems almost impossible to imagine as incompatible passions and
desires explode into our public life. Even scientists, who claim to
speak for the realities of the natural world, are distrusted by fellow
citizens who assume they are as corrupted by their own passions
and interests as everyone else. At a time when mastery seems so
close at hand, as through the manipulation of the gnomic stuff of
life itself, the climactic conditions required for human life (to say
nothing of conditions for the bulk of species we share the biosphere
with)[138] appear to be threatened by our ever-increasing scientific

proficiency.[139] Nature appears more alien and inhospitable than ever. In a world producing radically divergent wants, desires, and identities, the ability to appeal to a natural moral standard has dissolved; the wants appear anarchic and self-justifying. The hope for moral lessons and the disciplining of passion by nature looks like a distant dream, and perhaps an impossible one for the democratic many.[140]

FOR ALL THAT, HOWEVER, the old desire to live by nature's standards refuses to die. During the Great Depression, John Crow Ransom, a member of the Southern Agrarians, praised the (near) subsistence economy of simple agrarianism both because it prevents antisocial competition between independent farmers and because it will never be able to produce enough surplus to cultivate crass consumerist materialism. The bulk of the land, he enthused, is actually "unfit for intensive money-making," yet because of its "very excellence and abundance, it is ideal for home-making."[141] Modest homesteads produce farmers who will be "the most innocent and esteemed members in the economic society because they alone will not injure each other through competition." This agrarianism will "restore to our economic life some of the humanity which it lacks today."[142] Here, during the height of industrial capitalism's greatest crisis in the twentieth century, the dream of a more stable and virtuous economy, with citizens shaped by the constraints of the natural landscape, was alive (if not well).

Likewise, the tradition of Progressive conservation produced, in Aldo Leopold's posthumous essay "The Land Ethic," a classic of modern environmentalism that subverts the anthropocentrism of the conservation tradition he grew out of. A product of Pinchot's Yale School of Forestry, a professional forester, and professor of game management at the University of Wisconsin, Leopold's conservation credentials were impeccable. Toward the end of his life, however, he became convinced (as we mentioned in chapter 1) that it was both possible and necessary to extend the boundaries of the moral community to include not only the human world but the natural environment as a whole—or, as he says, "soils, waters, plants, and animals, or collectively: the land."[143] This extension of moral consideration, he thought, is both "an evolutionary possibility and an ecological necessity."[144] His lifelong study made him sensitive to the essential ecological interrelationships and interdependencies of the various components of the land, while also driving home that many ecological goods lay entirely outside the realm of economic value and concern.[145] To the degree that conservation has been captured by economic interests, it will be blind to a host of ecologically essential goods. Only an extension of moral concern to the land as a whole will allow for a full and satisfactory understanding of our moral obligations. To make this move was to fundamentally alter our understanding of the human relationship to the nonhuman world: "In short, a land ethic changes the role of Homo sapiens from conqueror of the land-community to plain member and citizen of it. It implies respect for his fellow-members, and also respect for the community as such."[146] When we remember that for Pinchot conservationism promised "the planned and orderly development of the earth and all it contains," and that the "earth and its resources belong of right to its people,"[147] we begin to get a sense of how far Leopold had moved from the sensibilities of conservationism's first generation. He suggests that conservation "is a state of harmony between men and land."[148] Whereas the emphasis for Pinchot had been control and use into the unlimited future, Leopold emphasizes forms of restraint as an ethical rather than an ecological imperative, and which may in fact be contrary to our utilitarian wants. The science of ecology and the practice of conservation suggest to Leopold an intrinsic value in the natural world that requires a significant reorientation of our moral sensibilities. He is less confident about the promise of scientific control than many of his conservationist colleagues,[149] but more confident that this knowledge can help promote "love, respect, and admiration for land, and a high regard for its [moral] value."[150]

Progressive conservationism and its modern environmental equivalent is, at its core, a survivalist doctrine. What is common to Ransom and Leopold, and all those who inherit their sensibilities about the possibility of discovering moral lessons in nature, is the insistence that nature is to be valued beyond concerns for our own survival. The greatest representative of this view today is Wendell Berry, who began his career as an essayist (he was already a writer of poems and fiction) by self-consciously drawing his inspiration from the great founder of this strain of environmentalism and nature thinking, Henry David Thoreau.[151] In 2012 Berry was awarded the United States' highest official honor for a contributor to the humanities by being selected by the National Endowment for the Humanities to deliver the Jefferson Lecture at the John F. Kennedy Center in Washington, DC. His address, "It All Turns on Affection," transformed this honorary occasion into a moment of profound protest against the main currents of American society, indeed, against the deepest tendencies of our modern culture.[152] Those familiar with Berry's work were unsurprised by his message; his words that evening were, in truth, deeply consistent with the steady stream of essays, poems, and fiction that have flowed from the tips of his pencils for decades. This familiarity, however, couldn't disguise the fact that Berry, one of our most trenchant contemporary critics, believes that America is built on a destructive and terribly mistaken set of economic priorities, and that these priorities reflect in turn a significant moral decay at the heart of our culture.

Berry sketches a contrast between the perspective of James B. Duke, the tobacco industrialist and founder of Duke University, and his own grandfather, a Kentucky farmer. He explains that his grandfather's hardships as a small farmer were exacerbated when, as a result of the monopoly of Duke's American Tobacco Company, he was forced to sell his 1906 tobacco crop for no profit. Duke was building a successful business empire precisely because he understood the logic of capitalism: to maximize profit, to defeat and destroy to the extent possible all competition, and to take one's profits and follow one's opportunities for future profits wherever they may lead. Duke's business enterprise was a form of "pillage in absentia." He "went, or sent, wherever the getting was good, and he got as much as he could take."[153] The desire was for power. The knowledge used to pursue this power was abstract "statistical" knowledge, in which commodities like tobacco are reduced to a common market calculation, in which individual farmers and farms and the land upon which these farmers and farms preside recede from the field of vision. The entire process, which enriched the industrialist and diminished family farms, was motivated, not to put too fine a point on it, by greed. Such greed is insatiable and drives the industrial process. It transforms our relationships with the world and shapes (or, more accurately, deforms) both our human relations and our relations with the land and the rest of creation.

In Berry's view, the contrast between Duke and his grandfather could not have been greater. Whereas Duke was driven by an insatiable desire for what he did not have, the grandfather was motivated by more modest joys found "in his place and his affection for it, in its pastures, animals, and crops."[154] Rather than always desiring more, Berry's grandfather embraced the limits of his world, and the boundaries these provided for his own enterprises and dreams. Instead of love of wealth and power, Berry's grandfather loved his farm and community. Rather than bending the world to his will, he thought of his life's work in terms of stewardship, of respecting and preserving what he took to be a natural health in the land for all the plants and creatures—including people—who live there. Insatiable greed powers the Dukes of the world, while love of place, affection for locality, and a contentment with what is brings satisfaction to men and women like Berry's grandfather, despite the hardships they endure. In the ruthless world of the national and international marketplace, people of this sort look like romantics, losers, and people left in the wake of progress. In their locality, they look like thoughtful and responsible custodians of the land and good neighbors. Duke and Berry's grandfather were both driven by love, but what they loved was profoundly different; the love of wealth and power reflects merely an inordinate love of self, while the love of place reflects a love of a whole community. The former finds meaning in the imposition of one's will on the world; the latter finds meaning by contributing to the flourishing of the entire—human and nonhuman—community.

Profoundly different forms of knowledge are required by these different sensibilities. Berry calls Duke's knowledge "statistical," or abstract knowledge that reduces the universe of objects to general categories. Such knowledge is analytically powerful and morally obtuse. The knowledge his grandfather cultivated was personal and particular, relating to the fundamentally unique qualities of a given place. This kind of knowledge is much less generalizable than statistical knowledge, but it is deep and complex. It also helps locate us within a place and is thus capable of generating affection and stimulating ethical concern beyond one's desire for power to command.[155] Statistical knowledge captures the logic of industrialism, the creation of productive systems that can be replicated in any place or context; personal knowledge is contextually bound to locality. Statistical knowledge reduces agriculture, for example, to a handful of universal rules and principles; particular or local agricultural knowledge is attuned to the unique quality of any given piece of land or region. The former seeks uniformity; the latter seeks to understand and encourage the unique and distinctive in each place. Statistical knowledge serves concentrated, centralized human power. Particular knowledge serves localities and natural health.

These two forms of knowledge have fundamentally different purposes. Local knowledge aims to preserve and maintain the land and all (plants, animals, and people) who live on it now and into the future. Only individuals with intimate knowledge of local flora and fauna, the peculiarities of local weather, soils, drainage, insects, and so forth, will find themselves in a position to maintain not land in general, but this land in this specific place. The goal of local knowledge is the stewardship of a complex and unique local ecology in the present and into a stable future. Such knowledge is conserving and conservative, preferring stability to change. Statistical knowledge, in contrast, aims to discover the laws of nature for the purpose of controlling the nonhuman world in the service of human desire and interests. Such knowledge is progressive, pragmatic, and entirely anthropocentric. Rather than conserving, it is transformational. Rather than aiming at the stability and flourishing of the local (human and nonhuman) community, it aspires to mastery of all natural processes. Local knowledge is bounded by the experience and observation of the individuals living within that community, and by the affection that grows for this community through the process of cultivating human lives and purposes within this local context. Scientific knowledge is bounded only by the ignorance not yet abolished by increasingly powerful scientific practice. These limitations promise to be overcome in time, so science will be limited only by the natural laws increasingly understood and refined though the scientific method: "Beginning in science and engineering, and continuing, by intimation, into other disciplines, we have progressed into the belief that humans are intelligent enough, or soon will be, to transcend all limits and to forestall or correct all bad results of the misuse of intelligence."[156] Local knowledge is modest and humble; scientific knowledge aggressive and self-confident. Service is the aim of the former; mastery the aim of the latter.

Berry admits to a profound skepticism about scientific ambition and optimism. In truth, he believes, the practical application of statistical knowledge has disastrous effects on the natural world, and there is every reason to believe these effects are only accelerating in tandem with our foolish self-confidence. Industrial society, the offspring of the statistical mind-set, is an increasingly obvious and severe ecological disaster. Our fantasy of mastery will inevitably, in Berry's view, come back to haunt us: "Truth will retaliate with ugliness, poverty, and disease."[157] The sickness of both the land and the human communities that depend on it is the necessary result of our increasingly radical application of statistical knowledge to all facets of our lives.

To reject this attitude is to recognize "human limits and the necessity of human scale."[158] In contrast to the view that nature can, over time, be effectively understood and thus successfully commanded, Berry suggests that nature is "the impartial mother of all creatures, unpredictable, never entirely revealed."[159] Nature will always be shrouded in mystery, and to deny this is to succumb to hubris, to lose an understanding of our own (limited) natural capacities. In truth, these capacities are much more suitably adapted to local, immediate, particular knowledge than to abstract, generalizable knowledge: "The reality that is responsibly manageable by human intelligence is much nearer in scale to a small rural community or urban neighborhood than to the 'globe.'"[160] Only at the local scale is our understanding both informed and chastened by affection. Statistical knowledge cannot generate a similar kind of love, as affection can only be stimulated and maintained by particular things (the love driving statistical knowledge is best represented by money, a completely generalized form of value). Without affection, our weaknesses and vices are unleashed in the service of wealth and power, without significant regard for either the land or other people. Local knowledge produces concern for and commitment to others as a moderating (if imperfect) break on our self-love; statistical knowledge encourages irresponsible hubris. For humans to live well is to live modestly, in Berry's view, even if such modesty appears as a foolish or romantic fatalism to the world that produced, encouraged, and lionized James B. Duke.[161]

Berry admits that the accomplishments of industrial society have "brought some increase in convenience and comfort and some easing of pain."[162] This may seem a grudging, even not fully honest, admission to many readers; there is no doubt that medical technologies alone, for all their admitted unintended consequences, have brought unimaginable and very welcome relief to the human estate, and promise much more in the future.[163] Regardless of whatever utility industrial society produces, however, Berry is clear: these goods are produced at the cost of ecological disaster and the subversion of the human community. Indeed, his claim is that at the deepest level, industrial society represents an alienation of people from the world and their natural condition. In the final sentence of the lecture, Berry suggests, "We do not have to live as if we are alone."[164] The industrial society we have embraced is not only dangerous, destructive, and antisocial, it is inhumane, and represents a failure to recognize humans' proper place in the world, our proper relations to one another, and to the land. To live more like his grandfather, rather than James B. Duke, is to live in relative health, harmony, and community with the rest of creation. The kind of mastery represented by Duke produces alienation from both the earth and from one another. To be receptive to the goods and lessons of the local landscape, as was Berry's grandfather, is to live a life integrated into both the human and ecological communities.

Many of the elements we find in Berry's lecture are familiar to a Thoreauvian strain in contemporary environmental literature: the belief in natural limits to human activity, the distrust of the urban and industrial, the promotion of the local and rural, the hostility to purely instrumental rationality, and, perhaps most importantly, the idea that we must claim (or reclaim) a more modest form of living for both our own health and the health of the natural world. The choice is stark. On the one side are the destructive forces of the modern world, driven by an aggressive and selfish humanism; on the other is a belief that nature can teach a more restrained yet rewarding form of living. Berry is self-consciously participating in a long intellectual tradition championing the latter view. But though there is a much richer communitarian sensibility in his writing than we find in *Walden*, what he shares with Thoreau is nonetheless overwhelming. If the mainstream of the conservation and modern environmental movement reflects the modern world's general values and attitudes, here is a less pervasive yet obviously vigorous counterpoint to these attitudes within the broader environmental tradition (and American society). The Thoreauvian belief that we can learn from, and properly frame our lives within, limits defined by nature lives on in Berry's life and work.

Most importantly, we find in Berry and those with similar sensibilities a forceful assault on the core Enlightenment commitments of contemporary society. Rationality, in this modern and (from Berry's view) perverse form, has been alienated from a morality informed by the natural order of creation and the love of things greater than ourselves. As we have become estranged from our natural condition, reason has been placed in the service of power and power alone. The outcome is both unhappy and dangerous, but the temptations of power are great and difficult to resist. This development, Berry assures us, is not inevitable,[165] but the very success of reason in reshaping the natural world to suit our purposes, or at least the illusion of such success, makes it extremely difficult to resist. The human ego has been unleashed on the world by modern science and Enlightenment reason, and the human community and also the natural world at large suffers as a result.[166] We will return to this matter below, but for now it is sufficient to note that for Berry, the logic of modern reason is selfish and cut off from moral life through its project of transcending the natural world. Moral life, in Berry's view, must be embedded in the natural, while the modern perspective so often suggests that the natural, instead, is to be mastered by humans for whatever purposes we deem fit. This is why he claims, early in *It All Turns on Affection*, that "the problem that ought to concern us first is the fairly recent dismantling of our old understanding and acceptance of human limits."[167] We can appreciate the radicalism of Berry's views when we recognize that he is making two claims that chafe against the modern sensibility: first, that there is, in fact, a natural moral order to which we are subject; second, that we will live less destructive, but also freer and more satisfying, lives if we abandon the fantasy of controlling or even escaping nature and, instead, submit to this natural moral reality (which requires, just so there is no confusion here, much more modest ways of living than have become the norm and aspiration in modern society).

It is striking, of course, that Berry's lecture, delivered on the occasion of his receiving one of America's highest honors, should be so critical of so much that is undeniably common, even essential, to American society (and modern society more generally). How does it happen that contemporary America, obsessed as it is with economic transformation, growth, and global hegemony, would pause to recognize a poet farmer who believes that "in such modest joy in a modest holding"—such as the farm held by his grandfather—"is the promise of a stable, democratic society, a promise not to be found in 'mobility'"?[168] These comments reflect opinions Berry has been defending for decades. As far as he obviously and self-consciously stands from the mainstream of our social and political culture, he equally obviously also taps into something essential in our experience, something we may faintly recognize and even long for, despite both the passion and fatalism with which we pursue the life he criticizes. The legacy of the Enlightenment, animated by the dream of mastering nature and alleviating man's estate, is a seemingly overwhelming force driving not only our modern economy but even the mainstream of the modern environmental movement. Yet Berry keeps alive an alternative tradition, grounded in the legacy of Jeffersonian agrarianism and the Thoreauvian turn to nature, that also continues to resonate within contemporary American society. Even as a dissenter within the literary and agricultural communities, he captures a longing that haunts our imagination even at this late date, a longing to be guided by nature, to live as if we are not alone.

Over the course of his long and prolific career, Berry has consistently sounded this direct challenge to the primary thrust of so much of contemporary liberal culture. He has repeatedly claimed that we lose our humanity when we are possessed by the impossible Enlightenment ambition of mastery, that it literally makes us tyrannical in our human relations and in our relations with the natural world. His idea, at its base, is that all of creation (including human beings) are transformed by such an attitude into superficial objects to be manipulated for the sake of progress, wealth, power, and domination. When humans are the only creators, there is no limit to their willfulness in transforming, reshaping, mastering the world around them.[169] There is no reason to think that the Dukes and other industrialists in the world, to say nothing of the engineers and scientists, will think of human beings (and the broader world at large) as anything other than part of the stage upon which they will make their mark. This sensibility is, Berry fears, fundamentally violent and aggressive in character.

In addition, the project is based on an illusion, a lie claiming that the world around us can be known in its entirety. Mystery, as we have seen, is for Berry a central and inevitable element of the human condition. Because of the basic limitations of human understanding, scientific progress can never overcome our uncertainty about meaning and our confusions about moral obligation.[170] The reductive powers of science are simply not equipped to address the inscrutability of animate creation. This fact alone should warn us that humans are not to be trusted with power beyond the local, where the effects of their acts are most obvious and individuals are most likely to be held responsible (by themselves and others). As the barber in Berry's fictitious Port William, Jayber Crow, comments, "I fear changes made by people with more power than I've got."[171]

Berry is committed by faith to the view that there is a moral universe beyond our own wills. In *The Art of the Commonplace* he notes, "It is not from ourselves that we will learn to be better than we are," and "Fidelity to human order . . . if it is fully responsible, implies fidelity also to natural order."[172] In *Citizenship Papers*, he writes in a similar vein: "The practical point is that if I believe life is a miracle, I will grant it a respect and a deference that I would not grant it otherwise. If I believe it is a miracle, then I cannot believe that I am superior to it, or that I understand it, or that I own it."[173] We must distrust and chasten the moral impulses driving modern politics, economics, and consumer society:

> The moral argument points to restraint: it is a conclusion that may be in some sense tragic, but there is no escaping it. Much as we long for infinities of power and duration, we have no evidence that these lie within our reach, much less within our responsibility. It is more likely that we will have either to live within our limits, within the human definition, or not live at all. And certainly the knowledge of these limits and of how to live within them is the most comely and graceful knowledge that we have, the most healing and the most whole.[174]

The utopian fantasy of the ecomodernist and transhumanist, even the nonutopian progressive humanism of more modest moderns, is a nightmare to Berry's mind.

Like Thoreau, Berry believes a meaningful human life must be informed and framed by nature, rather than defining itself through a struggle to overcome nature. We must treat the natural world with care and respect not merely because of our need to protect, sustain, or repair the conditions for our own survival. In addition, we need to understand that the meaning of our own lives is contingent upon the constraints of nature—including, significantly, the constraint of death. Berry writes in a poem, "If we have become incapable / of denying ourselves anything, / then all that we have / will be taken from us."[175] As his compelling fictional character Hannah Coulter suggests, "You mustn't wish for another life. You mustn't want to be somebody else. What you must do is this: 'Rejoice evermore. Pray without ceasing. In every thing give thanks.' I am not all the way capable of so much, but those are the right instructions."[176] There is no lack of sorrow, misbehavior, even violence and hatred, in Berry's novels and stories. But his most powerful and moving characters, such as Hannah Coulter, accept their lot and attempt to live as respectfully with the land and others as possible. Indeed, their human dignity grows from their acceptance of and gratitude for their lives as they are given. This requires a modesty in their ambition, and a deep sense that their humanity grows not from self-assertion and autonomy (a liberal ideal Berry loathes)[177] but instead through their cooperation with and service to others. It requires love—the only immoderate force in Berry's moral universe—of the created world as it is given.

THE DIFFERENCES IN TONE between Berry and Thoreau are real enough, most importantly when we notice the contrast between Thoreau's emphasis on individual independence and Berry's rich exploration of communal life and human interdependencies. Despite this obvious difference, however, they both speak clearly to the need to respect and learn from what they understand to be the natural context in which a rewarding human life is to be lived.

As we briefly suggested in chapter 2, the Thoreauvian challenge to Enlightenment humanism is infused with a religious sensibility. Thoreau was himself by no means a conventional Christian, and he bragged in *Civil Disobedience* about having formally renounced membership in the church (thereby releasing himself from the obligation to support the clergy through his taxes).[178] Despite his rebellion from Concord's religious institutions and conventions, however, we find a noticeably religious quality in *Walden*. He criticizes the degree to which the Christianity practiced around him constitutes a kind of grim endurance and consolation, predicated on a tragic conception

of life. He complains, "There is nowhere recorded a simple and irrepressible satisfaction with the gift of life, any memorable praise of
God." To become "worthies of the world" requires that we embrace
and enjoy the life given us; this alone, he believes, would constitute
the legitimate and appropriate praise of God.[179] He speaks reverently
of Walden itself, as when he calls it "God's drop."[180] He suggests that
from God's perspective, we are similar to the insects observed from
our own human perspective.[181] Perhaps most tellingly, he speaks of
his quest to know God and the eternal: "God himself culminates
in the present moment"; "in dealing with truth we are immortal,"
and "need fear no change nor accident"; "So our human life but dies
down to its root, and still puts forth its green blade to eternity"; in
solitude we come close to God, "whose work we are."[182] These sentiments are poetically expressed and convey no conventional Protestant teaching or doctrine; they reflect Thoreau's ecumenical mining
of world philosophical and religious traditions. The point is simply
that Thoreau conveys a faith that nature has moral content, that we
are only a part of this moral universe, that we can learn from this
moral universe, that we owe it fidelity, and that if we recognize and
act on these truths our lives will be rejuvenated, perhaps even saved.
Some such religious sensibility is essential to the Thoreauvian tradition. Sometimes this takes the form of bumper-sticker slogans ("My
church is nature"), but it also takes more conventionally religious
forms, such as in Berry's Christian theism.[183]

Sometimes a belief in a natural human condition can lead to a
facile moral complacency in the face of environmental crises. If a
respect for the lessons of nature is required for the most meaningful
human lives, perhaps our environmental problems will simply force
us to a better world. Paul Gilding, for example, views the environmental crises as a prelude to much better, more humane and satisfying forms of life: "It is the crisis itself that will push humanity to its
next stage of development and allow us to realize our evolutionary
potential. It will be a rough ride, but in the end, we will arrive at a
better place."[184] The beauty of the environmental crisis, for Gilding,
is that it will force us to live as we should have lived all along. We
may resist and initially resent the need to live with less wealth and

fewer consumer goods. However, this forced reality will be a blessing in the end, since it will compel us to abandon our currently morally vacuous lifestyles and settle into economies and communities
much better suited to our "evolutionary potential": "Let's be blunt
and clear that this is going to involve those of us in the rich countries
having less—not just less growth, but less than we have now. Less
stuff, less money, less capacity to build wealth and consume. How
tragic is this? Not very tragic, really, not even sad."[185] We'll discover,
perhaps to our surprise, that our lives will be much happier and
satisfying than they currently are: "The good news gets better and
better. The values and beliefs we need to leave behind are actually
ones we don't really like, like aggressive pursuit of self-interest, and
the ones we need to emphasize and grow are ones we already have
and feel good about—values like having strong communities and
leading meaningful lives."[186] In this telling, the story is just too good
to be true: there is no human tragedy, no need for sacrifice, no loss
or irreparable damage. It turns out that nature will force us to live
according to our natures if we want to or not, and once it does we
will simply be grateful for whatever we leave behind as a result of
environmental disasters. Justice and personal satisfaction will both
grow naturally from these crises.

Thoreau and Berry provide a stern warning about such complacency. We have seen that for Thoreau, the goods of nature cannot be
forced upon us; they must be freely chosen to be enjoyed. Hannah
Coulter suggests a similar point at the end of the novel when she
comments, "We are waiting. For what? For the catastrophe that will
force us to become a community again? For the catastrophe that
will end everything?"[187] Such wishes are dangerous, self-defeating,
illusory, and ultimately undermine life itself. The problems we face
may present us with the occasion to seriously reconsider how to live
in the world. To expect nature to compel us to create a better world
is to abdicate our freedom and moral responsibility, to speak nothing of courting the very disasters we must try to avoid.

A surprising truth about the religious quality in the Thoreauvian tradition is that this does *not* distinguish it from utilitarian humanism nearly as much as we might expect. Although the *content*

of faith differs between the Thoreauvian and mainstream Enlightenment views, the *fact* of faith does not. At its foundation, the modern
view assumes a moral teleology—which we saw in our discussion
of Doudna when she unselfconsciously assumed that human nature
strives to know, control, and master nature—just as much as Wendell Berry does. This teleology is taken just as much on faith by the
humanist as is Berry's Christianity. Berry writes of how his grandfather's approach to the land "all turns on affection," and he observed
that what differentiated his grandfather from Duke was the different
objects of their love. Stating the differences as charitably as possible,
we might say that Berry's grandfather loved God's creation, above
all, while Duke loved his own creative power. In *The City of God*,
Augustine suggests that regimes are best differentiated by what it is
the communities in question love, and this observation seems to the
point here.[188] Each community will view outsiders with suspicion,
of course: the Thoreauvian will accuse the utilitarian of selfishness
and idolatry, the utilitarian will accuse the Thoreauvian of romantic
misanthropy, and both will rightly identify dangers in the opposing
camp.[189] In the final analysis, however, it would be a mistake to view
one of the positions as less committed to reason than the other. Both
employ reason within the context of an assumed moral universe.

This perfect misunderstanding was nicely captured in an exchange of letters between Berry and economist Edmund Phelps in
the pages of the *New York Review of Books*. Responding to a review
by Phelps, Berry complained that economists have no conception
of the land except as "natural resources," that they view agricultural
efficiency and innovation as unmitigated goods without accounting
for the environmental destructiveness of modern practices.

> It is a fact that industrial land use from mining to farming is
> massively destructive of everything involved, of land and people
> and of all that pertains to both. Everything in "the economy" is
> affected by this willing destructiveness. If Mr. Phelps thinks that
> such an economy can be righted by adding "imagination and
> creativity" to it, then you farm-raised city people ought to have
> some questions for him.

Phelps answers, correctly, that "Mr. Berry's complaint ... is with modernity itself," and suggests that "those of us born into vitalist and expressionist cultures must hope that governments will draw back from shutting down the modernist project of exploring, experimenting, and imagining—of voyaging into the unknown—that has been essential for rewarding lives." For Phelps, Berry's distrust of the progress and vitality of modern society would commit citizens to a "rural life of mercantile times, with its routine and isolation." Berry's world is incomparably confining and stultifying when placed beside the dynamism and excitement of a modern (urban) economy, with all its risks, changes, and unpredictability. To Berry, Phelps is committed to an inhumane and wildly destructive economy; to Phelps, Berry would consign us to a world few energetic, thoughtful, and free individuals would willingly chose. To Berry, freedom means independence and self-sufficiency; to Phelps, it means exploration of unknown possibilities, the invention of new worlds and human experiences.[190] The gap between these perspectives is not to be bridged by an appeal to reason alone. What is at stake are profoundly different sensibilities and affections. These individuals are simply in love with different things, and unable to sympathize with what it is the other is drawn to.

Somewhat surprisingly, as we discussed in chapter 2, there is a politically disengaged quality to the Thoreauvian environmental tradition, and this reflects the hope, as I have described it here, that we can listen to nature and learn our deepest moral lessons in this way (undistracted by the world of politics, in which opinion crowds out the claims of truth). One of Berry's most insightful critics, Kimberly Smith, has noted how he, like Thoreau, is much more concerned with reforming the citizenry's moral character than with conventional political participation. In contrast to more conventional populists, Berry "is considerably less optimistic about the potential of politics and government to solve our problems."[191] The hope, for both Thoreau and Berry, is less to mobilize a political movement around policy goals than it is to persuade their audience to stop loving those things that alienate them and make them desperate, to begin loving those things they believe are life-affirming and worthy of their affection. This, too, reflects what we might think of as more of a religious than political sensibility, and leads some environmentalists to at times become impatient with the long view taken by this tradition.[192] The emphasis here, as we have had occasion to mention before, is much more on moral transformation than on an immediate political strategy and mobilization.

There is one final significant tension between the message we receive in *Walden* and what we find in sympathetic contemporary writers. Recall Charles Fish's admiration for the agricultural household built and nurtured by his grandmother and uncles, and also recall his recognition that they represented a shadow of a world fading from the modern social environment. Berry also clearly recognizes the difficulty of retaining the agrarianism he champions. The problem is even deeper, however, than the practical matters of transitioning away from market society back to relatively or significantly self-sufficient agrarian communities—and these practical matters, of course, are formidable enough. The question, we might say, is whether or not we would expect enough free individuals to love a world shaped, limited, and given meaning by nature to assure that this world could be reproduced from generation to generation. Would free individuals willingly choose to live such lives?

In *Hannah Coulter*, Berry directly faces the problem: Hannah's children do not choose to live their adult lives in their parents' world; they use their educations to pursue what have become more conventional American careers away from Port William.[193] In his nonfiction, Berry writes of the ways in which schooling, no longer significantly controlled by localities, encourages children to aspire to lives beyond their local communities: "If we want our rural economy to survive, we must learn to educate our children, as Wes Jackson has said, not for 'upward mobility' but for homecoming. We must not depend on the school system for this. The school system educates for export."[194] But the sadness of Berry's great novel suggests a more subtle and disturbing suspicion on his part: that reasonable, free individuals can make choices to move away from the kind of world and life he has portrayed, defended, and advocated. For all of Charles Fish's admiration for his relatives and their agrarian commitments, his philosophical inclinations led him away from Vermont. This can be true of both artistic and service-oriented individuals; seductions of wealth and power are not the only reasons young adults can be led away from the local to the broader cosmopolitan world. There are human goods of great value in modern urban life that free individuals may choose to pursue for both virtuous and less virtuous reasons. At the very least, we must recognize that the forces working against embracing nature's limits are not only practical but also moral. Human modesty and limitation is a hard sell in the contemporary world, where individual striving is not only stimulated but admired as a virtue of free people. By the twenty-first century, the world of Port William looks, in the words chosen as the title of a collection of Berry's stories about this imagined town, like "that distant land."

Here the optimism of *Walden* contrasts with the melancholy of our contemporaries such as Berry and Fish. Thoreau's good news is not about a remembered "distant land," but about a land yet to be cultivated. The desire for liberation should drive us to the modesty of a life bounded and informed by nature. Only such a life will allow us to be fully aware of our choices, liberated from the seductions and impulses of what Thoreau calls "all that [is] not life."[195] Thoreau promises a new day, fully awake, in which we will disentangle ourselves from both the alienation and injustices of the lives we find ourselves living at present. His moral teleology suggests that we will be more alive and content to the degree that we allow nature rather than convention and opinion to define the moral parameters of our lives. It is essential to remember this deep confidence in Thoreau's appeal to nature. More than a century and a half after the publication of *Walden*, it is easy to believe that the Enlightenment logic of "nature as resources" has simply overwhelmed the "nature as tutor" option for the vast majority of us. The spirit of *Walden*, however, is overwhelmingly hopeful that free individuals will choose a simpler, more aware and independent life not because they are forced to by necessity, or even because they are "genetically wired" to prefer such a thing.[196] They will choose it because their lives will be more their own, more meaningful, and have greater integrity. To believe in the lessons of nature requires a skepticism about the modern moral intuition that in the final analysis human survival and well-being is the good that trumps all others. Such respect for nature is difficult for any individual to embrace; it is even more difficult for free people to reproduce from generation to generation. A promise of *Walden*, against the odds, is that free people can be persuaded, and that if they are, both their private and their public lives will gain immeasurably. This is the foundational American text for keeping this hope alive in a world constantly and powerfully pushing back against it.

CONCLUSION

Thoreau's primary objective in *Walden* is to encourage us to become morally conscientious and independent. This is not simply a matter of asserting oneself; one does not gain moral integrity simply by stating one's opinion or demanding recognition and respect. Two preliminary conditions, Thoreau believes, are required by anyone who will become fully responsible, and both of these are difficult but (in his view) attainable. The first is to extricate yourself from relationships that make you dependent on injustice. As he says in *Civil Disobedience*, our first duty is to make sure that we do not build our own lives on the exploitation of others:

> It is not a man's duty, as a matter of course, to devote himself to the eradication of any, even the most enormous wrong; he may still properly have other concerns to engage him; but it is his duty, at least, to wash his hands of it, and, if he gives it no thought longer, not to give it practically his support. If I devote myself to other pursuits and contemplations, I must first see, at least, that I do not pursue them sitting upon another man's shoulders.[1]

Thoreau insists that we become conscious of the degree to which we exploit unjust relations for our own advantage, often without being fully honest with ourselves or even fully aware of this. His solution is equally uncompromising: we must pursue what he calls voluntary poverty,[2] and we must withdraw our support from any government that supports injustice. Only by becoming as economically independent as possible can we stop "sitting upon another man's shoulders" when the broader economy is, say, a slave (or some other deeply exploitative) economy. In addition, only by being willing to live simply do we cease to require the protection and patronage of a government whose business includes protecting significant forms of unjust power.

Even if we successfully cultivate these two preconditions for moral independence, there is still more work to do. We are now in a position to honestly evaluate our obligations. Thoreau offers the natural world and liberal learning as the two paths to moral knowledge that are uncorrupted by the interests and rhetoric of contemporary partisanship. These are the tools available to help us behold, again in the language of *Civil Disobedience*, the place where truth "comes trickling into this lake or that pool," and we will be able to "gird up" our "loins once more," and continue our "pilgrimage toward its fountain-head."[3] Thoreau's primary worry is that in our practical affairs we become corrupted by self-interest to the point where we refuse to take this pilgrimage, or we even become blind to its possibility. We have much more to fear from conformity, cowardice, and a lack of faith in our ability to shape a life of meaning and moral integrity, Thoreau seems to believe, than we do from genuine conflict about the principles of moral life. *Walden* teaches that if we appropriately prepare ourselves to (morally) awaken, the nature of our condition is such that the truth is available to be grasped.[4] Our problems are fear and a lack of imagination, rather than deficits of intellect or judgment or access to moral reality. All normal people are able to grasp the moral imperatives of a fully satisfying and responsible life. This achievement, however, requires discipline, commitment, and a willingness to take responsibility for oneself. As much as anything else, Thoreau is asking us to find ways to be brutally honest with ourselves, to expose our own rationalizations and corrupting interests. His optimism lies in his belief that we can in fact shed these interests that distort our judgment, and in his faith that the resulting clarity of vision will be invigorating and liberating.

In addition, *Walden* offers hints about the influence individuals of character could have on our common life. I argued in chapter 2 that Thoreau doesn't give us a fully developed political program, but that he believes reform of individuals in their private life will offer significant public benefits. To try to translate his ethical views directly into a political theory or strategy, I suggested, is neither helpful nor what Thoreau had in mind. There are hints, however, if only hints, about what a rejuvenated public life could look like, at least on the local level. As I'll suggest below, there may be a bit more here than first meets the eye.

For many, there is both a lot to like and a lot to be unsure about in Thoreau's vision. His insistence on moral responsibility, his optimism about all normal individuals' possibility for achieving this, his sense that such a life is not only responsible but also deeply satisfying and a blessing to society at large, all have attractive qualities. The pull we feel from these claims has nothing to do with their originality. Thoreau's artistry, of course, is unique and the personality behind this artistry is eccentric and idiosyncratic. But this is to be expected: all "poets," in Thoreau's understanding, find their own "genius," that is, their own forms of expression. But the truths they express are universal and timeless, and Thoreau makes no claim to originality on this score. On the contrary, his views reflect what he takes to be the natural truths found in the great ancient traditions he mines (Greek, Latin, Indian, and Chinese), and the great modern writers he respects (like Coleridge and Raleigh)—and also in the acts of John Brown, whom he champions, along with other heroes ancient and modern. His aspiration is to participate in the grand tradition of philosophy and poetry, of human insight across time and place.

This is where many of us may begin to have doubts. Thoreau's commitment is to a natural moral order, which to many moderns looks hopelessly romantic and unpersuasive. Our fear is that Thoreau may have it exactly wrong: he believes that with the cultivation of character, we will find a universal and natural moral order, but we suspect that even with the best intentions, people of goodwill and fine character will still be tainted by self-interest[5] and, regardless, will disagree profoundly about the nature of moral life and its requirements. Thoreau promotes courage and commitment, but many of us suspect that tolerance and moral modesty may also be a requirement of democratic life. He found the natural world and the world of great literature an everlasting and trustworthy moral resource, but we suspect that nature is morally silent[6] and the world of even the greatest literature is shaped, at least in part, by privilege and prejudice.

Indeed, there are those who are deeply skeptical about the kind of moral reorienting Thoreau is proposing in the first place. Steven Pinker's comments about *Walden* in his most recent book alerts us to this:

> Evidence-free pronouncements about the misery of mankind are an occupational hazard of the social critic. In the 1854 classic *Walden*, Henry David Thoreau famously wrote, "The mass of men lead lives of quiet desperation." How a recluse living in a cabin on a pond could know this was never made clear, and the mass of men beg to differ. . . . Thoreau was a victim of the Optimism Gap (the "I'm OK, They're Not" illusion), which for happiness is more like a canyon. People in every country underestimate the proportion of their compatriots who say they are happy, by an average of 42 percentage points.[7]

There's a lot Pinker gets wrong in this comment: Thoreau does in fact speak as one who has known loss and discontentment;[8] he was not a simple recluse, as we know from his description of the visitors to Walden Pond, to say nothing of his biography as a village man. Thoreau makes clear that he is speaking only to those who are actually discontented and makes no claim to teach those not afflicted by this problem.[9] But Pinker is right that Thoreau thought desperation and discontentment, such as he had himself experienced, were widespread; Pinker believes the empirical data suggests that people are much happier than Thoreau and those who have followed him assume.[10] Perhaps they are. The Enlightenment program Pinker enthusiastically defends has no doubt been very successful in curing the sick, increasing the food supply, building safer and more comfortable buildings, and even promoting a more widespread peace than has been before experienced either between or within societies. These are obviously not small things. Pinker is certainly energetic in demonstrating the ways in which human utility has been promoted in the modern world. He is decidedly less persuasive, however, concerning matters of human meaning and attachment. Pinker enthuses that we have been "forced into cosmopolitanism."[11] He is delighted to report that the "biggest breakthrough" of the Scientific Revolution has been to "refute the intuition that the universe is saturated with purpose."[12] He has little to say about the loss of two resources people have conventionally looked to for comfort and meaning (other than to criticize them as profoundly regressive and a threat to progress): local community and religious traditions. To value the latter is to reject reason,[13] and the cosmopolitanism he promotes is apparently, to his mind, so obviously more desirable than what must only look like parochialism to Pinker that he doesn't even think to seriously address the issue at all. Opponents of Enlightenment progress are either reactionary tribalists, threatening to undo the humane work of scientific modernity with contemporary authoritarian populism,[14] or intellectuals, who seem to find a perverse solace and inspiration in their opposition to progress.[15]

The most significant issue raised by Pinker is obviously not his quick and superficial comment about Thoreau's lack of data concerning the lives and attitudes of his neighbors. Rather, it has to do with his vigorous defense of the kind of utilitarian sensibility Thoreau just as vigorously criticized. For Pinker, the only explanations for why people have rejected modern science and progress—or even feel uneasy about them—is either moral regression to a primitive psychology or intellectual self-absorption. There are momentary hints of doubt; Pinker admits that "a modicum of anxiety may be the price we pay for the uncertainty of freedom."[16] Overall, however, "Enlightenment is working,"[17] and any attempt to put ethical breaks on this movement is itself unethical, since it threatens to disrupt the progress of ameliorating the human condition.[18] In the final analysis, Pinker's position is identical to David Deutsch's (who provides one of the book's epigraphs) and that of the "ecomodernists" (Pinker prefers to call ecomodernism "Enlightenment Environmentalism" or "Humanistic Environmentalism"):[19] the problems we face, from climate change to depression, can only be addressed with the same scientific commitments others fear have caused (at least some of) the problems in the first place. The premise of *Walden*— that we are beset by moral confusion, a sense of despair about our own freedom, misplaced ambition, and an irresponsible acceptance of the (unjust) world as it is—is criticized as self-indulgent and regressive. If we embrace Enlightenment, these problems of agency, freedom, and responsibility will dissolve in the good work of modern life, which promises ever-increasing happiness, comfort, prosperity, peace, justice, and individual freedom. The only danger is in doubting or subverting Enlightenment commitments.

Thoreau's challenge to this view is certainly not a simple rejection of reason, science, or the solving of practical problems. Thoreau was not only a skilled and practical artisan (carpenter, inventor in the family pencil business, and highly regarded professional surveyor); he was also a significant naturalist contributing to the scientific observation and research of his generation and maintaining a close attention to the most advanced scientific writings of the time.[20] His complaint was with those who believed pragmatism and science would give us the values we need to frame and govern our lives in the most meaningful ways. This led him to his polemical attack on J. A. Etzler in "Paradise (To Be) Regained," where he claims that utopian engineering distracts us from our most important moral concerns.[21] Concern for the body is certainly not to be ignored; the first and longest chapter of *Walden*, after all, is "Economy." Care for the body, however, is not the proper end of human thriving, but rather the beginning. "In the long run men hit only what they aim at. Therefore, though they should fail immediately, they had better aim at something high."[22] This comment is found in a passage in which Thoreau expresses his distrust of the factory production of clothing (a battle long lost by our own time), but the point is a general one for him: that the purpose of utility is to serve ends higher than utility. He is clear that "till we have secured" the food, shelter, clothing, and fuel we need to keep our body protected and healthy, we will not be "prepared to entertain the true problems of life with freedom and a prospect of success."[23] The danger is to confuse these preconditions for a humane life with the humane life itself. That would constitute a corruption of human purposes rather than their fulfillment. Being too aggressive toward nature may also be a predictable consequence of inflating the value of utility, and such aggression can encourage behavior that constitutes a threat to the natural world upon which we depend.[24]

Here lies the fundamental disagreement between those, such as Pinker, who view science as the whole of rationality[25] and those such as Thoreau who believe we must subordinate material science to moral considerations found outside of science. Pinker is persuaded that the progress promoted by Enlightenment generates the morally admirable qualities of reason, tolerance, cosmopolitanism, and liberality. It turns out that "knowledge and sound institutions lead to moral progress."[26] In fact, he believes even materialism and consumerism are being mitigated by the fruits of Enlightenment; Pinker observes what he calls *dematerialization*, the turning away of young people from owning cars and other conventional consumer goods valued by earlier generations.[27] The Thoreauvian is skeptical. It is hard to believe that an obsession with thousand-dollar iPhones and upscale craft beer is a sign that materialism is losing its grip. It looks instead as though consumerism is finding new objects of desire, rather than leaving the desire for objects behind.[28] More significantly, to the Thoreauvian the Enlightenment commitments defended by Pinker appear to require the discipline of moral considerations and sensibilities it is itself incapable of generating. In Wendell Berry's language, it is difficult to see how Enlightenment thinking can generate love of place or commitment to others. Pinker's claim is that Enlightenment thinking generates social, material, political, and technological conditions that are best for all. The Thoreauvian fears that it reduces both the earth and other people to the status of objects, existing for the purpose of serving individuals' wants and desires. How could such an attitude prevent the kind of selfish preoccupation that has haunted both advocates and critics of democracy from the time of Plato? What will generate solidarity and commitment in such a world? Love and sacrifice must be drawn from moral resources beyond pleasure. This is not to suggest that the "bourgeois" concern for pleasure or utility is to be fully rejected. It is to say, rather, that utility is unsatisfactory if it is thought to constitute the entirely of moral life or its highest purpose.

We have seen that Thoreau was no simple primitivist. Oliver Wendell Holmes was close to the truth when he suggested that Thoreau was "half college-graduate and half Algonquin," but then seems to have lost his own insight when he later suggested that Thoreau was a "nullifier of civilization."[29] The claim in *Walden* is that we need to use the fruits of civilization wisely and prudently—that we needed to combine the "hardiness" of "savages" with the "intellectualness" of "the civilized man."[30] Thoreau was not a Luddite, but rather an advocate of voluntary poverty, the prudential use of wealth, technology, and "civilization" in order to prepare ourselves to live independently, thoughtfully, creatively. We don't find here rejection of Enlightenment, per se, but there is a warning against being too self-congratulatory about our own contemporary social wisdom (what he refers to contemptuously as the "mere smoke of opinion"[31]) and losing our critical capacities to learn from the long history of human wisdom and experience. There is certainly a warning against the materialism of contemporary society, including our overwhelming preoccupation with wealth and pleasure. And again, the unoriginality (in content, not form) of these arguments in *Walden* reflects Thoreau's respect for earlier thinkers and also what he takes to be the best parts of the "civilization" of his own moment.

Perhaps the most important message in relation to Pinker's defense of Enlightenment is Thoreau's suspicion that a preoccupation with or reliance on appeals to utility leads to a significant moral blindness. The logic of scientific discovery, as we saw in earlier discussions, generates its own momentum if human utility and scientific progress are self-validating. Such an attitude, we suggested in chapter 3, is just as likely to lead to fatalism and the eclipse of reason as it is to the promotion of significant and meaningful moral evaluation.

This is why we saw that no less an advocate of humanism than Luc Ferry recognizes that science, even more than nature, may be what most needs to be tamed and disciplined today.[32] Thoreau's thinking constitutes a form of humanism—human thriving and satisfaction is the goal—but it teaches a chastened and situated humanism, one that recognizes other great values that need to be recognized and respected. There is no sign that the views Pinker, or Deutsch, or the ecomodernists defend can moderate or chasten human aggression toward the natural world. At the end of the day, this world is merely clay to be shaped by increasingly skilled human hands in response to whatever these humans happen to desire or think they need. The Thoreauvian tradition is uneasy with this moral commitment, and for good reason. This critical tradition represents not so much a simple romance with nature, an irrational or superstitious or atavistic distrust of scientific reason, but a sober recognition of the potentially tyrannical and unrestrained potential of Enlightenment reason if left to its own devices.

MARK LILLA HAS RECENTLY commented that "democracies without democrats do not last."[33] Lilla reminds us of the ancient concern that without citizens of appropriate character and commitment, democracies are at risk of subverting themselves. I criticized Thoreau in chapter 2 for not giving us a fully developed understanding of how to move from his personal morality to a satisfactory political ethics. It is true that he helps us think about how we might have the integrity and independence of thought to recognize injustice and live a morally responsible personal life. He also gives us good reason to think that such individuals may provide a responsible foundation for democratic life, especially when we are confronted by significant wrongs and injustices. But I observed that the very independence and moral self-confidence Thoreau promotes can also lead to a moral posture that makes it difficult to cooperate with others, indeed, which may make it difficult to think of disagreement as anything other than a sign of corruption on the part of one's opponents (a pathology we see all too frequently in our contemporary political life). Because Thoreau thought that by far our biggest moral misunderstandings grew from cowardice and the corrupting influences in our lives, he was not particularly worried about our ability to understand our moral obligations—assuming we could minimize our fears and corrupt interests. He was much less worried about honest disagreement (at least as honest as can reasonably be expected) than democrats actually have good reason to fret about.

This problem is much more significant than Thoreau imagined. It is not just that we have reason to suspect (and we do) that "conscience" is never sufficient to produce moral certainty. An additional problem is that the conditions of our lives are such that it is actually very difficult to gain the kind of knowledge responsible citizenship requires. For Thoreau, we are almost all the way home, morally, when we succeeded in extricating ourselves from injustice. We may object that Thoreau was not entirely honest about the degree to which our lives are necessarily and inevitably intertwined with the whole of the social fabric around us—true enough in Thoreau's lifetime, and even more so today, given the complexity and interdependence of modern life. More importantly, we may appeal to ideas as old as those found in Aristotle's *Politics* and object that Thoreau had an insufficient understanding of civic knowledge and obligation. From this ancient perspective, if citizens are to contribute significantly to an understanding of our real political options, they must not position themselves as autonomous, disinterested critics. Rather, they must be civically engaged; they must actually take their turns at both ruling and being ruled.[34] The idea is that if citizens never have the experience of exercising collective responsibility, it will be very difficult for them to understand or properly evaluate the exercise of authority by others. If, for example, I have no personal history that could illuminate the complexity and paradoxes of political decision-making, or the kind of tradeoffs public policy requires us to consider, "ruling" or exercising political authority will be, for all practical purposes, quite mysterious to me. When authority acts contrary to my interests or my will, those wielding this authority are likely to appear as simply malevolent or foolish. Because my scope of vision is so limited, it will be impossible for me to understand the full context within which a decision is made, or even to understand that a broader context might exist even if it is not fully visible from my vantage point. Yascha Mounk observes, "Voters do not like to think that the world is complicated."[35] This disposition, however, does nothing to change the reality that the world has become increasingly, even alarmingly, complicated. As contemporary political life requires technocrats of ever-expanding sophistication, populists of the Left and Right are blind to this truth, persuaded that expertise is a mere pretense for the irresponsible and likely self-interested exercise of power. How could their own experience demonstrate the contrary to them?

This problem cannot be solved by simply bringing more information to voters, by making them better informed about "the facts." What we face is a deficit in our experiences and relationships even more than a deficit of analytical acuity or background knowledge.[36] Until one has exercised even modest authority, or at least been able to observe such authority exercised by people close and well known to you, the ideas of authority and responsibility are mere abstractions. It is only by having political experience, if only in a small way, that one begins to understand the problems that those with authority face. Only when we have such knowledge can we meaningfully evaluate the acts of those who govern. During the Obama administration, many on the Left simply had no conception of the kind of compromises that would be required to pursue the administration's agenda, and the result was an absurd ease with which many critics could flippantly accuse the president of abandoning his principles. Even more alarmingly, the early years of the Trump administration are witnessing the dismantling of technocratic expertise at the heart of the federal government (most worryingly at the State Department and the EPA). President Trump's populist political base is virulently hostile to claims about complexity and the expertise required to manage our national affairs; experts are thought to be little more than an ideological or self-interested political clique (the "deep state"). When there is a significant gap between the rulers and the ruled, when the overlap, no matter how imperfect, declines to the point of vanishing, both rulers and ruled lose their moorings.

Rulers become increasingly remote and thus more likely to pander to the simplistic or false beliefs of the many, just as they are likely to become increasingly corrupt by virtue of the gap between the reality of governing and what the many see and understand. Those without political experience develop profoundly distorted understandings of political reality. Both rulers and ruled become irresponsible as the chasm between their experiences and responsibilities grows.

To the degree that these observations are true, this suggests that the conditions of modern society may create a significant obstacle to the exercise of responsible democratic power. As society becomes increasingly complex (producing the need for administrative expertise in virtually every facet of governance) and the centers of power become ever-more remote from most citizens' daily lives, the epistemological conditions for civic education become just that much further removed from the experience (and therefore the understanding) of everyday citizens.[37] As I noted in the introduction, a general concern about the "virtue" or civic education of democratic citizens is ancient and elemental in the history of democratic regimes. What we may be witnessing in our own time is an exacerbation or extension of this problem, a set of modern conditions that make responsible democratic leadership and citizenship even more difficult than we might expect when the opportunities for genuine civic experience and understanding are more widely accessible.

These worries are not necessarily news. James Madison and the Federalists hoped to cure "the mischiefs of faction" through the innovations of a large, federal, and representative republic designed precisely for the purpose of insulating representatives, to a significant degree, from the passions of the demos. But if U.S. citizens are not to rule themselves directly, this raises the problem of how they are to have the experiences necessary to provide a significant civic education. One major answer to this problem has been the establishment of public schooling for children, the development of a system of compulsory education that would, above all, provide the civic lessons required by future citizens. We know that these civic concerns were first and foremost in the mind of the great representative of this movement in the nineteenth century, Horace Mann, and continued to be of the highest consideration in the work of the twentieth century's most influential theorist of democratic education, John Dewey. To the degree that the Aristotelian tradition of thinking about citizenship has merit, however, the problem of civic education is not primarily a matter of improving classroom civic instruction for our school children (don't get me wrong: that could never hurt). Tom Nichols, who has bemoaned the populist attack on expertise in our current political environment, writes, "Experts have a responsibility to educate. Voters have a responsibility to learn."[38] True as this may be, it doesn't get to the heart of the problem, at least to the degree that civic education requires knowledge that grows from political responsibility and experience. As political authority becomes both more remote and more complex, such opportunities for ruling recede for all but political professionals.[39] Schooling is not the primary problem, and therefore not the primary solution.[40] Sharing collective power and authority among citizens is. Without mechanisms to achieve this goal, political understanding becomes abstract and brittle. Ideology and passion rush in where practical knowledge can't be found. Both rulers and ruled become corrupted by their disconnection from one other.[41]

A second solution to the problem of civic education grew more organically as American civil society developed a rich array of voluntary associations and organizations. Alexis de Tocqueville famously suggested that without religious and civic associations—from churches to fraternal and civic organizations—there would be insufficient experiences in American democratic life to tie citizens to one another: "In democratic countries the science of association is the mother science; the progress of all the others depends on the progress of that one."[42] His observation is that in a democracy the size and scope of a modern nation state, local political and prepolitical associations become essential for providing civic experiences.[43] Without these groups and organizations democracies are in danger of producing individuals who are socially isolated and preoccupied with their own private affairs.[44] The consequence of such privacy and individualism will likely be dangerously irresponsible and factious government.[45] Some of the most important contemporary social science demonstrates both the significance of a healthy associational life for creating public trust ("social capital") and the civic responsibility required by modern democratic citizenship, as well as reasons to fear that this civil society is in decline and being replaced by increasingly privatized and isolated ways of living.[46]

So how, as Lilla asks, are we to create democrats? Thoreau may give us more help here than is commonly recognized. First, it is essential that we learn to reflect, to think, to withdraw from the hustle and bustle of daily battles and business to allow for a new and less partisan view of the affairs of the world. Walden Pond is a perfect symbol for this task, being both partially removed yet close to and nonetheless connected to the life of Concord Village. Thoreau is obviously not didactically presenting the only method for encouraging this reflection; he is not suggesting we all literally recreate his retreat in the woods. Rather, he is providing an example of how he worked to find a place of partial remove, a space for reflection and meditation, which would help him resist the immediate pull of unconsidered or passion-driven opinion. We may not have Walden Pond to retreat to, but Thoreau does imply that all of us can learn to use the natural world as a tonic and a refuge, a counterpoint to the conventions and opinions of human society. This business of reflection will require, second, that we confront the degree to which we are implicated in the wrongs we profess to hate. Thoreau is a tough teacher on this score: he will not allow us to forget that our comforts and pleasures are often privileges built on the exploitation of others, and he is right to suggest that it takes courage to look squarely at this reality. Third, becoming aware of our complicity in injustices requires that we act to do what we can to disengage with or alter these institutions, relationships, and practices to the degree possible. If we are to become responsible individuals, we must take all three of these tasks seriously. Becoming such individuals is also the precondition, Thoreau insists, of becoming responsible democrats.

This Thoreauvian program is essential, but it is not enough by itself. Thoreau's insistence on the withdrawal from unjust institutions is too dogmatic; there are certainly times when such a withdrawal is appropriate, but there are others when engagement is what is required. The pursuit of economic simplicity is an appropriate way of withdrawing from the most overbearing and damaging elements of the market and insisting on an economy that serves purposes higher than utility. But engagement, and not merely withdrawal, will also be necessary in political life. Thoreauvian ethics can connect with this engagement at the local level, and this is no small matter. His moral ideal suggests that the preconditions for democracy are found locally among responsible individuals and good neighbors. He says little about what the duties of good neighbors are, but he does imply that these have to do with engagement at the level of voluntary associations in what we today call civil society and with face-to-face politics. Both of these foci are indeed essential to anyone concerned with the revitalization of contemporary democracy. The creation or re-creation of vital political competition at the local level is essential to rebuilding meaningful political debate and engagement.[47] Only face-to-face political associations, promoting grassroots responsibility, compromises, and loyalties, have any chance of resisting the power of impersonal (and often cynically manipulated) social media campaigns. That is, only revitalized political parties and party competition have any chance of resisting the kind of social media–driven hostile political takeover experienced by the Republicans (and almost experienced by the Democrats) in 2016.[48] Civil society also needs to be revitalized, in order to produce opportunities for neighbors from different walks of life to routinely rub shoulders in the course of their daily lives. Thoreau intuits what has become clear in much of the most important social science of the contemporary era: that a healthy and democratic civil society and local politics is required for the sake of healthy democratic institutions more generally.

If a political strategy is to be developed to complement a Thoreauvian ethics, it will have to be more open to compromise and negotiation than Thoreau tended to be (in his significantly less democratic political environment). Democracy requires a level of moral modesty, a willingness to assume goodwill on the part of one's opponents, which is in tension with Thoreau's faith in the infallibility of a properly cultivated conscience. His own counsel of neighborliness and local engagement can encourage the growth of democratic practices within the context of this neighborliness. Such relationships can act to mitigate the dangers of self-righteousness and intolerance of different opinions to the degree that they cultivate trust and mutual regard among citizens. Our neighborhoods and communities have become so homogeneous that social trust has become more tribal than civic, and our democratic practices at the moment reflect this disaster. Thoreauvian commitments point us in directions for beginning to rebuild the local foundations of democratic practice. Even if Thoreau did not take us all the way to thinking about how these practices must evolve, he gives us much essential advice nonetheless.

TWO DAYS AFTER THE election of Donald Trump, Zadie Smith was awarded the Welt Literature Prize in Berlin. The talk she gave, later published under the title "On Optimism and Despair," is among the most sober and insightful reflections on contemporary public affairs found within the great sea of recent punditry, alarmed warnings, and strategic analyses offered in response to the rise of ethno-nationalist populism across the liberal democratic world.[49] She notes that as an artist concerned primarily with the "intimate lives of people," she is not by nature a political person. In these dark political times, she has often been asked about what is assumed to be the "failure of multiculturalism," and the appearance that we have now become so divided that our differences have become impossible for us to overcome for the sake of living together peacefully and equitably:

> In this argument it is the writer who is meant to be the naïve child, but I maintain that people who believe in fundamental and irreversible changes in human nature are themselves ahistorical and naïve. If novelists know anything it's that individual citizens are internally plural: that they have within them the full range of behavioral possibilities. They are like complex musical scores from which certain melodies can be teased out and others ignored or suppressed, depending, at least in part, on who is doing the conducting. At this moment, all over the world—and most

recently in America—the conductors standing in front of this human orchestra have only the meanest and most banal melodies in mind. Here in Germany you will remember these martial songs; they are not a very distant memory. But there is no place on earth where they have not been played at one time or another. Those of us who remember, too, a finer music must try now to play it, and encourage others, if we can, to sing along.[50]

There is both a great realism and a great optimism in Smith's comments. Yes, the hateful melodies currently coursing through our public life reflect real, dangerous, and recognizable human possibilities. But there are other possibilities, attractive ones, and these have precedents too. There is no inevitability to either set of circumstances. What is required of free citizens is to attempt to play the attractive, peaceful, "finer music" that is available to us.

Easier said than done. There are a great many thoughtful and conflicting recommendations for approaching this work. We saw earlier that Steven Levitsky and Daniel Ziblatt believe we must reestablish democratic norms in our national politics if we are to break out of our current dysfunction. Yascha Mounk argues that liberal democracy today suffers from dividing these two values and practices—liberalism and democracy—and suggests that the cure for our ills must be found in reestablishing the practical link between liberal respect for individual rights and democratic respect for majority rule and party competition.[51] Mark Lilla argues that by emphasizing identity politics, liberalism has made politics expressive rather than persuasive, and has opened the door to all manner of hateful (racist and nationalist) politics on the Right. What is needed, he believes, is the reassertion of a unifying liberalism of common interests and values, in order to heal the polarization of contemporary democracy.[52] President Obama, in his Farewell Address, also emphasized the need for cultivating a sense of political solidarity.[53] Others are uncertain about the democratic project altogether. Samuel Beckett once claimed that "people are bloody ignorant apes"; the degree we believe this is so is the degree to which we will be very skeptical about the prospects for the successful democratic participation of such creatures.[54] Tom Nichols believes we are "a country obsessed with the worship of its own ignorance," and that "Americans ... have become almost childlike in their refusal to learn enough to govern themselves or to guide the policies that affect their lives."[55] Jason Brennan finds the whole democratic project divisive and a threat to individual liberty, and recommends limiting political power in any form as much as possible.[56] Bryan Caplan thinks there is little reason to believe that voters will ever become knowledgeable enough to be entrusted with political power.[57]

Smith's comment expresses an optimism not found in the most skeptical of these critics of democracy, but she tells us little about the strategy for changing the "music" being conducted in contemporary liberal democracies. What she offers, instead, is something very much like what Thoreau had in mind in *Walden*. She reminds us that we can change, and that these changes can have a significant effect on the world in which we live. Her overall interest as an artist, much like Thoreau's, is focused more on private than public life, but the artist's insight is that choices are available to free people that can influence both the public and private spheres for the better. For all his cantankerousness, Thoreau was remarkably optimistic about our ability to change, to morally reshape our lives for greater integrity and satisfaction. He thought free people were capable of moderation, of living with discipline and within limits set by nature and morality. He also believed that we would find such lives satisfying and a pleasure.[58] We may have our doubts.[59] But for all these doubts, it is helpful to be reminded to have courage, to maintain our integrity to the best of our ability, and to remember our responsibility toward the truth, the earth, and our neighbors. Such lessons, at a moment of political anger, uncertainty, tribal conflict, populist vindictiveness, and environmental irresponsibility, must be at the heart of any attempt to restore our democratic health.

NOTES

Introduction

1. Henry David Thoreau, *Walden*, in *A Week on the Concord and Merrimack Rivers; Walden, or, Life in the Woods; The Maine Woods; Cape Cod* (New York: Library of America, 1985), 389.

2. Ibid., 586.

3. Ibid., 581.

4. Ibid., 547, 570.

5. Ibid., 551.

6. Ibid., 394.

7. Ibid., 587.

8. Ibid., 329.

9. Ibid., 328. This is an unfortunate trope found in a number of Thoreau's writings. It added rhetorical punch to his social critique, but at the significant cost of trivializing—or at least not taking as seriously as he should—the brutality and criminality of American slavery.

10. Ibid., 325.

11. Ibid., 326.

12. And, in honesty, he gives us reason to worry about this from time to time during flights of particularly exaggerated rhetoric. Consider, for just one example, his comment in the opening pages of *Walden* that, "I have lived some thirty years on this planet, and I have yet to hear the first syllable of valuable or even earnest advice from my seniors. They have told me nothing, and probably cannot tell me any thing, to the purpose" (ibid., 330).

13. Ibid., 335.

14. In a famous and cryptic passage, Thoreau writes, "I long ago lost a hound, a bay horse, and turtledove, and am still on their trail" (ibid., 336). We know from his biography that his losses included his brother, who died young from a tetanus infection, a young woman who

refused his marriage proposal, and even his first profession as a school teacher; for comments about this last matter, see ibid., 377.

15. Ibid., 384.

16. Ibid., 361.

17. Ibid., 331.

18. Ibid., 338.

19. Ibid., 579.

20. Ibid., 580.

21. Ibid., 586.

22. Brian Walker, "Thoreau's Alternative Economics: Work, Liberty, and Democratic Cultivation," *American Political Science Review* 92, no. 4 (1998): 845–56.

23. *Walden*, 389.

24. Ibid., 350.

25. Ibid., 409–10. Here, and throughout the text, for quoted material, if I have not noted otherwise (by saying "my emphasis"), the italics are in the original text. This is true throughout the book.

26. Ibid., 443.

27. Henry David Thoreau, *Civil Disobedience*, ed. Bob Pepperman Taylor (Peterborough, ON: Broadview Press, 2016), 42.

28. Jane Bennett, "On Being a Native: Thoreau's Hermeneutics of Self," *Polity* 22, no. 4 (1990): 559.

29. Plato, *The Republic*, trans. G. M. A. Grube, rev. C. D. C. Reeve (Indianapolis: Hackett, 1992), bk. 7, 227–28.

30. Ibid., 232.

31. Ibid., 231.

32. Ibid., 234.

33. Ibid., 232.

34. Mann's son accompanied Thoreau on his final journey, west to Minnesota, where Thoreau was seeking a cure for the tuberculosis that would soon kill him.

35. Horace Mann, *Lectures on Education* (Boston: Lemuel N. Ide, 1850), 171.

36. See John Locke, *Second Treatise on Government* (Indianapolis: Hackett, 1980), chap. 2, sec. 6.

37. Ralph Waldo Emerson, "Napoleon; or, the Man of the World," chapter 6 of *Representative Men*, in *Essays and Lectures* (New York: Library of America, 1983), 727.

38. Ibid., 742.

39. Ibid., 743.

40. Ibid., 745.

41. Andrew Delbanco, *The Death of Satan* (New York: Farrar, Straus and Giroux, 1995), 105–6. A similar point is made by Andrew Shankman, *Crucible of American Democracy* (Lawrence: University Press of Kansas, 2004), 230–33.

42. Gordon Wood, *Empire of Liberty* (New York: Oxford University Press, 2009), 736.

43. Lance Banning, *Jefferson and Madison* (Madison, WI: Madison House, 1995), 90.

44. James Fenimore Cooper, *The American Democrat* (New York: Penguin, 1989), 141.

45. Bryan Caplan, *The Myth of the Rational Voter* (Princeton, NJ: Princeton University Press, 2007), 19.

46. The original poem had also requested that "God shed His grace on thee / Till selfish gain no longer stain, / The banner of the free!" Thanks to Francis Gregory Gause for this observation.

47. Under the stress of the Cold War, the Pledge of Allegiance was amended to include reference to God in order to further differentiate American values from communism and the Soviet Union. See discussion in Danielle Allen, *Talking to Strangers* (Chicago: University of Chicago Press, 2004), 13. For a fascinating book-length study of the Pledge, see Richard Ellis, *To the Flag* (Lawrence: University Press of Kansas, 2005).

48. Theodore Roosevelt declares, for example, that "people who say they have not time to attend to politics are simply saying that they are unfit to live in a free community"; Roosevelt, *The Works of Theodore Roosevelt* (New York: Charles Scribner's Sons, 1926), 13:282. Florence Kelly, in 1899, charged: "Under the guise of republican freedom, we have degenerated into a nation of mock citizens"; quoted in Eric Foner, *The Story of American Freedom* (New York: W. W. Norton, 1998), 124. Foner discusses the growth of the "cult of the flag" and the emergence of "The Star-Spangled Banner" in the 1890s (see 134).

49. William James, *Writings 1902–1910* (New York: Library of America, 1987), 1289.

50. Mark Twain, *The Autobiography of Mark Twain* (Berkeley: University of California Press, 2010), 1:259–60.

51. For a significantly less amused reflection on American impulsiveness and irresponsibility, see John Updike, *Rabbit Run* (New York: Random House, 1960).

52. Herb London, "If We Don't Shape Up, Who'll Ship Out?," *Burlington* [VT] *Free Press*, April 6, 2002, 6A.

53. Stephen Carter, *Integrity* (New York: Basic Books, 1996), 221.

54. Stephen Carter, *Civility* (New York: Basic Books, 1998), 17.

55. Robert Dahl, *On Political Equality* (New Haven, CT: Yale University Press, 2006). See, for example, 104–5: "It is by no means unlikely that advanced capitalism will foster a revolt against our worship of consumption and our focus on ever-increasing gains for consumers. For a growing number of persons, the goal of consumer satisfaction may yield to the goal of civic participation. The now dominant culture of consumerism may then give way to a culture of citizenship that would promote, among other ends, greater political equality among Americans."

56. Alan Wolfe, *Does American Democracy Still Work?* (New Haven, CT: Yale University Press, 2006). Wolfe claims, for example, that "George W. Bush has been the most ideological politician ever to hold the office of president of the United States" (178), and that we are now witnessing "politics without civility" (180). Little did he imagine how much worse this incivility could become.

57. Michael Sandel, *Democracy's Discontent* (Cambridge, MA: Harvard University Press, 1996), 3, 6.

58. Jean Bethke Elshtain, *Democracy on Trial* (New York: Basic Books, 1995), 1–2.

59. Saul Levmore and Martha Nussbaum, eds., *The Offensive Internet* (Cambridge, MA: Harvard University Press, 2010).

60. Mark Lilla, "The Tea Party Jacobins," *New York Review of Books*, May 27, 2010, 56.

61. In April 2018, the Trump administration began forcibly separating children from parents who brought them across the U.S. border, only suspending this policy in June in response to widespread political outrage; on October 24, Gregory Alan Bush shot and killed two African American shoppers in a grocery store in Kentucky after failing to gain entry (because the doors were locked) to a predominately black church with the clear intention of killing parishioners; on October 26, Cesar Sayoc was arrested for sending pipe bombs through the mail to as many as a dozen prominent Democrats and Trump critics (including George

Soros, President Obama, Vice President Biden, Secretary of State Clinton, Rep. Maxine Waters, senators Kamala Harris and Corey Booker, and actor Robert De Niro); on October 27, Robert Bowers entered a synagogue in Pittsburgh, yelled "All Jews must die," and killed eleven congregants.

    62. See Glenn Kessler, Salvador Rizzo, and Meg Kelly, *Washington Post* Fact Checker Analysis, "President Trump Has Made More Than 5000 False or Misleading Claims," September 13, 2018: https://www .washingtonpost.com/politics/2018/09/13/president-trump-has-made -more-than-false-or-misleading-claims/?utm_term=.8d463b07190a. According to Bob Woodward, President Trump's former chief economic advisor, Gary Cohen, described Trump as "a professional liar"; Woodward, *Fear* (New York: Simon and Schuster, 2018), 209.

    63. Cass R. Sunstein, *#Republic* (Princeton, NJ: Princeton University Press, 2017), ix.

    64. Catherine Rampell, "Americans Believe Crazy, Wrong Things," *Washington Post*, January 4, 2017, https://www.commercial-news.com /opinion/rampell-americans-believe-crazy-wrong-things/article_9533 c479-9ae3-54d3-a270-00f4486b46c9.html.

    65. Daniel Akst, *We Have Met the Enemy* (New York: Penguin, 2011), 153.

    66. Ibid., 4.

    67. Ibid., 244.

    68. Ibid., 242.

    69. Ibid., 241.

    70. Jonathan Franzen, *Freedom* (New York: Farrar, Straus and Giroux, 2010), 181.

    71. Ibid., 193.

    72. Ibid., 241.

    73. Ibid., 503.

    74. Wood, *Empire of Liberty*, 115.

    75. Walt Whitman, "Democratic Vistas," in *Complete Poetry and Collected Prose* (New York: Library of America, 1982), 957.

    76. Ibid., 952. It is important to note that Whitman is using "men" as a gender-neutral pronoun; part of the perfection encouraged by democracy would include the equality of the sexes (ibid., 970).

    77. Ibid., 980.

    78. The phrase is from Lincoln's 1862 annual message to Congress.

79. Alexis de Tocqueville, *Democracy in America* (Chicago: University of Chicago Press, 2000), 227. Gordon Wood has written that early Americans "had an extraordinary emotional need to exaggerate their importance in the world" (*Empire of Liberty*, 622).

80. After the American Revolution, more Americans (per capita) could vote than in any other nation. Being the most democratic nation at the end of the eighteenth century, of course, does not make the United States the originator or inventor of democracy (it has, of course, much more ancient roots than this). See Shankman, *Crucible of American Democracy*, 20.

81. Amartya Sen, the Nobel-winning economist, is just one of the many commentators since Tocqueville's time to be annoyed by this American sense of exceptionalism, this belief that the United States constitutes the true home of the democratic experience. He argues that democracy is neither the sole invention of America or of the West as a whole. See Sen, "Humanity and Citizenship," in Martha Nussbaum, et al., *For Love of Country?* (Boston: Beacon Press, 1996), 111–18. In a similar vein, the great American historian Richard Hofstadter once commented, "Part of our trouble is that our sense of ourselves hasn't diminished as much as it ought to"; quoted in Jill Lepore, *The Whites of Their Eyes* (Princeton, NJ: Princeton University Press, 2010), 68.

82. For a French reflection on these matters, consider Michel Houellebecq's meditation on the vacuous and deadening pleasures and freedoms of secular European society in his recent novel, *Submission* (New York: Farrar, Straus and Giroux, 2015).

83. Alexander Hamilton, James Madison, and John Jay, *The Federalist Papers*, ed. Clinton Rossiter (New York: Mentor, 1999), 46.

84. Ibid., 51.

85. Ibid., 50.

86. Ibid., 290.

87. Mann, *Lectures on Education*, 238–39.

88. President Barack Obama, Farewell Address, January 10, 2017, https://www.nytimes.com/2017/01/10/us/politics/obama-farewell-address-speech.html.

89. Quoted in Sunstein, *#Republic*, 157.

90. Michael Oakeshott thought of the American founding as an "instructive chapter" in the style of politics he calls "Rationalism," which is distinguishable, in part, by the belief that "political machinery can take

the place of moral and political education." He agrees with Mann that such a belief is a mistake. See Oakeshott, *Rationalism in Politics and Other Essays* (London: Methuen, 1962), 26, 6.

91. "If a man does not keep pace with his companions, perhaps it is because he hears a different drummer. Let him step to the music which he hears, however measured or far away" (*Walden*, 581).

92. "This world is a place of business. What an infinite bustle! I am awaked almost every night by the panting of the locomotive. It interrupts my dreams. There is no Sabbath. It would be glorious to see mankind at leisure for once. It is nothing but work, work, work. . . . I think there is nothing, not even crime, more opposed to poetry, to philosophy, ay, to life itself, than this incessant business"; Thoreau, "Life without Principle," in *Collected Essays and Poems* (New York: Library of America, 2001), 348–49.

93. *Walden*, 396, 352.

94. Brad S. Gregory, for example, laments that "capitalism has colonized the desires of the vast majority of modern Europeans and North Americans, regardless of their metaphysical beliefs, in ways that conduce to self-interested conformity," and that the "ubiquitous practices of consumerism are more than anything else the cultural glue that holds Western societies together"; Gregory, *The Unintended Reformation* (Cambridge, MA: Harvard University Press, 2012), 229, 236.

95. Rod Dreher comments critically on what he takes to be "the end point of modernity: the autonomous, freely choosing individual, finding meaning in no one but himself"; Dreher, *The Benedict Option* (New York: Sentinel, 2017), 44.

96. Patrick J. Deneen, *Conserving America?* (South Bend, IN: St. Augustine's Press, 2016), 3.

97. For my more developed critical reading of *Walden*, see Bob Pepperman Taylor, *America's Bachelor Uncle: Thoreau and the American Polity* (Lawrence: University Press of Kansas, 1996), chap. 5. For my readings of Thoreau's *Civil Disobedience*, see Taylor, *The Routledge Guidebook to Thoreau's "Civil Disobedience"* (London: Routledge, 2015), and the introduction to my Broadview edition of Thoreau, *Civil Disobedience*.

98. Rosenblum is following Stanley Cavell here; he had referred to *Walden* as a "sacred text"; see Cavell, *The Senses of Walden* (Chicago: University of Chicago Press, 1981), 14. Nancy L. Rosenblum, *Good*

Neighbors: The Democracy of Everyday Life (Princeton, NJ: Princeton University Press, 2016), 223.

Chapter I. Simplicity

1. John Adams, *A Defence of the Constitutions of Government of the United States of America* (Philadelphia: Printed by H. Sweitzer for William Cobbett, 1797), 2:387.
2. Thoreau, *Walden*, 334.
3. Thoreau, *Civil Disobedience*, 48.
4. Ibid., 48–49.
5. Thoreau, "Life without Principle," 350.
6. *Walden*, 378.
7. Ibid., 334.
8. Ibid., 586.
9. Ibid., 387.
10. Ibid., 335.
11. Ibid., 374.
12. Ibid., 377.
13. Ibid., 378.
14. "Life without Principle," 348–49.
15. *Walden*, 584.
16. "It is the luxurious and dissipated who set the fashions which the herd so diligently follow" (ibid., 351).
17. Ibid., 394.
18. Ibid., 396, 352.
19. Ibid., 395.
20. Ibid., 460.
21. Ibid., 350.
22. *Civil Disobedience*, 48–49.
23. *Walden*, 459.
24. "Life without Principle," 350.
25. *Walden*, 362.
26. Ibid., 359.
27. He was also actively involved in his family's pencil-manufacturing business.
28. *Walden*, 366.
29. Henry D. Thoreau, *The Journal of Henry D. Thoreau*, ed. Bradford Torrey and Francis H. Allen, 14 vols. (Boston: Houghton Mifflin, 1949), 1:278.

30. Ibid., 2:47.

31. Thoreau, untitled poem, in *Collected Essays and Poems*, 637.

32. *Walden*, 336.

33. Ibid., 398, 399.

34. Ibid., 400.

35. Ibid., 399.

36. Matthew 6:24.

37. *Walden*, 402.

38. Ibid., 331.

39. Ibid., 582–83.

40. Ibid., 587.

41. "Life without Principle," 362.

42. *Walden*, 584.

43. The project is also in danger of being both too self-congratulatory and too demanding to maintain its relevance to a large audience. One is reminded of the cook in a Joseph Conrad novella, who heroically yet sanctimoniously prepares hot food for the crew during a storm when their ship was nearly capsized. "Like many benefactors of humanity, the cook took himself too seriously, and reaped the reward of irreverence"; Joseph Conrad, *The Nigger of the Narcissus* (New York: Doubleday, Doran and Co., 1929), 84.

44. *Civil Disobedience*, 40–41.

45. Ibid., 55.

46. *Walden*, 333.

47. Ibid., 347.

48. Ibid., 384.

49. Ibid., 387.

50. For the most developed account of Thoreau as a virtue ethicist, see Philip Cafaro, *Thoreau's Living Ethics* (Athens: University of Georgia Press, 2004).

51. *Walden*, 386.

52. Ibid., 384.

53. Ibid., 485.

54. Ibid.

55. Ibid., 487.

56. Ibid., 486.

57. Ibid., 487.

58. Ibid., 489.

59. Ibid.

60. Ibid., 486.

61. Ibid., 489.

62. Gavin Jones, *American Hungers: The Problem of Poverty in U.S. Literature, 1840–1945* (Princeton, NJ: Princeton University Press, 2007), 34.

63. Lawrence Buell, "Downwardly Mobile for Conscience's Sake: Voluntary Simplicity from Thoreau to Lily Bart," *American Literary History* 17 (Winter 2005): 653.

64. *Walden*, 350.

65. Ibid., 365.

66. *Journal*, 1:412.

67. Henry David Thoreau, *Familiar Letters of Henry David Thoreau*, ed. F. B. Sanborn (Boston: Houghton, Mifflin, 1894), 265.

68. Mark Sundeen, *The Unsettlers* (New York: Riverhead, 2016), 114.

69. Ibid., 61.

70. For an interview with Hughes (from April 25, 2011), see https://www.motherearthnews.com/nature-and-environment/sustainable-communities/possibility-alliance-ze0z11zmar.

71. See Sundeen, *Unsettlers*, 117. One needn't appeal only, or even necessarily, to high-brow arts in this context; imagining the loss of the electric guitar in the unsettlers' world is enough to give many of us pause.

72. Ibid., 9.

73. Andrew Bacevich, *The Limits of Power* (New York: Henry Holt, 2008), 16.

74. Deneen, *Conserving America?*, 7.

75. "Most of all, perhaps the very act of acquiring so much stuff has turned us ever more into individuals and ever less into members of a community, isolating us in a way that runs contrary to our most basic instincts"; Bill McKibben, *Deep Economy* (New York: Henry Holt, 2007), 37.

76. Jedediah Purdy, *After Nature* (Cambridge, MA: Harvard University Press, 2015), 256.

77. Ann Patchett, "My Year of No Shopping," *New York Times*, December 15, 2017, https://www.nytimes.com/2017/12/15/opinion/sunday/shopping-consumerism.html. "The unspoken question of shopping is 'What do I need?' What I needed was less" (ibid.).

78. Here are just a few representative titles: Marie Kondo, *The Life Changing Magic of Tidying Up* (Berkeley, CA: Ten Speed Press, 2014); Richard Carlson, *Don't Sweat the Small Stuff and It's All Small Stuff* (New York: Hyperion 1997); Cristin Frank, *Living Simple, Free and Happy* (Blue Ash, OH: Betterway Home Books, 2013); Emily Ley, *A Simplified Life* (Nashville, TN: Thomas Nelson, 2017); Elaine St. James, *Living the Simple Life* (New York: Hyperion, 1996); and a current favorite, Mark Manson, *The Subtle Art of Not Giving a Fuck* (New York: HarperCollins, 2016).

79. Plato, *The Republic*, 47–48.

80. See Michael Walzer, *Exodus and Revolution* (New York: Basic Books, 1986).

81. See "Dedication to the Republic of Geneva," in Jean-Jacques Rousseau, *Discourse on the Origin of Inequality*, in *The Basic Political Writings* (Indianapolis: Hackett, 1987), 32.

82. Aldo Leopold, "The Land Ethic," in *A Sand County Almanac* (New York: Ballantine Books, 1966), 240.

83. For a taste of this literature, see J. Baird Callicott, *In Defense of the Land Ethic* (New York: SUNY Press, 1989), and Callicott, *Beyond the Land Ethic* (New York: SUNY Press, 1999); Bryan G. Norton, "The Constancy of Leopold's Land Ethic," *Conservation Biology* 2 (March 1988): 93–102; Lewis Hinchman, "Aldo Leopold's Hermeneutic of Nature," *Review of Politics* (Spring 1995): 225–49; Larry Arnhart, "Aldo Leopold's Human Ecology," in *Conservation Reconsidered*, ed. Charles Rubin (Lanham, MD: Rowman and Littlefield, 2000), 103–32.

84. Leopold, "Land Ethic," 262–63.

85. For a more developed discussion of this tension in Leopold's work, see Bob Pepperman Taylor, "Aldo Leopold's Civic Education," in *Democracy and the Claims of Nature*, ed. Ben A. Minteer and Bob Pepperman Taylor (Lanham, MD: Rowman and Littlefield, 2002), 173–87.

86. Leopold, *Sand County Almanac*, 6.

87. Ibid., 76.

88. See his discussion of the need for wilderness sport as a form of adventure in Aldo Leopold, *The River of the Mother of God and Other Essays* (Madison: University of Wisconsin Press, 1991), 124–25. In this collection, he also writes of the way conservation provides us the "opportunity of personal contact with natural beauty" (ibid., 193).

89. Ibid., 94.

90. Leopold, *Sand County Almanac*, 109.

91. See Leopold, *River of the Mother of God*, 98–105; Leopold, *Sand County Almanac*, 119.

92. "Wilderness and economics are, in every ordinary sense, mutually exclusive" (Leopold, *River of the Mother of God*, 125).

93. Aldo Leopold, *For Health of the Land* (Washington, DC: Island Press, 1999), 148.

94. Leopold, *River of the Mother of God*, 137.

95. Leopold, *Sand County*, xviii.

96. Ibid.

97. Ibid., xix.

98. George Scialabba, *What Are Intellectuals Good For?* (Boston: Pressed Wafer, 2009), 165.

99. Christopher Lasch, *The True and Only Heaven* (New York: W. W. Norton, 1991), 17.

100. See Christopher Lasch, *The Revolt of the Elites* (New York: W. W. Norton, 1995), 8.

101. Lasch, *True and Only Heaven*, 528.

102. Ibid., 529; see 14, and also 169.

103. Ibid., 530.

104. Ibid., 532.

105. Jill Lepore, "The War and the Roses," *New Yorker*, August 8, 2016, 31.

106. Lasch, *Revolt of the Elites*, 6.

107. Ibid., 9.

108. Ibid., 28.

109. Ibid., 246.

110. Richard Rorty, "Two Cheers for Elitism," *New Yorker*, January 30, 1995, 86.

111. Ibid., 87.

112. It should be noted that Lasch's own reading of Thoreau is very different than mine. Although he was no admirer of Thoreau, the conceptual point made here remains. That is, even if Lasch is right that Emerson has more to say about limits than Thoreau (and I don't believe he is), the more important issue in this context is simply that he is promoting a brief for a recognition of the value of moderation and the acceptance of limits. See Lasch, *True and Only Heaven*, chap. 6.

113. See Richard Rorty, *Achieving Our Country* (Cambridge, MA: Harvard University Press, 1998), chap. 1.

114. McKibben, *Deep Economy*, 120.

115. Alan L. Mittleman, *Human Nature and Jewish Thought* (Princeton, NJ: Princeton University Press, 2015), 184.

116. Yuval Noah Harari, *Homo Deus* (New York: Harper, 2017), 202.

117. "Farmers toil. Nature laughs. Farmers weep. There's your history of agriculture in a nutshell"; Kristin Kimball, *The Dirty Life* (New York: Scribner, 2010), 207.

118. Ibid., 158.

119. Dreher, *The Benedict Option*, 191–92.

120. John Dewey, *The Public and Its Problems*, ed. Melvin Rogers (Athens, OH: Swallow Press, 2016).

121. Nora Hanagan, "From Agrarian Dreams to Democratic Realities: A Deweyan Alternative to Jeffersonian Food Politics," *Political Research Quarterly* 68 (2015): 39.

122. Dewey's term, coined in *The Public and Its Problems*, for our complex, heterogeneous, industrially based society (Dewey, *The Public and Its Problems*, chap. 5).

123. Louise O. Fresco, *Hamburgers in Paradise* (Princeton, NJ: Princeton University Press, 2016), 230.

124. "In the end, barring disaster on a global scale, we will be able to feed present and future generations in ways that are sustainable and healthy as well as balanced and equitable" (ibid., xiv).

125. Ibid., 240.

126. Mark Denny, *Making the Most of the Anthropocene* (Baltimore: Johns Hopkins University Press, 2017), 54.

127. Ibid., 126.

128. For a thoughtful and informative response to this common observation about the lower yields of organic agriculture compared to conventional farming, see John P. Reganold and Jonathan M. Wachter, "Organic Agriculture in the Twenty-first Century," *Nature Plants*, article no. 15221 (February 2016), 1–8; for a popular account of this scholarly review article, see John Reganold, "Can We Feed 10 Billion People on Organic Farming Alone?," *The Guardian*, August 14, 2016, https://www .theguardian.com/sustainable-business/2016/aug/14/organic-farming -agriculture-world-hunger. Reganold and Wachter review the scholarly literature comparing organic and conventional agriculture along four metrics of sustainability—production (yields), environment, economics, and the well-being of society—and find the positive contributions

of organic agriculture much more significant and promising than the many critics such as Fresco would suggest. When we take into account the environmental, social justice, and economic effects of conventional agriculture, organic farming promises a much higher social profit than inspection of yield rates alone would suggest. The authors conclude that a much more extensive organic system, combined with a much more modest level of conventional practices, would be able to feed the projected populations—even more confidently if consumers in the developed world ate an increasingly less meat-intensive diet.

129. One hundred and sixty-two years after *Walden* was published, a best-selling self-help book appeared in which the following (kind of) Thoreauvian point is made in decidedly non-Thoreauvian language: "This, in a nutshell, is what 'self-improvement' is really about: prioritizing better values, choosing better things to give a fuck about. Because when you give better fucks, you get better problems. And when you get better problems, you get a better life" (Manson, *The Subtle Art of Not Giving a Fuck*, 89). Such is the continuity, and the transformation, of our self-help literature over the centuries.

130. Amartya Sen, *Development as Freedom* (New York: Anchor, 1999), 292.

131. "The conditions of bourgeois society are too narrow to comprise the wealth created by them. And how does the bourgeoisie get over these crises? On the one hand by enforced destruction of a mass of productive forces; on the other, by the conquest of new markets, and by the more thorough exploitation of the old ones. That is to say, by paving the way for more extensive and more destructive crises, and by diminishing the means whereby crises are prevented. The weapons with which the bourgeoisie felled feudalism to the ground are now turned against the bourgeoisie itself"; Karl Marx and Frederick Engels, *Manifesto of the Communist Party*, in *Selected Works* (Moscow: Progress Publishers, 1977), 1:114.

132. Bill McKibben, *Enough* (New York: Times Books, 2003), 205.

133. Ibid., 178.

134. See, for example, this report from Kate Snow and Cynthia Mc-Fadden, "Generation at Risk: America's Youngest Facing Mental Health Crisis," NBC News, December 10, 2017, https://www.nbcnews.com /health/kids-health/generation-risk-america-s-youngest-facing-mental -health-crisis-n827836.

135. Steven Pinker believes the world bequeathed to us by the Enlightenment has produced ever-increasing human utility and promises to continue to do so indefinitely (if we will only let it). We will turn to his argument in the conclusion. See Pinker, *Enlightenment Now* (New York: Viking, 2018).

Chapter 2. Different Drummers

1. Thoreau, *Walden*, 355.

2. It is true that Thoreau occasionally helped move people along the Underground Railroad, and, as a fellow traveler to the abolition movement, he occasionally gave aid to abolition organizations and activities in forms other than speeches and essays. For example, a week after his release from jail, he hosted the Concord Female Anti-Slavery Society at his Walden Pond cabin. Such activities, however, were generally hidden from sight in his role as a writer and lecturer. For Thoreau's hosting of his sisters' abolition organization's celebration of the second anniversary of West Indian emancipation, see Sandra Harbert Petrulionis, *To Set This World Right* (Ithaca, NY: Cornell University Press, 2006), 60.

3. *Walden*, 496.

4. Ibid.

5. Ibid., 572.

6. Ibid., 376.

7. Ibid., 573.

8. Ibid., 460.

9. Ibid., 459.

10. Ibid., 573.

11. Ibid., 380.

12. Ibid., 381.

13. Ibid.

14. Ibid., 459.

15. Thoreau, *Civil Disobedience*, 43.

16. *Walden*, 536.

17. Ibid., 532.

18. Ibid., 514.

19. Ibid., 329.

20. Henry David Thoreau, "Paradise (To Be) Regained," in *Collected Essays and Poems*, 137.

21. Ibid.

22. Henry David Thoreau, "Slavery in Massachusetts," in *Collected Essays and Poems*, 342.

23. "I find it wholesome to be alone the greater part of the time. To be in company, even with the best, is soon wearisome and dissipating. I love to be alone. I never found the companion that was so companionable as solitude. We are for the most part more lonely when we go abroad among men than when we stay in our chambers. A man thinking or working is always alone, let him be where he will" (*Walden*, 430).

24. Henry David Thoreau, *Letters to Various Persons* (Boston: Houghton, Mifflin, 1885), 108.

25. *Walden*, 434.

26. In a letter to his English friend Cholmondeley in 1855, Thoreau says he has little to do with the nation's politics, and dreams instead of a "glorious *private life*" (Thoreau, *Familiar Letters*, 297).

27. Thoreau, "Life without Principle," 359.

28. Thoreau, *Journal*, 1:239.

29. "Life without Principle," 357.

30. Henry David Thoreau, "A Plea for Captain John Brown," in *Collected Essays and Poems*, 404.

31. "Slavery in Massachusetts," 341.

32. "Will mankind never learn that policy is not morality—that it never secures any moral right, but considers merely what is expedient? . . . What is wanted is men, not of policy, but of probity—who recognize a higher law than the Constitution, or the decision of the majority" (ibid., 343).

33. "The chief want" of every state is a "high and earnest purpose in its inhabitants" ("Life without Principle," 365).

34. *Walden*, 459.

35. Henry David Thoreau, "Natural History of Massachusetts," in *Collected Essays and Poems*, 21.

36. "A Plea for Captain John Brown," 407; "Slavery in Massachusetts," 337.

37. Ibid., 344.

38. Henry David Thoreau, "A Yankee in Canada," in *Collected Essays and Poems*, 311.

39. Thoreau, *Civil Disobedience*, 55.

40. Ibid., 37.

41. Ibid., 40.

42. Ibid., 38.

43. Ibid. 53.

44. Ibid.

45. Ibid., 42.

46. "They only can force me who obey a higher law than I" (ibid., 50). Thoreau was not alone in his views here. Emerson writes, in "Politics" (published in 1844, four years before Thoreau delivered the lectures, in 1848, that would become *Civil Disobedience*), of the moral superiority of the individual to the state; see Emerson, "Politics," in *Essays and Lectures*, 567.

47. *Civil Disobedience*, 46.

48. "Slavery in Massachusetts," 346.

49. "I had never respected the Government near to which I had lived, but I had foolishly thought that I might manage to live here, minding my private affairs, and forget it. . . . I dwelt before, perhaps, in the illusion that my life passed somewhere only *between* heaven and hell, but now I cannot persuade myself that I do not dwell *wholly within* hell. . . . I feel that, to some extent, the State has fatally interfered with my lawful business" (ibid., 345).

50. Ibid., 343.

51. Ralph Waldo Emerson, "Thoreau," in *Thoreau: A Century of Criticism*, ed. Walter Harding (Dallas: Southern Methodist University, 1954), 25. Emerson's son, Edward, would also reflect on the friendly relationships between Thoreau and children; see Harold Bloom, ed., *Henry David Thoreau* (New York: Bloom's Literary Criticism, 2008), 70.

52. *Journal*, 3:194.

53. Ibid., 11:326.

54. *Civil Disobedience*, 52.

55. Emerson, "Thoreau," 23.

56. "There was somewhat military in his nature, not to be subdued, always manly and able, but rarely tender, as if he did not feel himself except in opposition" (ibid., 25).

57. In *Civil Disobedience*, Thoreau brags about having refused to pay the tax that went to support the local clergy (49).

58. Emerson, "Thoreau," 37, 38.

59. Two critics, one from the nineteenth century and one from the twenty-first, probably suffice to make the point of how early and recently such criticisms have been voiced. James Russell Lowell, Thoreau's contemporary, found occasion only three years after Thoreau's death to

write: "He seems to us to have been a man with so high a conceit of himself that he accepted without questioning, and insisted on our accepting, his defects and weaknesses of character as virtues and powers peculiar to himself" (see Harding, *Thoreau: A Century of Criticism*, 45). More recently, Kathryn Schulz has penned a comparably blistering assessment of Thoreau's moral character, claiming he was "self-obsessed: narcissistic, fanatical about self-control, adamant that he required nothing beyond himself to understand and thrive in the world" (see Kathryn Schulz, "Pond Scum: Henry Thoreau's Moral Myopia," *New Yorker*, October 19, 2015, 40). Two classic attacks on Thoreau's moral integrity from the twentieth century are Vincent Buranelli, "The Case against Thoreau," *Ethics* 67, no. 4 (1957): 257–68, and George Hochfield, "Anti-Thoreau," *Sewanee Review* 96, no. 3 (1988): 433–43.

60. The Rev. Martin Luther King Jr., "A Legacy of Creative Protest," in *Thoreau in Our Season*, ed. John Hicks (Amherst: University of Massachusetts Press, 1967), 13.

61. Hannah Arendt, "Civil Disobedience," in *Crises of the Republic* (New York: Harcourt Brace Jovanovich, 1972), 60–61.

62. Ibid., 55.

63. Wen Stephenson, *What We're Fighting for Now Is Each Other* (Boston: Beacon Press, 2015), 15.

64. Ibid., 29.

65. Ibid., ix, xv.

66. "It's hard to shake the feeling that I'm in need of salvation" (ibid., 2).

67. Ibid., 8.

68. Ibid., 20.

69. See, e.g., ibid., 24, 35.

70. Ibid., 37–38.

71. Ibid., 58.

72. Ibid., 208, 187, 91.

73. Ibid., 178.

74. Max Weber, "Politics as a Vocation," in *From Max Weber*, ed. H. H. Gerth and C. Wright Mills (New York: Oxford University Press, 1978), 121.

75. Recall his comment in *Civil Disobedience* that it would be better to let the nation dissolve than allow slavery to continue for another day: "This people must cease to hold slaves, and to make war on Mexico, though it cost them their existence as a people" (41).

76. Weber, "Politics as a Vocation," 121.

77. Ibid., 123.

78. Ibid., 126.

79. Ibid.

80. Ibid., 127.

81. Critics of Brown, Thoreau claims, do not understand this truth about moral life. "Such do not know that like the seed is the fruit, and that, in the moral world, when good seed is planted, good fruit is inevitable, and does not depend on our watering and cultivating; that when you plant, or bury, a hero in his field, a crop of heroes is sure to spring up. This is a seed of such force and vitality, that it does not ask our leave to germinate" ("A Plea for Captain John Brown," 402).

82. Weber, "Politics as a Vocation," 122.

83. Constantin Fasolt, *The Limits of History* (Chicago: University of Chicago Press, 2004), 137, 138.

84. Ibid., 143.

85. Philip F. Gura, *Man's Better Angels* (Cambridge, MA: Belknap Press, 2017), 266.

86. Andrew Delbanco, *The Abolitionist Imagination* (Cambridge, MA: Harvard University Press, 2012), 47, 48.

87. Ibid., 49.

88. Ibid., 163.

89. See the essays by Delbanco's critics in ibid.

90. See, e.g., the suggestion by Manisha Sinha that the moral ambivalence Delbanco praises in novelists Melville and Hawthorne was, in reality, racial hostility to equality (ibid., 96).

91. Barack Obama, Nobel Lecture, December 10, 2008, https://www.nobelprize.org/nobel_prizes/peace/laureates/2009/obama-lecture_en.html.

92. Adam Gopnik says he "can't help noting that anti-liberal polemics . . . always have more force and gusto than liberalism's defenses have ever had. . . . The middle way is not the way of melodrama. . . . 'Illiberalism' is the permanent fact of life. Moments of social peace and coexistence, however troubled and imperfect, are the brief miracle that needs explaining, and protecting" (Gopnik, "The Liberal Imagination," *New Yorker*, March 20, 2017, 93). If Gopnik is right, moral outrage will always find liberal moderation an easy and appealing target.

93. Ta-Nehisi Coates, *We Were Eight Years in Power* (New York: One World, 2017), 212.

94. Delbanco, *Abolitionist Imagination*, 53.

95. Weber, "Politics as a Vocation," 128.

96. Ibid., 127.

97. Steven Levitsky and Daniel Ziblatt, *How Democracies Die* (New York: Crown, 2018).

98. Ibid., 8.

99. See ibid., 204, for the impact of the civil rights movement in breaking the accord between the major parties. One nice illustration of the Republican attack on norms prior to the Trump presidency is House Majority Leader Tom DeLay's response to President George W. Bush's insistence that he (Bush) would be a "uniter," not a "divider." DeLay reportedly responded to Bush: "We don't work with Democrats. There'll be none of that uniter-divider stuff" (ibid., 152). In a sense, onetime Trump advisor Steve Bannon's politics, as summarized by journalist Michael Wolff, is the logical end of this Republican anger: "The new politics was not the art of compromise but the art of conflict"; Wolff, *Fire and Fury* (New York: Henry Holt, 2018), 63.

100. Levitsky and Ziblatt, *How Democracies Die*, 222.

101. Ibid., 171.

102. See Harry V. Jaffa, "Thoreau and Lincoln," in *A Political Companion to Henry David Thoreau*, ed. Jack Turner (Lexington: University Press of Kentucky, 2009), 178–204.

103. Abraham Lincoln, *The Portable Abraham Lincoln* (New York: Penguin, 1992), 68.

104. Abraham Lincoln, *Speeches and Writings, 1859–1865* (New York: Library of America, 1989), 19.

105. See Manisha Sinha, "Did the Abolitionists Cause the Civil War?" in Delbanco, *Abolitionist Imagination*, 81–108.

106. David Bromwich, *Moral Imagination: Essays* (Princeton, NJ: Princeton University Press, 2014), 158. This hatred was real enough. Yet, for Thoreau and many others, it was hard not to simply be pessimistic about the possibility of a successful transition from a slave to a free and democratic society by political means alone.

107. For a taste of this literature, see John Patrick Diggins, "Thoreau, Marx, and the 'Riddle' of Alienation," *Social Research* 39 (Winter 1972): 571–98; Heinz Eulau, "Wayside Challenger: Some Remarks on the Politics of Henry David Thoreau," in *Thoreau: A Collection of Critical Essays*, ed. Sherman Paul (Englewood Cliffs, NJ: Prentice-Hall, 1962), 117–30; and Jaffa, "Thoreau and Lincoln."

108. See, e.g., Jane Bennett, *Thoreau's Nature* (Thousand Oaks, CA: Sage, 1994); Shannon Mariotti, *Thoreau's Democratic Withdrawal* (Madison: University of Wisconsin Press, 2010); Nancy Rosenblum, "Thoreau's Militant Conscience," *Political Theory* 9 (1981): 81–110; Brian Walker, "Thoreau on Democratic Cultivation," *Political Theory* 29 (2001): 155–89. For a quick introduction to this literature, see Turner, *A Political Companion to Henry David Thoreau*. For a recent contribution that is skeptical of these developments, see Jonathan McKenzie, *The Political Thought of Henry David Thoreau* (Lexington: University Press of Kentucky, 2016).

109. This is a more pessimistic conclusion about Thoreau's political contribution than I had reached in an earlier work, but not necessarily one that is incompatible with the general thrust of that earlier reading. See Bob Pepperman Taylor, *America's Bachelor Uncle*, conclusion.

110. *Walden*, 389.

111. Nancy Rosenblum, *Good Neighbors* (Princeton, NJ: Princeton University Press, 2016), 231.

112. See quote in note 33, above.

113. *Civil Disobedience*, 56.

114. Emerson, "Politics," 559.

115. Ralph Waldo Emerson, "Culture," in *Essays and Lectures*, 1020.

116. Emerson, "Politics," 567.

117. Ibid., 570.

118. Ibid., 569.

119. *Civil Disobedience*, 57.

120. Ibid., 38.

121. "The State never intentionally confronts a man's sense, intellectual or moral, but only his body, his senses" (ibid., 50).

122. Ibid., 40.

123. Ibid., 39.

124. Ibid., 50.

125. "O for a man who is a *man*, and, as my neighbor says, has a bone in his back which you cannot pass your hand through!" (ibid., 42).

126. Danielle Allen, "Charlottesville Is Not the Continuation of an Old Fight. It is Something New," *Washington Post*, August 13, 2017, https://www.washingtonpost.com/opinions/charlottesville-is-not -the-continuation-of-an-old-fight-it-is-something-new/2017/08/13 /971812f6-8029-11e7-b359-15a3617c767b_story.html?utm_term= .3c7b43f7582e.

127. Manisha Sinha, "Did the Abolitionists Cause the Civil War?" in Delbanco, *Abolitionist Imagination*, 95.

128. J. M. Coetzee, *Diary of A Bad Year* (New York: Viking, 2007), 3.

129. See Garry Wills, "Big Rocket Man," *New York Review of Books*, December 21, 2017, 8.

130. Shane Goldmacher, "America Hits New Landmark: 200 Million Registered Voters," *Politico*, October 19, 2016, https://www.politico .com/story/2016/10/how-many-registered-voters-are-in-america-2016 -229993.

131. This growing remoteness of the centers of power from common citizens is obviously not unique to the United States. In many ways it simply reflects modern technological realities and the contemporary nature of both political and economic institutions. In Pankaj Mishra's words, "the burden of personal inadequacy and estrangement has been increased by the unavoidable awareness of an unlimited horizon of global complications: the information we have and are constantly stimulated by is much greater than the range of what we can do"; Mishra, *The Age of Anger* (New York: Farrar, Straus and Giroux, 2017), 338–39.

132. It is interesting to note that the American obsession with gun ownership has grown in response to the feeling of alienation and powerlessness before the national state. How else to explain the fantasy that we can protect ourselves with private arms against an overbearing state and treasonous elites?

133. Anyone who looks to the populist rebellion that produced the Trump presidency as evidence for democratic efficacy will have a hard time explaining the speed and ease with which the Trump administration has pursued plutocratic policies diametrically opposed to the interests of the populist base that supported (and continues to support) the president.

134. John B. Judis, *The Populist Explosion* (New York: Columbia Global Reports, 2016), 16.

135. Judis, for example, argues that calling populist movements "fascists exaggerates the danger they pose—they don't threaten to wage war or disband parliaments" (ibid., 157). It would be interesting to know how long one could be persuaded by this analysis, in light of President Trump's military bellicosity (especially toward North Korea) and his assaults on the media, the Department of Justice, and the intelligence agencies. It is true that Trump ran for office more as an isolationist and

nationalist than an imperialist, and that his rhetoric could plausibly be thought to have aimed at fulfilling the promises of democracy (against a "rigged system") more than about attacking it directly. His behavior as president, however, provides significant reason to worry more about the fascistic elements of his politics—the racialism, the appeals to violence, the uncompromising threats to all opponents—than Judis sensed when he was writing prior to the 2016 election.

136. Contrast, for example, Ta-Nehisi Coates, "The First White President," in *We Were Eight Years in Power*, epilogue, 341–67, with Joan C. Williams, *White Working Class* (Boston: Harvard Business Review, 2017). The most sophisticated study of the motivations of Trump voters in 2016 suggest that Coates's racial explanation is closer to the truth than Williams's explanation based upon social class grievance. See Diana C. Mutz, "Status Threat, Not Economic Hardship, Explains the 2016 Presidential Vote," *Proceedings of the National Academy of Sciences* 115, no. 19 (2018): E4330–E4339, http://www.pnas.org/content/early/2018/04/18/1718155115.

137. "It is no time, then, to be judging according to [a judge's] precedents, but to establish a precedent for the future. I would much rather trust to the sentiment of the people. In their vote, you would get something of some value, at least, however small; but, in the other case, only the trammeled judgment of an individual, of no significance, be it which way it might." "The city does not *think* much. On any moral question, I would rather have the opinion of Boxboro than of Boston and New York put together. . . . When, in some obscure country town, the farmers come together to a special town meeting, to express their opinion on some subject which is vexing the land, that, I think, is the true Congress, and the most respectable one that is ever assembled in the United States" ("Slavery in Massachusetts," 338, 339).

138. Dreher, *The Benedict Option*, 9.

139. Ibid., 99.

140. Ibid., 121.

141. Ibid., 159.

142. *Walden*, 459.

143. *Civil Disobedience*, 52–53.

144. Marc J. Dunkelman, *The Vanishing Neighbor* (New York: W. W. Norton, 2014), 73.

145. Ibid., 190.

146. Michael Sandel, *What Money Can't Buy* (New York: Farrar, Straus and Giroux, 2012), 203.

147. Danielle Allen writes: "Perhaps the single most important thing we could do to reverse inequalities that abound in our society would be to repeal zoning laws and other measures that dramatically segregate people by income and ethnicity. Increased social connectedness across lines of socioeconomic and ethnic difference would generate egalitarian effects"; Allen, *Our Declaration* (New York: W. W. Norton, 2015), 244.

148. Scialabba, *What Are Intellectuals Good For?*, 20.

149. Alexis de Tocqueville visited the United States to study just these democratic elements of American society fifteen years before Thoreau moved to his cabin by Walden Pond.

150. *Walden*, 409.

151. Ibid., 409–10.

152. For more on these matters, see Taylor, *America's Bachelor Uncle*, 70–73.

153. "Life without Principle," 362.

154. *Walden*, 395.

155. Ibid., 334.

156. "Total Noise, the seething static of every particular thing and experience, and one's total freedom of infinite choice about what to choose to attend to and represent and connect, and how, and why, etc." (David Foster Wallace, "Deciderization 2007—A Special Report," 2, http://neugierig.org/content/dfw/bestamerican.pdf). This essay was written as the introduction for David Foster Wallace, ed., *The Best American Essays 2007* (New York: Mariner Books, 2007).

157. Franklin Foer, *World without Mind* (New York: Penguin, 2017), 8.

158. David Brooks, "How Evil Is Tech?," *New York Times*, November 20, 2017, https://www.nytimes.com/2017/11/20/opinion/how -evil-is-tech.html.

159. Wolff, *Fire and Fury*, 114.

160. According to Barbara Ehrenreich, "A 2015 study found that the average adult attention span had shrunk from twelve seconds a dozen years ago to eight seconds, which is shorter than the attention span of a gold-fish"; Ehrenreich, *Natural Causes* (New York: Hachette Book Group, 2018), 73.

161. Bryan Caplan, *The Case against Education* (Princeton, NJ: Princeton University Press, 2018), 6.

162. Ibid., 206.

163. Ibid., 237.

164. Ibid., 242.

165. "Literature [has] been made a kind of data to illustrate, supposedly, some graceless theory that stood apart from it, and that would be shed in a year or two and replaced by something post- or neo- and in any case as gracelessly irrelevant to a work of language as whatever it displaced. I think this phenomenon is an effect of the utilitarian hostility to the humanities and to art, an attempt to repackage them, to give them some appearance of respectability. And yet the beautiful persists, and so do eloquence and depth of thought, and they belong to all of us because they are the most pregnant evidence we can have of what is possible in us"; Marilynne Robinson, *What Are We Doing Here?* (New York: Farrar, Straus and Giroux, 2018), 33.

166. "*Most* of what schools teach has no value in the labor market. Students fail to learn *most* of what they're taught. Adults forget *most* of what they learn" (Caplan, *The Case against Education*, 68).

167. "Ultimately, I believe the best education policy is no education policy at all: the separation of school and state" (ibid., 6).

168. Robinson, *What Are We Doing Here?*, 39.

169. Patrick J. Deneen, *Why Liberalism Failed* (New Haven, CT: Yale University Press, 2018), 111.

170. Marilynne Robinson, *The Death of Adam* (Boston: Houghton Mifflin, 1998), 7.

171. Horace Mann, that great nineteenth-century advocate of public education, of the "common school," only strategically turned to promoting the economic benefits of democratically distributed education when he felt that politically his appeals to moral and civic principles were falling on deaf ears. See my discussion in Bob Pepperman Taylor, *Horace Mann's Troubling Legacy* (Lawrence: University Press of Kansas, 2010), 66, and chap. 3 more generally.

172. Robinson, *The Death of Adam*, 142.

173. Marilynne Robinson, *The Givenness of Things* (New York: Farrar, Straus and Giroux, 2015), 27.

174. Marilynne Robinson, *When I Was a Child I Read Books* (New York: Farrar, Straus and Giroux, 2012), 159.

175. "The dominant view now is that [education's] legitimate function is not to prepare people for citizenship in a democracy but to prepare them to be members of a docile though skilled working class" (Robinson, *What Are We Doing Here?*, 94).

176. "The most difficult struggle of our civilization has been to find the means to create autonomy for ordinary lives, so that they might not be plundered or disposed of according to the whims of more powerful people"; Marilynne Robinson, *Mother Country* (New York: Farrar, Straus and Giroux, 1989), 105.

177. Wyatt Mason, "The Revelations of Marilynne Robinson," *New York Times Magazine*, October 1, 2014, https://www.nytimes.com/2014/10/05/magazine/the-revelations-of-marilynne-robinson.html.

178. Wendell Berry, *The Long-Legged House* (Berkeley: Counterpoint, 2012), 86.

Chapter 3. Learning from Nature

1. Thoreau, *Walden*, 394.
2. Thoreau, "Walking," in *Collected Essays and Poems*, 251.
3. *Walden*, 579.
4. Ibid., 482.
5. Thoreau, *Autumnal Hints*, in *Collected Essays and Poems*, 393.
6. *Walden*, 384.
7. Ibid., 353, 354. In "A Winter Walk," Thoreau suggests that nature is the model for all art. See *Collected Essays and Poems*, 92.
8. *Walden*, 451.
9. Ibid., 551.
10. Ibid., 503.
11. Ibid., 329.
12. Thoreau, *Essays and Poems*, 516.
13. *Walden*, 422.
14. Ibid., 400.
15. Ibid., 399.
16. "We should be blessed if we live in the present always" (ibid., 572).
17. Thoreau, "Life without Principle," 362.
18. *Walden*, 393, 584.
19. Ibid., 488.
20. "Walking," 239.

21. *Walden,* 575.

22. "How can you expect the birds to sing when their groves are cut down?" (ibid., 476). Our agriculture deforms us, he suggests, by knowing nature only from the perspective of a robber (454). The final passages of "The Ponds" are devoted to an attack on the misuse of nature, the marketization of nature, and the misunderstanding of its deepest values (see ibid., 478–82). See also Thoreau, "Huckleberries," in *Collected Essays and Poems,* 500.

23. This lesson was basic to Emerson's *Nature,* which moves us from thinking of nature as "commodity" to seeing that nature can represent higher aesthetic and moral goods.

24. *Walden,* 453.

25. Letter from Thoreau to Harrison G. O. Blake, August 9, 1850, in Thoreau, *Letters to Various Persons,* 63.

26. See *Walden,* 578.

27. "Huckleberries," 495.

28. *Walden,* 490.

29. Henry David Thoreau, *The Maine Woods,* in *A Week on the Concord and Merrimack Rivers; Walden, or, Life in the Woods; The Maine Woods; Cape Cod,* 685. "Every creature is better alive than dead, men and moose and pine-trees, and he who understands it aright will rather preserve its life than destroy it" (ibid.). "It is the living spirit of the [pine] tree, not its spirit of turpentine, with which I sympathize, and which heals my cuts. It is as immortal as I am, and perchance will go to as high a heaven, there to tower above me still" (ibid.).

30. Henry David Thoreau, *A Week on the Concord and Merrimack Rivers,* in *A Week on the Concord and Merrimack Rivers; Walden, or, Life in the Woods; The Maine Woods; Cape Cod,* 284.

31. Thoreau, "The Last Days of John Brown," in *Collected Essays and Poems,* 422.

32. Thoreau, *Journal,* 9:121.

33. And of Emerson's transcendentalism, so important as an influence on Thoreau also.

34. "All nature is my bride" (*Journal,* 9:337).

35. *Walden,* 490, 493, 497, 498.

36. Ibid., 496.

37. Kimberly K. Smith, *African American Environmental Thought* (Lawrence: University Press of Kansas, 2007), 8.

38. Ibid., 95.

39. Samuel Danforth, "A Brief Recognition of New-Englands Errand into the Wilderness" (1670), http://digitalcommons.unl.edu/cgi/viewcontent.cgi?article=1038&context=libraryscience, 11.

40. Ibid., 14.

41. Ibid., 19.

42. Ibid., 19–20.

43. Thomas Paine, *Common Sense* (London: Penguin, 1988), 120.

44. Perry Miller, *Nature's Nation* (Cambridge, MA: Harvard University Press, 1967), 9.

45. Ralph Waldo Emerson, "Literary Ethics," in *Essays and Lectures*, 101.

46. Emerson, *Nature*, in *Essays and Lectures*, 48.

47. "Everywhere we have met thousands of Democrats, Independents, and Republicans from all economic conditions and walks of life bound together in that community of shared values of family, work, neighborhood, peace and freedom. They are concerned, yes, but they are not frightened. They are disturbed, but not dismayed. They are the kind of men and women Tom Paine had in mind when he wrote—during the darkest days of the American Revolution—'We have it in our power to begin the world over again'"; Ronald Reagan, Nomination Acceptance Speech, Republican National Convention, Detroit, Michigan, July 17, 1980, http://www.4president.org/speeches/reagan1980convention.htm.

48. Thomas Jefferson, *Notes on the State of Virginia* (Chapel Hill: University of North Carolina Press, 1982), 165.

49. Thomas Jefferson to John Jay, August 23, 1785, in Jefferson, *Writings* (New York: Library of America, 1984), 818.

50. Charles Fish, *In Good Hands* (New York: Kodansha International, 1996), 16.

51. Ibid., 45.

52. Ibid., 100.

53. Wendell Berry, *The Unsettling of America* (Berkeley, CA: Counterpoint, 1996), 5.

54. Ibid., 8–9.

55. Ibid., 9.

56. Carl Becker, "Kansas," in *Every Man His Own Historian* (New York: Appleton, Century, Crofts, 1935), 6.

57. Ibid., 9.

58. Ibid.

59. Ibid., 12.

60. Ibid., 18.

61. Tocqueville, *Democracy in America*, 460.

62. Emerson, *Nature*, 21.

63. Ibid., 28.

64. Ibid., 41.

65. Ibid., 10.

66. Miller, *Nature's Nation*, 203.

67. George Perkins Marsh, *Man and Nature* (Cambridge, MA: Harvard University Press, 1965), 37.

68. Ibid., 36.

69. Ibid., 43.

70. Gifford Pinchot, *Breaking New Ground* (New York: Harcourt, Brace, 1947), xvi.

71. Ibid., 324.

72. Ibid., 77.

73. Ibid., 29; also see 28.

74. Ibid., 353.

75. Ibid., 505.

76. Ibid., 190.

77. Samuel P. Hays, *Conservation and the Gospel of Efficiency* (Cambridge, MA: Harvard University Press, 1959), 2.

78. Ibid., 125.

79. Miller, *Nature's Nation*, 203.

80. Perry Miller, "The Responsibility of Mind in a Civilization of Machines," *American Scholar* 31 (1961): 58–59.

81. Ibid., 67.

82. For a much more positive evaluation of Thoreau's influence in his age and our own, see Laura Dassow Walls, *Henry David Thoreau: A Life* (Chicago: University of Chicago Press, 2017).

83. See, e.g., Naomi Klein, *This Changes Everything* (New York: Simon and Schuster, 2014).

84. Ted Nordhaus and Michael Shellenberger, *The Death of Environmentalism*, January 25, 2005, https://changethis.com/manifesto/show/12.Environmentalism.

85. Ibid., 33.

86. Ibid., 26.

87. Ted Nordhaus and Michael Shellenberger, *Break Through* (Boston: Houghton Mifflin, 2007), 15.

88. Ibid., 13.

89. Ibid., 16.

90. Ibid., 18.

91. Ibid., 144.

92. Ibid., 186.

93. Ibid., 271. They are referring to Stewart Brand.

94. Ibid., 211.

95. Ibid., 249–50.

96. Ibid., 270.

97. Quoted in Felicity Barringer, "Paper Sets Off Debate on Environmentalism's Future," *New York Times*, February 6, 2005, http://www.nytimes.com/2005/02/06/us/paper-sets-off-a-debate-on-environmentalisms-future.html?mcubz=1&_r=0.

98. See Marsh, *Man and Nature*.

99. See Bill McKibben, *The End of Nature* (New York: Random House, 1989).

100. Bruno Latour, *Facing Gaia* (Cambridge, MA: Polity, 2017), 142.

101. See interview with Stewart Brand, *Edge*, August 18, 2009, https://www.edge.org/conversation/stewart_brand-we-are-as-gods-and-have-to-get-good-at-it. In contrast, Latour writes: "It would be absurd . . . to think that there is a collective being, human society, that is the new *agent* of geohistory, as the proletariat was thought to be in an earlier epoch. In the face of the old nature—itself reconstituted—there is literally *no one* about whom one can say that he or she is *responsible*. Why? Because there is no way to *unify* the Anthropos as an actor endowed with some sort of moral or political consistency, to the point of charging it with being a character capable of acting on this new global stage. No business-as-usual anthropocentric character can participate in the Anthropocene: this is where the whole interest of the notion lies" (Latour, *Facing Gaia*, 121).

102. "An Ecomodernist Manifesto," April 2015, http://www.ecomodernism.org/.

103. Ibid., 12.

104. Ibid., 18.

105. Ibid., 25.

106. Ibid., 31.

107. "In the Anthropocene, humans do not disturb nature. We reshape it. . . . Only to the extent that humanity is able to engineer, design,

and conserve nature more actively than ever before will humanity or nonhuman nature thrive in the Anthropocene"; Erle C. Ellis, "Too Big for Nature," in *After Preservation*, ed. Ben A. Minteer and Stephen J. Pyne (Chicago: University of Chicago Press, 2015), 29.

108. Paul Kingsnorth writes, "It was, perhaps, inevitable that a utilitarian society would generate a utilitarian environmentalism. . . . I can't speak with a straight face about saving the planet when what I really mean is saving myself from what is coming"; Kingsnorth, *Confessions of a Recovering Environmentalist* (Minneapolis: Graywolf Press, 2017), 79–80.

109. Clive Hamilton, *Defiant Earth* (Cambridge, MA: Polity, 2017), 27.

110. Ibid., 41–43.

111. Pope Francis, *Encyclical Letter "Laudato Si'": On Care for Our Common Home* (Huntington, IN: Our Sunday Visitor Publishing, 2015).

112. The geological epoch that commenced 11,700 years ago, at the end of the last major glacial epoch.

113. Hamilton, *Defiant Earth*, 48.

114. Ibid., 73.

115. For a defense of the "technofix" approach to the problems of the Anthropocene that is, oddly, flip in presentation but sober and thoughtful in content, see Mark Denny, *Making the Most of the Anthropocene* (Baltimore: Johns Hopkins University Press, 2017).

116. David Deutsch, *The Beginning of Infinity* (New York: Viking, 2011).

117. Ibid., 59.

118. Ibid., 55.

119. Ibid., 423.

120. Ibid., 371.

121. Ibid., 50.

122. Ibid., 213.

123. Harari, *Homo Deus*, 22.

124. Biologist Laura Deming quoted in Mark O'Connell, *To Be a Machine* (New York: Doubleday, 2017), 190.

125. Ibid., 171.

126. Ibid., 50, 145.

127. Don DeLillo, *Zero K* (New York: Scribner, 2016), 66. The character also muses, "Isn't it a human glory to refuse to accept a certain fate?" (253).

128. Max More, "A Letter to Mother Nature: Amendments to the Human Constitution," May 25, 2009, http://strategicphilosophy .blogspot.com/2009/05/its-about-ten-years-since-i-wrote.html.

129. Dara Horn shrewdly observes, "Of all the slightly creepy aspects to this trend, the strangest is the least noticed: the people publicly championing life extension are mainly men." For her discussion of why men are more drawn to this fantasy than are women, see Horn, "The Men Who Want to Live Forever," *New York Times*, January 25, 2018, https://www.nytimes.com/2018/01/25/opinion/sunday/silicon-valley -immortality.html. See, too, Madeline Miller, *Circe* (New York: Little, Brown, 2018), a novel about the goddess Circe's choice to become mortal.

130. Jennifer A. Doudna and Samuel H. Sternberg, *A Crack in Creation* (Boston: Houghton Mifflin Harcourt, 2017), 228, 229.

131. Ibid., 239.

132. Ibid., 246.

133. Quoted in ibid., 218.

134. Ibid., 209.

135. Ibid., 239.

136. It is noteworthy that modern wealth is equally detached from political affiliation and control. For a particularly disturbing illustration of this, see Evan Osnos's description of how a crass cosmopolitan survivalism is infecting especially the technological community in Silicon Valley and the East Coast financial community. The growing market in converted and fortified abandoned missile siloes and remote luxury compounds in New Zealand is remarkable for both the degree to which the commercial and technological elite are susceptible to a fantasy of lone-survival and the way in which survival is imagined as completely uninformed by political identity, solidarity, or cooperation. As one hedge-fund manager commented at the World Economic Forum, "I know hedge-fund managers all over the world who are buying airstrips and farms in places like New Zealand because they think they need a getaway [in the event of social breakdown or cataclysmic warfare]" (Evan Osnos, "Survival of the Richest," *New Yorker*, January 30, 2017, 40).

137. The extreme language Dave Foreman uses to condemn this development reflects his frustration with the degree to which utilitarian humanism has, for so many, washed away concern for the rest of the natural world: "Such uncaring, careless, carefree brushing away of all

other Earthlings but for the ecosystem services they give the last surviving ground ape is—how can I can I say this—wicked. It is awash in sin, it is treason to life, to Earth, and to all other Earthlings" (Dave Foreman, "The Anthropocene and Ozymandias," in Minteer and Pyne, *After Preservation*, 56).

138. See Elizabeth Kolbert, *The Sixth Extinction* (New York: Henry Holt, 2014).

139. Even as strong an advocate of Enlightenment humanism as Luc Ferry worries about this: "Today it is no longer nature that engenders the major risks for humankind, but scientific investigation; thus it is no longer nature that we have to tame, but rather science"; Ferry, *What Is the Good Life?* (Chicago: University of Chicago Press, 2005), 275.

140. "It's the devil's bargain ...—medicine and electricity and rocket science in exchange for an empty heaven"; John Updike, *Villages* (New York: Alfred A. Knopf, 2004), 198.

141. John Crow Ransom, *Land* (Notre Dame, IN: University of Notre Dame Press, 2017), 29. Ransom never found a publisher for this manuscript during his lifetime. Long believed lost, it has only recently been rediscovered and published.

142. Ibid., 28.

143. Leopold, "Land Ethic," 239.

144. Ibid.

145. Ibid., 246–51.

146. Ibid., 240.

147. Pinchot, *Breaking New Ground*, 353, 505.

148. Leopold, "Land Ethic," 243.

149. "The ordinary citizen today assumes that science knows what makes the community clock tick; the scientist is equally sure that he does not. He knows that the biotic mechanism is so complex that its workings may never be fully understood" (ibid., 240–41).

150. Ibid., 261.

151. The Thoreauvian tropes and themes are especially obvious in Berry's first collection of essays, *The Long-Legged House* (Berkeley, CA: Counterpoint, 2012).

152. Wendell Berry, *It All Turns on Affection* (Berkeley, CA: Counterpoint, 2012).

153. Ibid., 11.

154. Ibid., 17.

155. "For humans to have a responsible relationship to the world, they must imagine their places in it. . . . As imagination enables sympathy, sympathy enables affection. And in affection we find the possibility of a neighborly, kind, and conserving economy" (ibid., 14).

156. Ibid., 19.

157. Ibid., 27.

158. Ibid., 31.

159. Ibid., 27. Recall Leopold's skepticism that we will be able to fully understand the land in all its complexity. See quote in note 149, above.

160. Berry, *It All Turns on Affection*, 25.

161. As I write, an advertisement for GMC automobiles asks viewers if they want to be merely good parents and decent people. The answer, obviously, is no, there are much higher aspirations to power, prestige, success, and comfort. See https://www.youtube.com/watch?v =AALuceCLDkk.

162. Berry, *It All Turns on Affection*, 29.

163. It is noteworthy that Berry's fiction is almost completely silent on the medical profession. The one mention of a hospital is found in the story "Fidelity" (included in the collection *That Distant Land*) where it is portrayed as a prison to be escaped by a dying man; see Wendell Berry, *That Distant Land* (Berkeley, CA: Counterpoint, 2004), 376. The doctor in the fictional world of Port William, Gib Holston, is rarely mentioned, is underdeveloped as a character, and has no obvious redeeming moral qualities (he is the town's only "professed atheist," has one eye, has at some point killed a man, is small of stature and quick to anger). He is an occasional companion to the admirable Wheeler Catlett, but only as "a digression, an indulgence perhaps, certainly a fascination of a sort, and a source of stories"; see Wendell Berry, *A Place in Time* (Berkeley, CA: Counterpoint, 2012), 160–63.

164. Berry, *It All Turns on Affection*, 38.

165. Ibid.

166. Philosopher Dale Jamieson comments, "It feels as though we are living through some weird perversion of the Enlightenment dream. Instead of humanity rationally governing the world and itself, we are at the mercy of monsters that we have created"; Jamieson, *Reason in Dark Times* (Oxford: Oxford University Press, 2014), 1.

167. Berry, *It All Turns on Affection*, 19.

168. Ibid., 17.

169. For a remarkable example of the commitment to overcoming nature, see Henry T. Greely's argument for eliminating sexual reproduction and replacing it with laboratory technologies in Greely, *The End of Sex* (Cambridge, MA: Harvard University Press, 2016). Greely writes: "The process of human reproduction is wasteful, expensive, and bizarrely complicated. Such a process surely must be the product of evolution, because no one would have designed it this way. And, for many people who want to be parents, it does not work. Ultimately, this book is about the ways we are likely to redesign that system, to make it less wasteful, expensive, and complicated" (44).

170. E. L. Doctorow suggests (through the voice of one of his characters), "Even if all the possible scientific questions are answered, *our problem is still not touched at all*"; Doctorow, *The City of God* (New York: Plume, 2000), 87. Doctorow has also noted, in an essay, that without some humility about our own understanding, we become quite dangerous creatures: "In the course of my own life I have observed that the great civilizer on earth seems to have been doubt"; Doctorow, *Reporting the Universe* (Cambridge, MA: Harvard University Press, 2003), 115.

171. Wendell Berry, *Jayber Crow* (Washington, DC: Counterpoint, 2000), 291.

172. Wendell Berry, *The Art of the Commonplace* (Berkeley, CA: Counterpoint, 2002), 29, 125.

173. Wendell Berry, *Citizenship Papers* (Washington, DC: Shoemaker and Hoard, 2003), 183.

174. Berry, *Unsettling of America*, 98.

175. Wendell Berry, *This Day* (Berkeley, CA: Counterpoint, 2013), 273.

176. Wendell Berry, *Hannah Coulter* (Berkeley, CA: Counterpoint, 2004), 113.

177. "Practically, there is only a distinction between responsible and irresponsible dependence" (Berry, *Art of the Commonplace*, 107).

178. "Some years ago, the State met me in behalf of the Church, and commanded me to pay a certain sum toward the support of a clergyman whose preaching my father attended, but never I myself . . . I declined to pay . . . I did not see why the schoolmaster should be taxed to support the priest, and not the priest the schoolmaster; for I was not the State's schoolmaster, but I supported myself by voluntary subscription. . . .

However, at the request of the selectman, I condescended to make some such statement as this in writing:—'Know all men by these presents, that I, Henry Thoreau, do not wish to be regarded as a member of any incorporated society which I have not joined.' This I gave to the town clerk; and he has it" (Thoreau, *Civil Disobedience*, 49).

179. *Walden*, 384.

180. Ibid., 477.

181. Ibid., 586.

182. Ibid., 399, 402, 570, 429.

183. "The ecological teaching of the Bible is simply inescapable: God made the world because He wanted it made. He thinks the world is good, and He loves it. It is His world; He has never relinquished title to it." "What the Bible proposes is a moral economy, the standard of which is the health of properties belonging to God"; Wendell Berry, *What Are People For?* (San Francisco: North Point Press, 1990), 97, 100.

184. Paul Gilding, *The Great Disruption* (New York: Bloomsbury, 2011), 2.

185. Ibid., 221.

186. Ibid., 254.

187. Berry, *Hannah Coulter*, 181.

188. Augustine, *City of God*, trans. Henry Bettenson (New York: Penguin, 1981), 890.

189. For the first view, simply recall Berry's charges against Duke. For the second, see Luc Ferry, *The New Ecological Order* (Chicago: University of Chicago Press, 1995).

190. *New York Review of Books*, October 22, 2015, 78.

191. Kimberly K. Smith, *Wendell Berry and the Agrarian Tradition* (Lawrence: University Press of Kansas, 2003), 183.

192. Smith, for example, is critical of what she takes to be Berry's inability to properly contend with many real and pressing national and international environmental problems. See ibid., 200.

193. It should be noted that Berry has had much more success keeping his own children at home in the local agrarian community than does his fictional hero.

194. Berry, *Citizenship Papers*, 82.

195. *Walden*, 394.

196. McKibben offers an underdeveloped evolutionary argument that we are "genetically wired" for the sociability of farmer's markets

and a "shift to economies that are more local in scale"; see Bill McKibben, *Deep Economy*, 105–9.

Conclusion

1. Thoreau, *Civil Disobedience*, 43.

2. For doubts about the morally satisfying nature of voluntary poverty, see J. M. Coetzee, *The Childhood of Jesus* (New York: Viking, 2013). The protagonist finds himself in a society priding itself on economic simplicity and finds this world bland and uninspiring: "You live on a diet of bread and water and bean paste and you claim to be filled. How can that be, humanly speaking? Are you lying, even to yourselves?" (30).

3. *Civil Disobedience*, 56.

4. He shared (and likely learned) this view from Emerson: "Undoubtedly we have no questions to ask which are unanswerable. We must trust the perfection of the creation so far, as to believe that whatever curiosity the order of things has awakened in our minds, the order of things can satisfy"; Emerson, *Nature*, 7.

5. "For purity of soul, as we know, is beyond everyone's reach"; José Saramago, *Blindness* (New York: Harcourt, 1997), 184.

6. Note how much stronger Thoreau's moralized claims about nature's resources are than what we find in contemporary appeals to nature's therapeutic value. See, e.g., Florence Williams, *The Nature Fix* (New York: W. W. Norton, 2017).

7. Steven Pinker, *Enlightenment Now* (New York: Viking, 2018), 268.

8. Remember Thoreau's reference to having "lost a hound, a bay horse, and a turtledove," and still being on their trail (*Walden*, 336).

9. "I do not mean to prescribe rules to strong and valiant natures, who will mind their own affairs whether in heaven or hell, and perchance build more magnificently and spend more lavishly than the richest, without ever impoverishing themselves, not knowing how they live,—if, indeed, there are any such, as has been dreamed; nor to those who find their encouragement and inspiration in precisely the present condition of things, and cherish it with the fondness and enthusiasm of lovers,—and, to some extent, I reckon myself in this number; I do not speak to those who are well employed, in whatever circumstances, and they know whether they are well employed or not;—but mainly to the mass of men

who are discontented, and idly complaining of the harness of their lot or of the times, when they might improve them" (ibid., 335).

10. "Are we really so unhappy? Mostly we are not" (Pinker, *Enlightenment Now*, 283).

11. Ibid., 11.

12. Ibid., 24.

13. See ibid., 30.

14. "Authoritarian populism can be seen as a pushback of elements of human nature—tribalism, authoritarianism, demonization, zero-sum thinking—against the Enlightenment institutions that were designed to circumvent them" (ibid., 333).

15. "Intellectuals hate progress. Intellectuals who call themselves 'progressive' *really* hate progress" (ibid., 39).

16. Ibid., 285.

17. Ibid., 324.

18. See his criticism of bioethics in ibid., 402.

19. Ibid., 122.

20. Thoreau's most recent biographer notes that late in his career, "Thoreau knew he was on the cutting edge of science, one of the first to apply Darwin's theories in the field"; Walls, *Henry David Thoreau*, 474.

21. Thoreau, "Paradise (To Be) Regained," 137.

22. *Walden*, 344.

23. Ibid., 332.

24. After publishing *Silent Spring* in 1962, Rachel Carson appeared on television along with a hostile representative of the insecticide industry, Robert White-Stevens. Carson commented, "Can anyone believe it is possible to lay down such a barrage of poisons on the surface of the earth without making it unfit for all life?" White-Stevens angrily responded, "Miss Carson maintains that the balance of nature is a major force in the survival of man, whereas the modern chemist, the modern biologist and scientist believes that man is steadily controlling nature." To which Carson replied, "Now, to these people, apparently, the balance of nature was something repealed as soon as man came on the scene. Well, you might just as well assume that you could repeal the law of gravity"; see Jill Lepore, "The Shorebird: Rachel Carson and the Rising of the Seas," *New Yorker*, March 26, 2018, 72.

25. John Dewey writes, "Science is a name for knowledge in its most characteristic form. It represents in its degree, the perfected

outcome of learning,—its consummation"; John Dewey, *Democracy and Education*, in *The Middle Works* (Carbondale: Southern Illinois University Press, 1985), 9:196.

26. Pinker, *Enlightenment Now*, 228.

27. Ibid., 135.

28. Mark Lilla bitingly suggests that college towns, the most representative enclaves for Pinker's Enlightenment cosmopolitanism, have become centers of a new consumerism: "Most have become meccas of a new consumerist culture for the highly educated, surrounded by techie office parks and increasingly expensive homes. They are places where you can visit a bookshop, see a foreign movie, pick up vitamins and candles, have a decent meal followed by an expresso, and perhaps attend a workshop and have your conscience cleaned"; Mark Lilla, *The Once and Future Liberal* (New York: Harper, 2017), 80–81.

29. Oliver Wendell Holmes, *Ralph Waldo Emerson* (Boston: Houghton, Mifflin, and Co., 1886), 72, 86.

30. *Walden*, 333.

31. Ibid., 329.

32. Ferry, *What Is the Good Life?*, 275.

33. Lilla, *The Once and Future Liberal*, 132.

34. A good citizen "must have the knowledge and ability both to be ruled and to rule." The citizen must "know the rule of free people from both sides"; Aristotle, *The Politics*, ed. and trans. C. D. C. Reeve (Indianapolis: Hackett, 1998), 73.

35. Yascha Mounk, *The People vs. Democracy* (Cambridge, MA: Harvard University Press, 2018), 38.

36. Perhaps the pragmatic point is a little more precise: that without the problems being an actual element of our experience, the background knowledge has no urgency or obvious relevance. One is much more apt to focus and learn when one is practically implicated in a situation.

37. The classic American text on this problem is Walter Lippmann, *Public Opinion* (New York: Macmillan, 1930). Lippmann writes, for example: "The world we have to deal with politically is out of reach, out of sight, out of mind. . . . The substance of the argument is that democracy in its original form never seriously faced the problem which arises because the pictures inside people's heads do not automatically correspond with the world outside" (29–31).

38. Tom Nichols, *The Death of Expertise* (New York: Oxford University Press, 2017), 11.

39. A parallel problem grows with our relationship to science and engineering. As the built environment increasingly becomes the purview of ever-more esoteric scientific knowledge and technologies, people outside these fields find themselves subject to the rule by scientific expertise in ways that are ever-more remote from their understanding or control. One of the most troubling meditations on this problem is provided by Margaret Atwood in her dystopian *MaddAddam* trilogy: *Oryx and Crake* (New York: Anchor, 2004); *The Year of the Flood* (New York: Anchor, 2010); *MaddAddam* (New York: Anchor, 2014).

40. Public schooling is most likely to provide meaningful civic education by bringing students from different walks of life together and assuring equal educational resources and opportunities for all students than it is through civic curricular programming. Our history of funding public education with local property taxes and the contemporary political movement to privatize schooling are both significant threats to this democratic mission. See Taylor, *Horace Mann's Troubling Legacy*, chap. 5.

41. "It is an unlivable paradox, knowing both that you're implicated in the authority of your government and that you have little say in which decisions you will eventually be credited with, at least in part"; Elizabeth Bruenig, "Our Democracy Has Much Bigger Problems Than Trump," *Washington Post*, May 2, 2018, https://www.washingtonpost .com/opinions/the-nation-is-mired-in-bitter-impotence/2018/05/02 /74decfdc-4e3b-11e8-af46-b1d6dc0d9bfe_story.html?utm_term= .d0e137df1f6f.

42. Tocqueville, *Democracy in America*, 492.

43. "It is . . . in the township that the force of free people resides" (ibid., 57).

44. "Thus not only does democracy make each man forget his ancestors, but it hides his descendants from him and separates him from his contemporaries; it constantly leads him back toward himself alone and threatens finally to confine him wholly in the solitude of his own heart" (ibid., 484).

45. "When the mass of citizens wants to be occupied only with private affairs, the smallest parties should not despair of becoming masters of public affairs" (ibid., 516).

46. Two founding classics of this literature are Robert Putnam, *Making Democracy Work* (Princeton, NJ: Princeton University Press, 1993), and Putnam, *Bowling Alone* (New York: Simon and Schuster, 2000).

47. This is why it is essential to dismantle the gerrymandered congressional districts throughout the country. Too many districts are currently so uncompetitive as to make party competition virtually irrelevant within them, thereby discouraging political participation.

48. The point is nicely captured in the claim one hears occasionally that Donald Trump is the first independent to be elected president. At the very least, he led a hostile takeover of the Republican Party, much as Bernie Sanders attempted on the Democratic side.

49. Zadie Smith, "On Optimism and Despair," *New York Review of Books*, December 22, 2016, 36–38.

50. Ibid., 38.

51. "Liberal democracy, the unique mix of individual rights and popular rule that has long characterized most governments in North America and Western Europe, is coming apart at its seams" (Mounk, *The People vs. Democracy*, 14).

52. Mark Lilla, "The End of Identity Liberalism," *New York Times*, November 18, 2016, https://www.nytimes.com/2016/11/20/opinion/sunday/the-end-of-identity-liberalism.html. See also Lilla, *The Once and Future Liberal*.

53. "Democracy does require a basic sense of solidarity. The idea that, for all our outward differences, we're all in this together, that we rise or fall as one"; President Barak Obama, Farewell Address, January 10, 2017, https://www.nytimes.com/2017/01/10/us/politics/obama-farewell-address-speech.html.

54. Quoted in Emrys Westacott, *The Wisdom of Frugality* (Princeton, NJ: Princeton University Press, 2016), 141.

55. Nichols, *The Death of Expertise*, ix, 217.

56. "Politics tends to make us hate each other, even when it shouldn't"; Jason Brennan, *Against Democracy* (Princeton, NJ: Princeton University Press, 2016), 231.

57. Bryan Caplan, *The Myth of the Rational Voter*.

58. The contrast with the most politically pessimistic environmentalists (especially "Malthusian" thinkers from the past generation) is striking here. For example, William Ophuls, writing in the 1970s, was persuaded that democratic citizens would never willingly submit to the limits

imposed by nature. Only a cadre of "ecological mandarins," wielding un-checked political power, would be able to sufficiently protect nature from the ravages of free people. "Only a government possessing great powers to regulate individual behavior in the ecological common interest can deal effectively with the tragedy of the commons"; William Ophuls, *Ecology and the Politics of Scarcity* (San Francisco: W. H. Freeman, 1977), 154. For more on this point, see Bob Pepperman Taylor, *Our Limits Transgressed* (Lawrence: University Press of Kansas, 1992), chap. 2.

59. Consider this deeply pessimistic assessment from Russell Banks's novel *Continental Drift*: "It's dreams. And especially the dream of the new life, the dream of starting over. The more a man trades off his known life, the one in front of him that came to him by birth and the accidents and happenstance of youth, the more of that he trades for dreams of a new life, the less power he has"; Banks, *Continental Drift* (New York: Harper and Row, 1985), 283.

BIBLIOGRAPHY

Adams, John. *A Defence of the Constitutions of Government of the United States of America.* Vol. 2. Philadelphia: Printed by H. Sweitzer for William Cobbett, 1797.

Akst, Daniel. *We Have Met the Enemy.* New York: Penguin, 2011.

Allen, Danielle. "Charlottesville Is Not the Continuation of an Old Fight. It is Something New." *Washington Post,* August 13, 2017. https://www.washingtonpost.com/opinions/charlottesville-is-not -the-continuation-of-an-old-fight-it-is-something-new/2017/08/13 /971812f6-8029-11e7-b359-15a3617c767b_story.html?utm_term= .3c7b43f7582e.

———. *Our Declaration.* New York: W. W. Norton, 2015.

———. *Talking to Strangers.* Chicago: University of Chicago Press, 2004.

Arendt, Hannah. *Crises of the Republic.* New York: Harcourt Brace Jovanovich, 1972.

Aristotle. *The Politics.* Edited and translated by C. D. C. Reeve. Indianapolis: Hackett, 1998.

Arnhart, Larry. "Aldo Leopold's Human Ecology." In *Conservation Reconsidered,* edited by Charles Rubin, 103–32. New York: Rowman and Littlefield, 2000.

Atwood, Margaret. *MaddAddam.* New York: Anchor, 2014.

———. *Oryx and Crake.* New York: Anchor, 2004.

———. *The Year of the Flood.* New York: Anchor, 2010.

Augustine. *City of God.* Translated by Henry Bettenson. New York: Penguin, 1981.

Bacevich, Andrew. *The Limits of Power.* New York: Henry Holt, 2008.

Banks, Russell. *Continental Drift.* New York: Harper and Row, 1985.

Banning, Lance. *Jefferson and Madison.* Madison, WI: Madison House, 1995.

Barringer, Felicity. "Paper Sets Off Debate on Environmentalism's Future." *New York Times*, February 6, 2005. http://www.nytimes.com /2005/02/06/us/paper-sets-off-a-debate-on-environmentalisms -future.html?mcubz=1&_r=0.

Becker, Carl. *Every Man His Own Historian*. New York: Appleton, Century, Crofts, 1935.

Bennett, Jane. "On Being a Native: Thoreau's Hermeneutics of Self." *Polity* 22, no. 4 (1990): 559–80.

———. *Thoreau's Nature*. Thousand Oaks, CA: Sage, 1994.

Berry, Wendell. *Citizenship Papers*. Washington, DC: Shoemaker and Hoard, 2003.

———. *Hannah Coulter*. Berkeley, CA: Counterpoint, 2004.

———. *It All Turns on Affection*. Berkeley, CA: Counterpoint, 2012.

———. *Jayber Crow*. Washington, DC: Counterpoint, 2000.

———. "Letter." *New York Review of Books*, October 22, 2015, 78.

———. *The Long-Legged House*. Berkeley, CA: Counterpoint, 2012.

———. *A Place in Time*. Berkeley, CA: Counterpoint, 2012.

———. *That Distant Land*. Berkeley, CA: Counterpoint, 2004.

———. *This Day*. Berkeley, CA: Counterpoint, 2013.

———. *The Unsettling of America*. Berkeley, CA: Counterpoint, 1996.

———. *What Are People For?* San Francisco: North Point Press, 1990.

Bloom, Harold, ed. *Henry David Thoreau*. New York: Bloom's Literary Criticism, 2008.

Brand, Stewart. Interview. *Edge*, August 18, 2019. https://www.edge .org/conversation/stewart_brand-we-are-as-gods-and-have-to-get -good-at-it.

Brennan, Jason. *Against Democracy*. Princeton, NJ: Princeton University Press, 2016.

Bromwich, David. *Moral Imagination: Essays*. Princeton, NJ: Princeton University Press, 2014.

Brooks, David. "How Evil Is Tech?" *New York Times*, November 20, 2017. https://www.nytimes.com/2017/11/20/opinion/how-evil-is -tech.html.

Bruenig, Elizabeth. "Our Democracy Has Much Bigger Problems Than Trump." *Washington Post*, May 2, 2018. https://www.washington post.com/opinions/the-nation-is-mired-in-bitter-impotence/2018 /05/02/74decfdc-4e3b-11e8-af46-b1d6dc0d9bfe_story.html?utm _term=.d0e137df1f6f.

Buell, Lawrence. "Downwardly Mobile for Conscience's Sake: Voluntary Simplicity from Thoreau to Lily Bart." *American Literary History* 17 (Winter 2005): 653–65.

Buranelli, Vincent. "The Case against Thoreau." *Ethics* 67, no. 4 (1957): 257–68.

Cafaro, Philip. *Thoreau's Living Ethics*. Athens: University of Georgia Press, 2004.

Callicott, J. Baird. *Beyond the Land Ethic*. New York: SUNY Press, 1999.

———. *In Defense of the Land Ethic*. New York: SUNY Press, 1989.

Caplan, Bryan. *The Case against Education*. Princeton, NJ: Princeton University Press, 2018.

———. *The Myth of the Rational Voter*. Princeton, NJ: Princeton University Press, 2007.

Carlson, Richard. *Don't Sweat the Small Stuff and It's All Small Stuff*. New York: Hyperion, 1997.

Carter, Stephen. *Civility*. New York: Basic Books, 1998.

———. *Integrity*. New York: Basic Books, 1996.

Cavell, Stanley. *The Senses of Walden*. Chicago: University of Chicago Press, 1981.

Coates, Ta-Nehisi. *We Were Eight Years in Power*. New York: One World, 2017.

Coetzee, J. M. *The Childhood of Jesus*. New York: Viking, 2013.

———. *Diary of a Bad Year*. New York: Viking, 2007.

Conrad, Joseph. *The Nigger of the Narcissus*. New York: Doubleday, Doran and Co., 1929.

Cooper, James Fenimore. *The American Democrat*. New York: Penguin, 1989.

Dahl, Robert. *On Political Equality*. New Haven, CT: Yale University Press, 2006.

Danforth, Samuel. "A Brief Recognition of New-Englands Errand into the Wilderness" (1670). http://digitalcommons.unl.edu/cgi/viewcontent.cgi?article=1038&context=libraryscience.

Delbanco, Andrew. *The Abolitionist Imagination*. Cambridge, MA: Harvard University Press, 2012.

———. *The Death of Satan*. New York: Farrar, Straus and Giroux, 1995.

DeLillo, Don. *Zero K*. New York: Scribner, 2016.

Deneen, Patrick J. *Conserving America?* South Bend, IN: St. Augustine's Press, 2016.

———. *Why Liberalism Failed*. New Haven, CT: Yale University Press, 2018.

Denny, Mark. *Making the Most of the Anthropocene*. Baltimore: Johns Hopkins University Press, 2017.

Deutsch, David. *The Beginning of Infinity*. New York: Viking, 2011.

Dewey, John. *Democracy and Education*. Vol. 9 of *Middle Works*. Carbondale: Southern Illinois University Press, 1985.

———. *The Public and Its Problems*. Edited by Melvin Rogers. Athens, OH: Swallow Press, 2016.

Diggins, John Patrick. "Thoreau, Marx, and the 'Riddle' of Alienation." *Social Research* 39 (Winter 1972): 571–98.

Doctorow, E. L. *The City of God*. New York: Plume, 2000.

———. *Reporting the Universe*. Cambridge, MA: Harvard University Press, 2003.

Doudna, Jennifer A., and Samuel H. Sternberg. *A Crack in Creation*. Boston: Houghton Mifflin Harcourt, 2017.

Dreher, Rod. *The Benedict Option*. New York: Sentinel, 2017.

Dunkelman, Marc J. *The Vanishing Neighbor*. New York: W. W. Norton, 2014.

"An Ecomodernist Manifesto." April 2015. http://www.ecomodernism.org/.

Ehrenreich, Barbara. *Natural Causes*. New York: Hachette Book Group, 2018.

Ellis, Richard. *To the Flag*. Lawrence: University Press of Kansas, 2005.

Elshtain, Jean Bethke. *Democracy on Trial*. New York: Basic Books, 1995.

Emerson, Ralph Waldo. *Essays and Lectures*. New York: Library of America, 1983.

———. "Thoreau." In *Thoreau: A Century of Criticism*, edited by Walter Harding, 22–40. Dallas: Southern Methodist University, 1954.

Eulau, Heinz. "Wayside Challenger: Some Remarks on the Politics of Henry David Thoreau." In *Thoreau: A Collection of Critical Essays*, edited by Sherman Paul, 117–30. Englewood Cliffs, NJ: Prentice-Hall, 1962.

Fasolt, Constantin. *The Limits of History*. Chicago: University of Chicago Press, 2004.

Ferry, Luc. *The New Ecological Order*. Chicago: University of Chicago Press, 1995.

———. *What Is the Good Life?* Chicago: University of Chicago Press, 2005.

Fish, Charles. *In Good Hands*. New York: Kodansha International, 1996.

Foer, Franklin. *World without Mind*. New York: Penguin, 2017.

Foner, Eric. *The Story of American Freedom*. New York: W. W. Norton, 1998.

Francis, Pope. *Encyclical Letter "Laudato Si'": On Care for Our Common Home*. Huntington, IN: Our Sunday Visitor Publishing, 2015.

Frank, Cristin. *Living Simple, Free and Happy*. Blue Ash, OH: Betterway Home Books, 2013.

Franzen, Jonathan. *Freedom*. New York: Farrar, Straus and Giroux, 2010.

Fresco, Louise O. *Hamburgers in Paradise*. Princeton, NJ: Princeton University Press, 2016.

Gilding, Paul. *The Great Disruption*. New York: Bloomsbury, 2011.

GMC Automobile Advertisement. https://www.youtube.com/watch?v=AALuceCLDkk.

Goldmacher, Shane. "America Hits New Landmark: 200 Million Registered Voters." *Politico*, October 19, 2016. https://www.politico.com/story/2016/10/how-many-registered-voters-are-in-america-2016-229993.

Gopnik, Adam. "The Liberal Imagination." *New Yorker*, March 20, 2017, 88–93.

Greeley, Henry T. *The End of Sex*. Cambridge, MA: Harvard University Press, 2016.

Gregory, Brad S. *The Unintended Reformation*. Cambridge, MA: Harvard University Press, 2012.

Gura, Philip F. *Man's Better Angels*. Cambridge, MA: Belknap Press, 2017.

Hamilton, Alexander, James Madison, and John Jay. *The Federalist Papers*. Edited by Clinton Rossiter. New York: Mentor, 1999.

Hamilton, Clive. *Defiant Earth*. Cambridge, MA: Polity, 2017.

Hanagan, Nora. "From Agrarian Dreams to Democratic Realities: A Deweyan Alternative to Jeffersonian Food Politics." *Political Research Quarterly* 68 (2014): 34–45.

Harari, Yuval Noah. *Homo Deus*. New York: Harper, 2017.

Harding, Walter, ed. *Thoreau: A Century of Criticism*. Dallas: Southern Methodist University Press, 1954.

Hays, Samuel P. *Conservation and the Gospel of Efficiency*. Cambridge, MA: Harvard University Press, 1987.

Hicks, John H., ed. *Thoreau in Our Season*. Amherst: University of Massachusetts Press, 1967.

Hinchman, Lewis P. "Aldo Leopold's Hermeneutic of Nature." *Review of Politics* (Spring 1995): 225–49.

Hochfield, George. "Anti-Thoreau." *Sewanee Review* 96, no. 3 (1988): 433–43.

Holmes, Oliver Wendell. *Ralph Waldo Emerson*. Boston: Houghton, Mifflin, and Co., 1886.

Horn, Dara. "The Men Who Want to Live Forever." *New York Times*, January 25, 2018. https://www.nytimes.com/2018/01/25/opinion /sunday/silicon-valley-immortality.html.

Houellebecq, Michel. *Submission*. New York: Farrar, Straus and Giroux, 2015.

Hughes, Ethan. Interview. April 25, 2011. https://www.motherearthnews .com/nature-and-environment/sustainable-communities/possibility -alliance-ze0z11zmar.

James, William. *Writings 1902–1910*. New York: Library of America, 1987.

Jamieson, Dale. *Reason in Dark Times*. Oxford: Oxford University Press, 2014.

Jefferson, Thomas. *Notes on the State of Virginia*. Chapel Hill: University of North Carolina Press, 1982.

———. *Writings*. New York: Library of America, 1984.

Jones, Gavin. *American Hungers: The Problem of Poverty in U.S. Literature, 1840–1945*. Princeton, NJ: Princeton University Press, 2007.

Judis, John B. *The Populist Explosion*. New York: Columbia Global Reports, 2016.

Kessler, Glen, Salvador Rizzo, and Meg Kelly. "President Trump Has Made More Than 5000 False or Misleading Claims." *Washington Post*, September 13, 2018. https://www.washingtonpost.com /politics/2018/09/13/president-trump-has-made-more-than-false -or-misleading-claims/?utm_term=.8d463b07190a.

Kimball, Kristin. *The Dirty Life*. New York: Scribner, 2010.

Kingsnorth, Paul. *Confessions of a Recovering Environmentalist*. Minneapolis: Graywolf Press, 2017.

Klein, Naomi. *This Changes Everything*. New York: Simon and Schuster, 2014.

Kolbert, Elizabeth. *The Sixth Extinction*. New York: Henry Holt, 2014.

Kondo, Marie. *The Life Changing Magic of Tidying Up*. Berkeley, CA: Ten Speed Press, 2014.

Lasch, Christopher. *The Revolt of the Elites*. New York: W. W. Norton, 1995.

———. *The True and Only Heaven*. New York: W. W. Norton, 1991.

Latour, Bruno. *Facing Gaia*. Cambridge, MA: Polity, 2017.

Leopold, Aldo. *For Health of the Land*. Washington, DC: Island Press, 1999.

———. *The River of the Mother of God and Other Essays*. Madison: University of Wisconsin Press, 1991.

———. *A Sand County Almanac*. New York: Ballantine Books, 1998.

Lepore, Jill. "The Shorebird: Rachel Carson and the Rising of the Seas." *New Yorker*, March 26, 2018, 64–72.

———. "The War and the Roses." *New Yorker*, August 8, 2016, 24–32.

———. *The Whites of Their Eyes*. Princeton, NJ: Princeton University Press, 2010.

Levitsky, Steven, and Daniel Ziblatt. *How Democracies Die*. New York: Crown, 2018.

Levmore, Saul, and Martha Nussbaum, eds. *The Offensive Internet*. Cambridge, MA: Harvard University Press, 2010.

Ley, Emily. *A Simplified Life*. Nashville, TN: Thomas Nelson, 2017.

Lilla, Mark. "The End of Identity Liberalism." *New York Times*, November 18, 2016. https://www.nytimes.com/2016/11/20/opinion/sunday/the-end-of-identity-liberalism.html.

———. *The Once and Future Liberal*. New York: Harper, 2017.

———. "The Tea Party Jacobins." *New York Review of Books*, May 27, 2010, 53–56.

Lincoln, Abraham. *The Portable Abraham Lincoln*. New York: Penguin, 1992.

———. *Speeches and Writings, 1859–1865*. New York: Library of America, 1989.

Lippmann, Walter. *Public Opinion*. New York: Macmillan, 1930.

Locke, John. *Second Treatise on Government*. Indianapolis: Hackett, 1980.

London, Herb. "If We Don't Shape Up, Who'll Ship Out?" *Burlington [VT] Free Press*, April 6, 2002, 6A.

Mann, Horace. *Lectures on Education*. Boston: Lemuel N. Ide, 1850.

Manson, Mark. *The Subtle Art of Not Giving a Fuck*. New York: HarperCollins, 2016.

Mariotti, Shannon. *Thoreau's Democratic Withdrawal*. Madison: University of Wisconsin Press, 2010.

Marsh, George Perkins. *Man and Nature*. Cambridge, MA: Harvard University Press, 1965.

Marx, Karl, and Frederick Engels. *Manifesto of the Communist Party*. In *Selected Works*, 1:98–137. Moscow: Progress Publishers, 1977.

Mason, Wyatt. "The Revelations of Marilynne Robinson." *New York Times Magazine*, October 1, 2014. https://www.nytimes.com/2014/10/05/magazine/the-revelations-of-marilynne-robinson.html.

McKenzie, Jonathan. *The Political Thought of Henry David Thoreau*. Lexington: University Press of Kentucky, 2016.

McKibben, Bill. *Deep Economy*. New York: Henry Holt, 2007.

———. *The End of Nature*. New York: Random House, 1989.

———. *Enough*. New York: Times Books, 2003.

Miller, Madeline. *Circe*. New York: Little, Brown, 2018.

Miller, Perry. *Nature's Nation*. Cambridge, MA: Harvard University Press, 1967.

———. "The Responsibility of Mind in a Civilization of Machines." *American Scholar* 31 (1961): 51–69.

Minteer, Ben A., and Stephen J. Pyne, eds. *After Preservation*. Chicago: University of Chicago Press, 2015.

Mishra, Pankaj. *The Age of Anger*. New York: Farrar, Straus and Giroux, 2017.

Mittleman, Alan L. *Human Nature and Jewish Thought*. Princeton, NJ: Princeton University Press, 2015.

More, Max. "A Letter to Mother Nature: Amendments to the Human Constitution." May 25, 2009. http://strategicphilosophy.blogspot.com/2009/05/its-about-ten-years-since-i-wrote.html.

Mounk, Yascha. *The People vs. Democracy*. Cambridge, MA: Harvard University Press, 2018.

Mutz, Diana C. "Status Threat, Not Economic Hardship, Explains the 2016 Presidential Vote." *Proceedings of the National Academy of Sciences* 115, no. 19 (2018): E4330–E4339. http://www.pnas.org/content/early/2018/04/18/1718155115.

Nichols, Tom. *The Death of Expertise*. New York: Oxford University Press, 2017.

Nordhaus, Ted, and Michael Shellenberger. *Break Through*. Boston: Houghton Mifflin, 2007.

———. *The Death of Environmentalism*. January 25, 2005. https://changethis.com/manifesto/show/12.Environmentalism.

Norton, Bryan G. "The Constancy of Leopold's Land Ethic." *Conservation Biology* 2 (March 1988): 93–102.

Oakeshott, Michael. *Rationalism in Politics and Other Essays*. London: Methuen, 1962.

Obama, Barack. Farewell Address. January 10, 2017. https://www.ny times.com/2017/01/10/us/politics/obama-farewell-address-speech .html.

———. Nobel Lecture. December 10, 2008. https://www.nobelprize.org /nobel_prizes/peace/laureates/2009/obama-lecture_en.html.

O'Connell, Mark. *To Be a Machine*. New York: Doubleday, 2017.

Ophuls, William. *Ecology and the Politics of Scarcity*. San Francisco: W. H. Freeman, 1977.

Osnos, Evan. "Survival of the Richest." *New Yorker*, January 30, 2017, 36–46.

Paine, Thomas. *Common Sense*. London: Penguin, 1988.

Patchett, Ann. "My Year of No Shopping." *New York Times*, December 15, 2017. https://www.nytimes.com/2017/12/15/opinion/sunday /shopping-consumerism.html.

Petrulionis, Sandra Harbert. *To Set This World Right*. Ithaca, NY: Cornell University Press, 2006.

Phelps, Edmund. "Letter." *New York Review of Books*, October 22, 2015, 78.

Pinchot, Gifford. *Breaking New Ground*. New York: Harcourt, Brace, 1947.

Pinker, Steven. *Enlightenment Now*. New York: Viking, 2018.

Plato. *The Republic*. Translated by G. M. A. Grube. Revised by C. D. C. Reeve. Indianapolis: Hackett, 1992.

Purdy, Jedediah. *After Nature*. Cambridge, MA: Harvard University Press, 2015.

Putnam, Robert. *Bowling Alone*. New York: Simon and Schuster, 2000.

———. *Making Democracy Work*. Princeton, NJ: Princeton University Press, 1993.

Rampell, Catherine. "Americans Believe Crazy, Wrong Things." *Washington Post*, January 4, 2017. https://www.commercial-news.com /opinion/rampell-americans-believe-crazy-wrong-things/article _9533c479-9ae3-54d3-a270-00f4486b46c9.html.

Ransom, John Crow. *Land*. Notre Dame, IN: University of Notre Dame Press, 2017.

Reagan, Ronald. Nomination Acceptance Speech, Republican National Convention, Detroit, Michigan, July 17, 1980. http://www.4presi dent.org/speeches/reagan1980convention.htm.

Reganold, John P., and Jonathan M. Wachter. "Organic Agriculture in the Twenty-first Century." *Nature Plants*, article no. 15221 (February 2016): 1–8.

Robinson, Marilynne. *The Death of Adam*. Boston: Houghton Mifflin, 1998.

———. *The Givenness of Things*. New York: Farrar, Straus and Giroux, 2015.

———. *Mother Country*. New York: Farrar, Straus and Giroux, 1989.

———. *What Are We Doing Here?* New York: Farrar, Straus and Giroux, 2018.

———. *When I Was a Child I Read Books*. New York: Farrar, Straus and Giroux, 2012.

Roosevelt, Theodore. *The Works of Theodore Roosevelt*. Vol. 13. New York: Charles Scribner's Sons, 1926.

Rorty, Richard. *Achieving Our Country*. Cambridge, MA: Harvard University Press, 1998.

———. "Two Cheers for Elitism." *New Yorker*, January 30, 1995, 86–89.

Rosenblum, Nancy. *Good Neighbors*. Princeton, NJ: Princeton University Press, 2016.

———. "Thoreau's Militant Conscience." *Political Theory* 9 (1981): 81–110.

Rousseau, Jean-Jacques. *The Basic Political Writings*. Indianapolis: Hackett, 1987.

Sandel, Michael. *Democracy's Discontent*. Cambridge, MA: Harvard University Press, 1996.

———. *What Money Can't Buy*. New York: Farrar, Straus and Giroux, 2012.

Saramago, José. *Blindness*. New York: Harcourt, 1997.

Schultz, Kathryn. "Pond Scum: Henry Thoreau's Moral Myopia." *New Yorker*, October 19, 2015, 40–45.

Scialabba, George. *What Are Intellectuals Good For?* Boston: Pressed Wafer, 2009.

Sen, Amartya. *Development as Freedom*. New York: Anchor, 1999.

———. "Humanity and Citizenship." In *For Love of Country?*, edited by Martha Nussbaum, 111–18. Boston: Beacon Press, 1996.

Shankman, Andrew. *Crucible of American Democracy*. Lawrence: University Press of Kansas, 2004.

Smith, Kimberly. *African American Environmental Thought*. Lawrence: University Press of Kansas, 2007.

———. *Wendell Berry and the Agrarian Tradition*. Lawrence: University of Kansas Press, 2003.

Smith, Zadie. "On Optimism and Despair." *New York Review of Books*, December 22, 2016, 36–38.

Snow, Kate, and Cynthia McFadden. "Generation at Risk: America's Youngest Facing Mental Health Crisis." NBC News, December 10, 2017. https://www.nbcnews.com/health/kids-health/generation -risk-america-s-youngest-facing-mental-health-crisis-n827836.

St. James, Elaine. *Living the Simple Life*. New York: Hyperion, 1996.

Stephenson, Wen. *What We're Fighting for Now Is Each Other*. Boston: Beacon Press, 2015.

Sundeen, Mark. *The Unsettlers*. New York: Riverhead, 2016.

Sunstein, Cass R. *#Republic*. Princeton, NJ: Princeton University Press, 2017.

Taylor, Bob Pepperman. "Aldo Leopold's Civic Education." In *Democracy and the Claims of Nature*, edited by Ben A. Minteer and Bob Pepperman Taylor, 173–87. Lanham, MD: Rowman and Littlefield, 2002.

———. *America's Bachelor Uncle: Thoreau and the American Polity*. Lawrence: University Press of Kansas, 1996.

———. *Horace Mann's Troubling Legacy*. Lawrence: University Press of Kansas, 2010.

———. *Our Limits Transgressed*. Lawrence: University Press of Kansas, 1992.

———. *The Routledge Guidebook to Thoreau's "Civil Disobedience."* London: Routledge, 2015.

Thoreau, Henry David. *Civil Disobedience*. Edited Bob Pepperman Taylor. Peterborough, ON: Broadview Press, 2016.

———. *Collected Essays and Poems*. New York: Library of America, 2001.

———. *Familiar Letters of Henry David Thoreau*. Edited F. B. Sanborn. Boston: Houghton, Mifflin, 1894.

———. *The Journal of Henry D. Thoreau*. 14 vols. Edited Bradford Torrey and Francis H. Allen. Boston: Houghton Mifflin, 1949.

———. *Letters to Various Persons*. Boston: Houghton, Mifflin, 1885.

———. *A Week on the Concord and Merrimack Rivers; Walden, or, Life in the Woods; The Maine Woods; Cape Cod*. New York: Library of America, 1985.

Tocqueville, Alexis de. *Democracy in America*. Translated by Harvey C. Mansfield and Delba Winthrop. Chicago: University of Chicago Press, 2002.

Turner, Jack ed. *A Political Companion to Henry David Thoreau*. Lexington: University Press of Kentucky, 2009.

Twain, Mark. *The Autobiography of Mark Twain*. Vol. 1. Berkeley: University of California Press, 2010.

Updike, John. *Rabbit Run*. New York: Random House, 1960.

———. *Villages*. New York: Alfred A. Knopf, 2004.

Walker, Brian. "Thoreau on Democratic Cultivation." *Political Theory* 29 (2001): 155–89.

———. "Thoreau's Alternative Economics: Work, Liberty, and Democratic Cultivation." *American Political Science Review* 92 (December 1998): 845–56.

Wallace, David Foster. "Deciderization 2007—A Special Report." http://neugierig.org/content/dfw/bestamerican.pdf. Also found in David Foster Wallace, ed., introduction to *The Best American Essays 2007*. New York: Mariner Books, 2007.

Walls, Laura Dassow. *Henry David Thoreau: A Life*. Chicago: University of Chicago Press, 2017.

Walzer, Michael. *Exodus and Revolution*. New York: Basic Books, 1986.

Weber, Max. *From Max Weber*. Edited by H. H. Gerth and C. Wright Mills. New York: Oxford University Press, 1978.

Westacott, Emrys. *The Wisdom of Frugality*. Princeton, NJ: Princeton University Press, 2016.

Whitman, Walt. *Complete Poetry and Collected Prose*. New York: Library of America, 1982.

Williams, Florence. *The Nature Fix*. New York: W. W. Norton, 2017.

Williams, Joan C. *White Working Class*. Boston: Harvard Business Review, 2017.

Wills, Garry. "Big Rocket Man." *New York Review of Books*, December 21, 2017, 8.

Wolfe, Alan. *Does American Democracy Still Work?* New Haven, CT: Yale University Press, 2006.

Wolff, Michael. *Fire and Fury*. New York: Henry Holt, 2018.

Wood, Gordon. *Empire of Liberty*. New York: Oxford University Press, 2009.

Woodward, Bob. *Fear*. New York: Simon and Schuster, 2018.

INDEX

Bob Pepperman Taylor is the Elliott A. Brown Green and Gold Professor of Law, Politics, and Political Behavior at the University of Vermont. He is the author and editor of a number of books, including *The Routledge Guidebook to Thoreau's "Civil Disobedience."*

CPSIA information can be obtained
at www.ICGtesting.com
Printed in the USA
LVHW080842190920
666542LV00023B/1121